Study Guide

Economics & Contemporary Issues
SEVENTH EDITION

Ronald L. Moomaw

Oklahoma State University

Kent W. Olson

Oklahoma State University

Prepared by

Kenny Christianson

Binghamton University

THOMSON

SOUTH-WESTERN

Australia · Brazil · Canada · Mexico · Singapore · Spain · United Kingdom · United States

THOMSON

SOUTH-WESTERN

Study Guide t/a Economics and Contemporary Issues, Seventh Edition
Ronald L. Moomaw and Kent W. Olson
Prepared by Kenny Christianson

VP/Editorial Director:
Jack W. Calhoun

VP/Editor-in-Chief:
Alex von Rosenberg

AssociateAcquisitions Editor:
Sarah Dorger

Developmental Editor:
Katie Yanos

Executive Marketing Manager:
Brian Joyner

Content Project Manager:
Margaret M. Bril

Manager of Technology, Editorial:
Vicky True

Technology Project Manager:
Dana Cowden

Senior Manufacturing Coordinator:
Sandee Milewski

Printer:
ePAC Technologies
San Leandro, California

Cover Designer:
Jennifer Lambert/Jen2Design

Cover Images:
© Getty Images, Inc.

For more information about our products,
contact us at:

Thomson Learning Academic Resource
Center

1-800-423-0563

Thomson Higher Education
5191 Natorp Boulevard
Mason, OH 45040
USA

TABLE OF CONTENTS

Economic Growth: An Introduction to Scarcity and Choice

Objectives of the Chapter

After you have mastered this chapter you will understand that:

1. Scarcity forces individuals and nations to make choices which involve opportunity costs.

2. The cost of producing any good or service increases as the output of that good increases The production of more consumption goods comes at the expense of capital goods.

3. Economic growth can result from resource accumulation, technological improvements, or improvements in efficiency.

4. Gains in productivity depend upon growth in the capital-labor ratio and technical change, which consists of technological improvement and efficiency improvement.

5. The main determinant of real wage growth is the effect of compound productivity growth.

6. Productivity growth has changed over time in the United States and is lower than in many other advanced countries despite the fact that productivity levels are higher.

7. A market orientation seems to be more successful in terms of economic growth.

8. Population growth in developing countries makes per capita economic growth difficult.

9. There is a correlation between economic freedom and economic growth. Those countries with the greatest increases in economic freedom have higher rates of economic growth.

Key Terms

land

labor

physical capital

human capital

opportunity cost

production possibilities curve

best technology

marginal cost

scarcity

marginal benefit

marginal product

technological improvement

efficiency improvement

capital intensity

technical change

economic freedom

True False Questions

For these statements, indicate whether they are true or false. Defend your answer.

1. Efficiency improvements will cause the production possibilities curve to shift out as economic growth occurs.

   TRUE or FALSE

2. Productivity growth is an important determinant of labor compensation.

   TRUE or FALSE

3. A major reason Germany and Japan have experienced high economic growth rates is rapid growth in capital intensity.

   TRUE or FALSE

4. Those countries with higher levels of economic freedom are likely to see lower rates of economic growth compared to countries with less economic freedom.

   TRUE or FALSE

5. An increase in an economy's resources will lead to an outward shift of the PPC.

   TRUE or FALSE

Multiple Choice

Check yourself. Choose the best answer. Answers are found at the end of the chapter.

1. The Declaration of Independence and Adam Smith's The Wealth of Nations
    a. both support the importance of economic freedom to economic prosperity.
    b. were both written by American economists.
    c. were both published in 1776.
    d. both support the efficiency of centralized planning.

2. Which of the following is an example of land?
    a. A van used in a delivery service.
    b. An oil reserve in Alaska.
    c. A computer used by a banker.
    d. A staffing coordinator at an employment agency.

3. The production possibilities curve shows:
    a. the minimum combinations of two goods or services that can be produced if there is unemployment in the economy.
    b. the maximum combinations of two goods or services that can be produced if there is unemployment in the economy.
    c. the minimum combinations of two goods or services that can be produced if resources are fully employed and the best technology is being used.
    d. the maximum combinations of two goods or services that can be produced if resources are fully employed and the best technology is being used.

4. When Perelandra produces an additional unit of housing, 4,000 bottles of wine must be sacrificed. The 4,000 bottles of wine represent:
    a. the marginal benefit of producing housing in Perelandra.
    b. the marginal cost of producing housing in Perelandra.
    c. the total sacrifice of producing housing in Perelandra.
    d. the best-technological combination of producing housing in Perelandra.

5. Suppose there is an efficiency improvement in production in the country of Narnia. We would expect:
    a. Narnia's production possibilities curve to shift leftward.
    b. Narnia's production possibilities curve to shift rightward.
    c. a movement along Narnia's production possibilities curve.
    d. a movement from inside Narnia's production possibilities curve to a point closer to its production possibilities curve.

6.

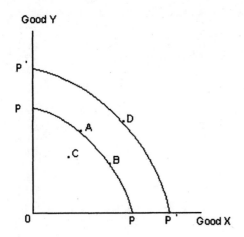

Suppose an economy's production possibilities curve is represented by curve PP. A combination of goods and services that is NOT being produced with the best technology would be represented by point:

a. A.
b. B.
c. C.
d. D.

7.

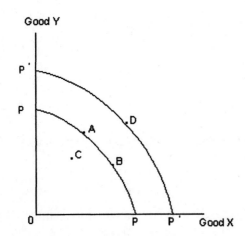

Suppose an economy's production possibilities curve is represented by curve P'P'. An efficient combination of goods and services would be represented:

a. by point A.
b. by point B.
c. by point C.
d. by point D.

8.

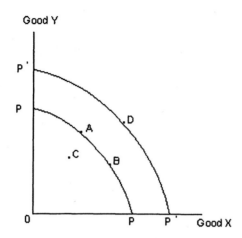

Suppose the economy's production possibilities curve is represented by curve PP. An increase in the number of capital goods would result in:

a. a shift from curve PP to curve P'P'.
b. a shift from curve P'P' to curve PP.
c. a movement from point A to point C.
d. a movement from point C to point A.

9.

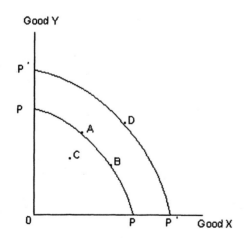

Suppose X represents capital goods and Y represents consumption goods. The cost of accumulating more capital goods would be represented as:

a. a movement from point A to point C.
b. a movement from point C to point A.
c. a movement from point A to point B.
d. a movement from point A to point D.

10.

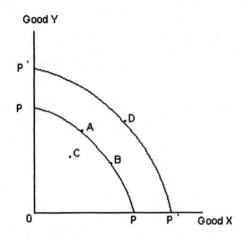

Suppose the economy's production possibilities curve is represented by curve PP. An efficiency improvement would be represented as:

a. a movement from point A to point C.
b. a movement from point B to point C.
c. a movement from point A to point B.
d. a movement from point C to point A.

11.

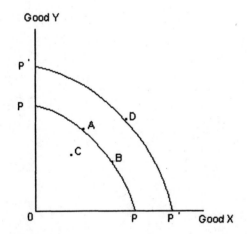

Suppose X represents capital goods and Y represents consumption goods. A movement from point A to point B:

a. is an increase in capital goods in the economy.
b. represents a decrease in the resources used to produce consumption goods.
c. will lead to higher rates of economic growth in the future.
d. all of the above.

12.

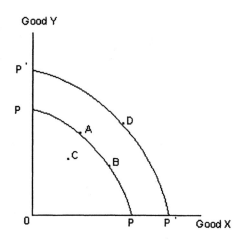

An increase in labor resources through immigration will lead to
a. a movement along the PPC curve from point A to point B.
b. a movement inside the PPC from point A to Point C.
c. a shift of the PPC from P'P' to PP.
d. a shift of the PPC from PP to P'P'.

13. The bowed out shape of the production possibilities curve implies that:
    a. in order to produce more of one good, we must sacrifice increasingly larger amounts of the other good.
    b. the economy is consistently operating with unemployed resources.
    c. the costs of production of all goods must be identical.
    d. full employment is attainable only if the prices of all goods are the same.

14. The PPC is downward-sloping due to
    a. scarcity
    b. increasing opportunity costs.
    c. the law of demand
    d. economic growth

15. Suppose the growth rate of capital exceeds the growth rate of labor. In this instance:
    a. the capital-labor ratio and the growth rate of real wages will decrease.
    b. the capital-labor ratio will increase and the growth rate of real wages will decrease.
    c. the capital-labor ratio and the growth rate of real wages will increase.
    d. the capital-labor ratio will fall and the growth rate of real wages will increase.

16. The decline in productivity growth over the 1973-1990 time period was largely the result of:
    a. an increase in capital intensity.
    b. a decline in technical change.
    c. a decline in capital intensity.
    d. a decline in technical efficiency.

17. Which of the following is an example of technological improvement?
    a. the elimination of price controls on wheat.
    b. an advance in engineering that allows the Pretty Dolls Toy Company to increase their rate of production.
    c. a court decision that breaks up a monopoly firm.
    d. a regulation that prohibits the production of genetically altered wheat.

18. Suppose the growth rate in labor productivity in Centralzia increased from 2% per year to 5% per year. Which of the following would we be likely to find?
    a. slower growth in supply of capital.
    b. slower growth in technical change.
    c. a decline in compensation per hour paid to labor.
    d. an increase in capital intensity.

19. Economic growth is depicted by a:
    a. movement toward the production possibilities curve.
    b. movement downward along the production possibilities curve.
    c. rightward shift in the production possibilities curve.
    d. change in the slope of the production possibilities curve.

20. Since 1960, the United States has had per capita GDP growth rates that were substantially higher than those of
    a. Japan
    b. Korea
    c. China
    d. Argentina

21. Some analysts hypothesize that productivity growth rates in the manufacturing sector have exceeded those in the service sector because the:
    a. labor force in the service sector is less well educated than in the manufacturing sector.
    b. the service sector is a much more competitive sector.
    c. the manufacturing sector has faced stiff foreign competition.
    d. rate of output in the manufacturing sector is difficult to measure.

22. Output per person in Japan is approximately equal to output per person in the United States because:
    a. Japanese employees are about as productive as employees in the United States.
    b. Japanese employees work longer hours than employees in the United States.
    c. Japanese firms have less government bureaucracy to contend with than do firms in the United States.
    d. The quality of the Japanese labor force is approximately equal to that of the labor force in the United States.

23. According to Maddison, technical change is occurring more rapidly in Japan than in the United States because of:
    a. the technical effect.
    b. the agricultural effect.
    c. the back-wash effect.
    d. the structural effect.

24. The structural effect refers to:
    a. shifts in economic activity from one sector to another.
    b. transfers in technology.
    c. increasing the capital-labor ratio in developing countries.
    d. increasing the quality of the labor force in developing countries.

25. Which of the following is an example of the technological diffusion effect?
    a. Foreign trade causes the break up of monopolies.
    b. Brazil adopts a new assembly method developed in Germany.
    c. Foreign trade causes firms to band together into large conglomerates.
    d. Costa Rica moves from an agriculture economy to a manufacturing economy.

26. The concept of opportunity cost suggests that:
    a. voluntary exchanges involve a loser and a winner.
    b. individuals must have perfect information on the benefits.
    c. dollar prices provide a perfect measure of the costs of producing all goods.
    d. in order to produce more of any particular good, something must be given up in return.

Fill-in Questions

1. In order to produce goods and services, an economy must have resources. There are three primary resources: land, labor, and capital. _____ includes all natural resources and raw materials. All physical and mental abilities used by people in the production process is _____ . _____ refers to the man-made, durable items used in the production process. As resources grow, so does an economy's ability to produce goods and services.

2. The _____ shows the maximum combination of goods and services that an economy can produce with its resources. If resources are fully employed and the _____ is being used, an economy will be producing at a point on its production possibilities curve.

3. As an economy moves down its production possibilities curve, it will get additional units of one good and give up units of another good. The value of what is sacrificed when making choices is referred to as _____ .

4. An economy should continue to produce additional units of a good as long as the _____ of the additional units exceeds the _____ . Recall that marginal cost will increase and marginal benefit will fall as we continuing producing additional units of a good. This occurs because _____ will fall.

5. All economies experience the problem of _____ . Because of this, we are interested in economic growth. Two sources of economic growth are technological improvements and efficiency improvements. _____ occurs when there is an improvement in the best technology. _____ occurs when there is a change from less than the best technology.

6. Productivity growth occurs when there is a growth in _____ , a growth in the ratio of capital to labor. Productivity is also affected by _____ . The latter is the result of technological and efficiency improvements. Productivity growth is important because it is an important determinant of labor compensation.

Problems Applying Economic Concepts

1. Use the information below to plot the economy's production possibilities curve.

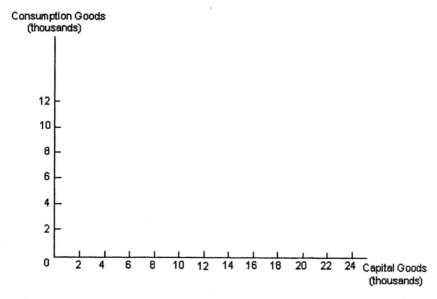

Consumption Goods	Capital Goods
10,000	0
8,000	3,000
6,000	5,000
4,000	6,500
2,000	7,500
0	8,000

2. Using the production possibilities curve you drew for question 1, show: a) a point at which the economy would produce if it were using the best technology, and b) a point at which the economy might produce if it was experiencing inefficiency.

3. Suppose that you have ten hours a day to devote to either studying or playing video games. Also assume that you can play two video games in one hour. For a fifteen-week semester, draw your PPC for studying and video games. Put "Video Games Played" on the vertical axis and "Hours Studying" on the horizontal axis. What is the opportunity cost of one hour of studying?

4. Using a production possibilities curve, show and explain why technological improvement is important for economic growth.

5. The economy of Galaopia produces two types of goods, consumption goods and capital goods. Economic studies show that at current production levels, the marginal benefit of an additional unit of consumption goods is $1,200 while the marginal cost is $1,000. Is Galaopia producing the best combination of goods and services?

6. Assume that the economy of Fruitland can produce two goods, apples (A) and bananas (B). The production of one apple requires one unit of labor (L) and two units of capital (K). One banana

requires two units of labor and one unit of capital. Fruitland is endowed with 600 units of labor and 600 units of capital.

a. Draw the production possibilities curve for Fruitland. Put apples (A) on the vertical axis. (HINT: For every 20 apples, determine how many bananas can be produced. How many apples and bananas can be produced if all resources are devoted to apples? If 20 less apples are produced, how many bananas can be produced? 40 less? Etc. Construct a table, and then graph it. It is helpful to include in your table the resources being devoted to the production of each good as well as the total amounts of labor and capital being used.)

b. Is the production of 200 apples and 200 bananas feasible? Efficient? What about 220 apples and 240 bananas?

c. What can be said about the utilization of resources when 100 apples and 100 bananas are produced?

d. What is the opportunity cost of increasing the production of apples from 280 to 300? From 0 to 20 units?

Problems Applying Economic Concepts Solutions

1.

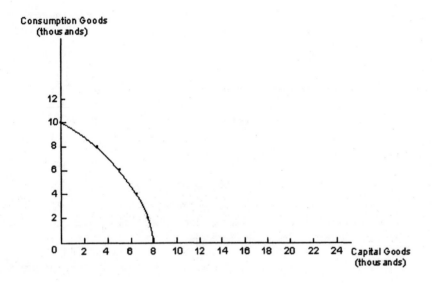

2.

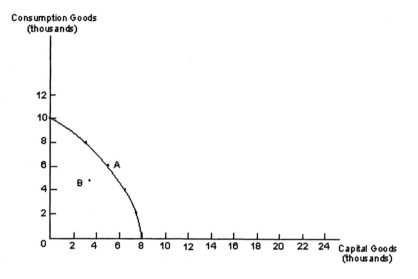

a. Point A shows a point at which the economy might produce if it were experiencing full employment and using the best technology. At this point (any point on the production possibilities curve) the maximum combination of goods and services is being produced.

b. Point B shows a point at which the economy might produce if it were inefficient. Any point inside the production possibilities curve is inefficient.

3. If you have ten hours a day to devote to video games or studying, that would be 70 hours per week. For 15 weeks, that would give a total of 1,050 hours. The PPC for video games and studying would look like this:

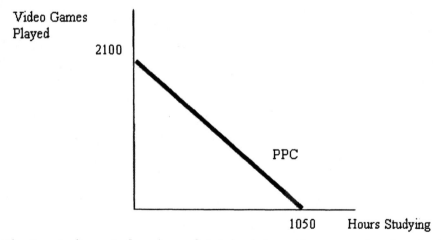

The opportunity cost of one hour of studying is two video games played, or the slope of the PPC.

4. Suppose the economy produces only two goods, food and clothing. The production possibilities curve PP shows the various efficient combinations of these two goods the economy can have. If technological

improvement occurs, the amount of output that can be obtained from the same quantity of resources will increase. This will shift the production possibilities curve from PP to P'P'. This shift shows that the same amount of resources can now produce more goods and services. Combinations of goods that were once unattainable are now available to the economy. This is the essence of economic growth.

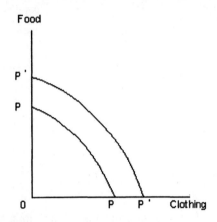

5. The best combination of goods and services occurs when the marginal benefit of an additional good is equal to its marginal cost. Here, the marginal benefit of an additional unit of consumption goods, $1,200, exceeds the marginal cost of the additional unit, $1,000. Galapia is not producing the best combination at this point. It should increase its production of consumption goods.

6. First, it is helpful to construct a table to keep track of the quantity of resources being used in the production of both goods. If 0 bananas are produced, there are 600 units of capital and 600 units of labor available for apple production. Since an apple requires two units of capital, then 600/2= 300 apples can be produced. Now suppose you want to produce 20 less apples. For 280 apples, 2 x 280 = 560 units of capital are required. This would leave 600 − 560 = 40 units of capital for banana production. Since each banana requires one unit of capital, with 40 units of capital then 40 bananas can be produced. Continue these calculations for 260 apples, 240 apples, etc. You can then derive the table presented below. Note that up to (200 apples, 200 bananas) capital is the economy's constraint. (It is all used up.) Since apples require more capital than bananas, when more apples are produced than bananas the economy runs out of capital. Once the economy produces more bananas than apples, it then runs out of labor. If 0 apples are produced, then 600 units of labor are available for bananas, from which 600/2 = 300 bananas can be produced.

   a.

You can then derive the following table:

APPLES	BANANAS	L(A)	L(B)	L	K(A)	K(B)	K
300	0	300	0	300	600	0	600
280	40	280	80	360	560	40	600
260	80	260	160	420	520	80	600
240	120	240	240	480	480	120	600
220	160	220	320	540	440	160	600
200	200	200	400	600	400	200	600
180	210	180	420	600	360	210	570
160	220	160	440	600	320	220	540
140	230	140	460	600	280	230	510
120	240	120	480	600	240	240	480
100	250	100	500	600	200	250	450
80	260	80	520	600	160	260	420
60	270	60	540	600	120	270	390
40	280	40	560	600	80	280	360
20	290	20	580	600	40	290	330
0	300	0	600	600	0	300	300

The production possibilities curve looks like this:

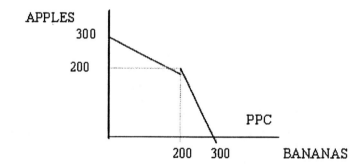

b. Yes, the production of 200 apples and 200 bananas is both feasible and efficient, since the point lies on the production possibilities curve. 220 apples and 240 bananas is unattainable (infeasible), since the point lies outside of the PPC. The economy does not have the resources or technology to produce this level of output.

c. When 100 of each are produced, the utilization of resources is inefficient, since the point lies inside the PPC. The economy can produce more of one or both goods without sacrificing the output of the other good.

d. From the table, the opportunity cost of increasing production of apples from 280 to 300 is the 40 bananas which must be given up (from 40 to 0). For 0 to 20 apples, the opportunity cost is the 10 bananas which must be given up (from 300 to 290).

Internet Exercises

1. To examine growth rates for different countries, go to the following website:
    http://www.cia.gov/cia/publications/factbook/rankorder/2003rank.html

2. To navigate the site, go to www.cia.gov (yes, the CIA), (1) then click on "World Factbook", (2) then click on "Guide to Rank Order Pages", (3) then click on "GDP – real growth rate." According to the table, what are the ten fastest-growing countries? What are the ten slowest-growing countries? Do you detect any patterns? How can the concepts outlined in the chapter help to explain these rankings?

Solutions

True False Questions

1. F, Efficiency improvements do result in economic growth, but they do not cause a shift in the production possibilities curve. Instead, with efficiency improvements, the economy moves from a point inside the production possibilities curve to a point on the curve.

2. T, Productivity growth limits how fast compensation per hour can grow. Compensation per hour typically grows at about the same rate as productivity. As labor productivity has fluctuated over the years, compensation has followed suit. Over the 1960-73 time period, productivity grew at about 3 percent annual. This matched the growth rate in labor compensation. When productivity fell over the 1973-90 time period, compensation fell as well.

3. T, Since 1950 productivity growth in Japan has been more than 2.5 times faster than in the U.S. Productivity growth in Europe has been more than 1.5 times faster than in the U.S. More than half of the convergence on productivity growth since 1973 has been the result of a more rapid growth of capital intensity. Europe and Japan have also received a greater boost from technical change, in particular efficiency improvements, than has the U.S.

4. F, Studies by Gwartney and others have found that there is a strong correlation between economic freedom and prosperity.

5. T, The quantity of resources is held constant along a given PPC, so an increase in resources means that now more combinations can be produced in the economy, so the PPC shifts outward.

Multiple Choice

1. C	10. D	19. C
2. B	11. D	20. D
3. D	12. D	21. C
4. B	13. A	22. B
5. D	14. A	23. D
6. C	15. C	24. A
7. D	16. B	25. B
8. A	17. B	26. D
9. C	18. D	

Fill-in Questions

1. Land; labor; Capital
2. production possibilities curve; best technology
3. opportunity cost
4. marginal benefit; marginal cost; marginal product
5. scarcity; Technological improvement; Efficiency improvement
6. capital intensity; technical change

An Introduction to Economic Systems and the Workings of the Price System

Objectives of the Chapter

After you have mastered this chapter you will understand:

1. The questions that an economic system must answer, the essential elements of a market economy, and the importance of coordination.

2. The meaning and importance of the division and specialization of labor and how specialization makes coordination more important.

3. The principle of comparative advantage means that specialization should occur where one has a lower opportunity cost.

4. That mutual benefits arise from specialization and trade when each party specializes according to comparative advantage.

5. The laws of demand and supply, the meaning of demand and supply prices, and how the laws of demand and supply interact to lead to market equilibrium.

6. The attributes of a price system--information, motivation, and rationing--that allow it to coordinate.

7. The relative success of a market economy's price system and a command economy's planning system in achieving coordination.

8. The experiences of transition economies in attaining the five important elements of a market economy.

Key Terms

relative price

comparative advantage

absolute advantage

quantity demanded

demand curve

demand price

law of demand

quantity supplied

supply curve

supply price

law of supply

excess demand

excess supply

equilibrium

scarcity

ration

economic profits

transition economies

True False Questions

For these statements, indicate whether they are true or false. Defend your answer.

1. In a command economy, economic decisions are made through the commands of millions of independent producers and consumers.

   TRUE or FALSE

2. Relative price measures what must be given up of one item in order to purchase a unit of another item.

   TRUE or FALSE

3. If relative price levels are unstable over time, decision-making costs can increase.

   TRUE or FALSE

4. If the price of apples increases from $0.25 to $0.50, then the relative price of apples in terms of bananas must have increased.

   TRUE or FALSE

5. A legal system that creates property rights and a system of contract enforcement is essential to a market economy.

   TRUE or FALSE

6. Adam Smith was the first to develop the principle of comparative advantage.

   TRUE or FALSE

7. Suppose that in Japan, the opportunity cost of a computer is 10 shirts, and in China, the opportunity cost of a computer is 15 shirts. Then China should specialize in computers, since they give up more shirts for each computer produced.

   TRUE or FALSE

8. A change in supply is represented as a movement along a given supply curve.

   TRUE or FALSE

9. Suppose the equilibrium price of CDs is $14.00 per CD. The current market price of CDs is $15.00 per CD. An excess demand for CDs will exist and price will tend to rise towards $15.00.

   TRUE or FALSE

10. Suppose that coffee and tea are substitutes. Then an increase in the price of coffee will lead to an increase in the price and quantity of tea.

    TRUE or FALSE

11. Because of government intervention, prices in a command economy tend to change more frequently than prices in a market economy.

    TRUE or FALSE

12. Most buyers and sellers in competitive markets are concerned that their decisions will affect the price of goods and services.

    TRUE or FALSE

13. Some analysts believe that too few bankruptcies have occurred in the transition economies.

    TRUE or FALSE

14. Command economies have generally performed as well as market economies.

    TRUE or FALSE

15. Of all of the transition economies in eastern Europe and the former Soviet Union, the Ukraine has been the most successful as measured along many dimensions of economic progress.

    TRUE or FALSE

Multiple Choice

Check yourself. Choose the best answer. Answers are found at the end of the chapter.

1. According to the authors, the essential features of a market system include:
   a. public ownership, involuntary market exchanges, and price stability.
   b. public ownership, voluntary market exchanges, and price instability.
   c. public ownership, voluntary market exchanges, and price stability.
   d. private ownership, voluntary market exchanges, and price stability.

2. One difference between a command economy and a market economy is that
   a. a market economy makes extensive use of central plans.
   b. economic decisions are decentralized in a command economy.
   c. prices are an important source of information in a market economy.
   d. a command economy generally leads to a more efficient allocation of resources.

3. The relative price of a good is:
   a. not a very accurate measure of how much must be given up in order to purchase an item.
   b. typically identical to the demand price of a good.
   c. a reliable measure of what must be given up to obtain a good.
   d. the price of a good in terms of dollars.

4. Suppose the price of a car is $20,000 and the price of a house is $120,000. Based on this information, we know that:
   a. the relative price of a car is 6 houses.
   b. the relative price of a car is 1/6 of a house.
   c. the relative rice of a car is $20,000.
   d. the relative price of cars has not been stable over time.

5. An economic system helps to determine:
   a. the level of employment in an economy.
   b. the quantities of goods and services produced in an economy.
   c. who receives the goods and services produced in an economy.
   d. all of these.

6. The division and specialization of labor is advantageous for an economy because:
   a. people are less skilled in production of a complete product.
   b. people have to spend more time shifting between tasks.
   c. property rights will become well established if there is specialization.
   d. they can lead to increased innovations.

7. According to the principle of comparative advantage, who should specialize in growing broccoli?
   a. Farmer Brown can grow either 100 bushels of broccoli or 200 bushels of onions on an acre of land.
   b. Farmer Jones can grow either 50 bushels of broccoli or 50 bushels of onions on an acre of land.
   c. Farmer Smith can grow either 200 bushels of broccoli or 300 bushels of onions on an acre of land.
   d. Farmer Doe can grow either 400 bushels of broccoli or 800 bushels of onions on an acre of land.

8. The principle of comparative advantage states that
   a. each party to a trade should specialize where it has the lowest opportunity cost.
   b. each party to a trade should specialize where it has the highest opportunity cost.
   c. each party to a trade should specialize where it has the lowest resource cost.
   d. specialization and trade are never beneficial.

9. In a competitive market, all buyers and sellers are:
   a. price setters.
   b. price takers.
   c. price givers.
   d. price insensitive.

10. Suppose the price of milk decreases from $2.89 per gallon to $2.78 per gallon. We would expect:
    a. an increase in the quantity of milk demanded.
    b. a decrease in the quantity of milk demanded.
    c. a decrease in the supply of milk.
    d. an increase in the demand for milk.

11. 10,000 hot fudge sundaes are currently on the market. $3.00 is the maximum price that anyone will pay for the 10,000th sundae. In this case, $3.00 is the:
    a. reserve price of hot fudge sundaes.
    b. demand price for hot fudge sundaes.
    c. supply price of hot fudge sundaes.
    d. stock price of hot fudge sundaes.

12. According to the law of supply:
    a. an increase in the price of a good will increase producer profits.
    b. an increase in the price of a good will decrease producer profits.
    c. an increase in the price of a good will increase quantity supplied.
    d. an increase in the price of a good will increase quantity demanded.

13. Suppose the market price of CDs is currently $17 per CD. The equilibrium price of CDs is $15 per CD. We know that:
    a. excess demand exists and there will be a tendency for price to rise.
    b. excess demand exists and there will be a tendency for price to fall.
    c. excess supply exists and there will be a tendency for price to rise.
    d. excess supply exists and there will be a tendency for price to fall.

14.

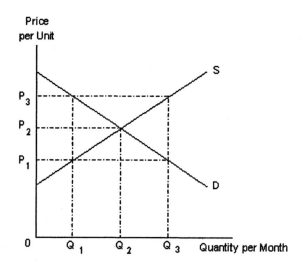

Refer to the diagram provided. The equilibrium price and quantity of CDs are:

a. P_1 and Q_2, respectively.
b. P_2 and Q_2, respectively.
c. P_2 and Q_3, respectively.
d. P_3 and Q_3, respectively.

15.

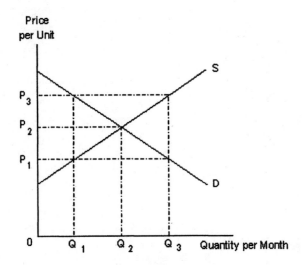

Refer to the diagram provided. If the price of CDs is currently P_3, we know that:

a. there is an excess demand of $Q_1 - Q_3$.
b. there is an excess demand of $Q_2 - Q_3$.
c. there is an excess supply of $Q_1 - Q_3$.
d. there is an excess supply of $Q_2 - Q_3$.

16.

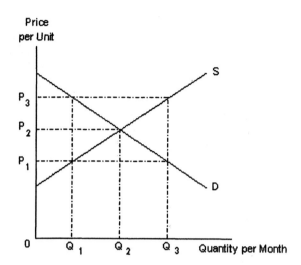

Refer to the diagram provided. If the price of CDs is currently P_1, we know that
a.   there will be a tendency for price to rise.
b.   there will be a tendency for price to fall.
c.   the market is in equilibrium.
d.   there is an excess supply of CDs.

17.

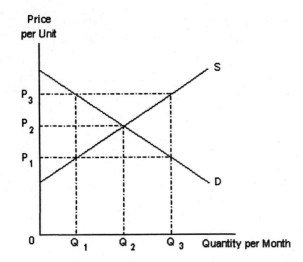

Refer to the diagram provided. If Q_3 units are offered on the market, the supply price is:

a. P_1
b. P_2
c. P_3
d. somewhere between P_1 and P_2.

18.

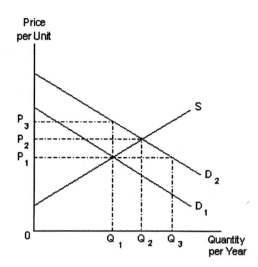

Refer to the diagram provided. Suppose demand increases from D_1 to D_2. Price and quantity will:

a. increase from P_1 and Q_1 to P_2 and Q_2, respectively.
b. increase from P_2 and Q_2 to P_3 and Q_3, respectively.
c. decrease from P_2 and Q_2 to P_1 and Q_1, respectively.
d. decrease from P_3 and Q_3 to P_2 and Q_2, respectively.

19.

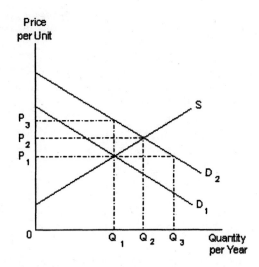

Refer to the diagram provided. If demand increases from D_1 to D_2, we know that initially:

a. an excess supply of Q_1 - Q_3 will exist.
b. an excess supply of Q_1 - Q_2 will exist.
c. an excess demand of Q_1 - Q_3 will exist.
d. an excess demand of Q_1 - Q_2 will exist.

20.

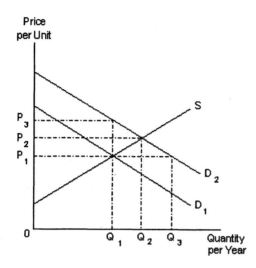

Refer to the diagram provided. Which of the following would cause demand to change from D_1 to D_2?

a. an increase in the price of the good.

b. a decrease in income.

c. an increase in income.

d. a news report saying that consumption of the good will increase the risk of heart attack by 3%.

21. Which of the following will lead to an increase in supply?

a. an increase in the price of the good

b. an increase in resource prices

c. an increase in consumer income

d. an increase in technology.

22. Prices in a command economy:

a. change in response to changes in market conditions.

b. are generally determined by the interaction of supply and demand.

c. generally change on an annual basis as government updates its plans for economic growth.

d. change infrequently because of both monetary and political costs.

23. Which of the following statements is correct?

a. Planners in a command economy are typically able to set prices that clear markets (quantity demanded = quantity supplied.)

b. If command economies are to move towards a market economy, there must be a legal system that generates a climate of trust.

c. It is relatively easy for planners in a command economy to change prices of goods and services.

d. Prices in former command economies were stable when price controls were removed.

24. In transition economies, inflation has occurred due to the fact that:
    a. prices were artificially high in the old command economies.
    b. prices were artificially low in the old command economies.
    c. prices accurately reflected scarcity in the old command economies.
    d. high and variable inflation existed in the old command economies.

25. In a voluntary exchange between two individuals:
    a. both parties expect to gain from the transaction.
    b. there will be both a winner and a loser.
    c. wealthy individuals gain at the expense of the less wealthy.
    d. the gains will exactly offset the losses.

26. Which of the following is NOT likely to be a problem with a command system of decision making?
    a. Collecting information.
    b. Providing incentives.
    c. Disseminating information.
    d. Increases in economic growth.

27. In a market economy, the scarcity of a good is measured by:
    a. the amount of time involved in producing it.
    b. the number of consumers or producers.
    c. its relative price.
    d. the excess supply relative to the excess demand.

28. The term quantity demanded refers to:
    a. the amount that buyers want to purchase at a given price.
    b. the amount that buyers can actually purchase at all prices.
    c. the amount that is available to be purchased.
    d. the positive relationship between price and demand.

29. The demand curve and the demand schedule describe the:
    a. quantity of the good demanded at each level of income.
    b. quantity of the good demanded at each price.
    c. relationship between equilibrium prices and quantities.
    d. relationship between quantities purchased and income.

30. The observation that people buy more at low prices than at high prices is known as the:
    a. the law of markets.
    b. the law of supply.
    c. the law of comparative advantage.
    d. the law of demand.

31. The market demand curve slopes downward because:
    a. quantities move in the same direction as prices.
    b. an increase in price leads to a decrease in demand.
    c. individual demand curves slope downward.
    d. it is independent of individual demand curves.

32. When a market is in equilibrium:
    a. all consumer needs have been satisfied.
    b. the good is no longer scarce.
    c. there is no longer any reason to ration the good.
    d. there is no reason for prices to change unless one of the factors held constant changes.

33. An excess supply:
    a. means that we have too much of the good to satisfy producers.
    b. occurs when there is too little supply.
    c. will persist only if prices are prevented from falling.
    d. will automatically trigger a decrease in supply.

34. Prices perform all of the following functions except:
    a. ensuring that income is equitably distributed.
    b. providing a coordinating mechanism between buyers and sellers.
    c. providing information concerning the relative scarcity of goods.
    d. influencing the incentives for buyers and sellers.

35. Which of the following is necessary for a market economy to function effectively?
    a. stable yet flexible prices
    b. property rights
    c. a legal system that generates a climate of trust
    d. all of the above

36. According to the discussion in the text,
    a. Russia has been the most successful country in the transition from central planning to capitalism.
    b. those countries that have been able to establish market incentives, such as Hungary and Slovenia, have been most successful in the transition to capitalism.
    c. the Ukraine has been the most successful country in eliminating corruption.
    d. Hungary and Slovenia will never be successful as capitalist countries.

Fill-in Questions

1. A market system relies heavily on prices in order to inform, ration, and motivate. In making decisions, it is most helpful to think of the price of a product as its _____ . This price measures what must be given up to purchase an item. In order for prices to inform, there must be reasonable price stability.

2. According to the principle of _____ , each party to a trade should specialize in the production of that good where it has a lower opportunity cost than the other party.

3. In a market system, price is determined by the interaction of demand and supply. A _____ shows the quantity of a product that will be demanded at various prices. A _____ shows the quantity of a product that will be supplied at various prices. The intersection of demand and supply determines the _____ price and quantity of a product.

4. Another way to look at demand and supply curves is in terms of demand price and supply price. _____ shows the price at which consumers will buy the exact quantity on the market. It is the maximum price that anyone will pay for the last unit. _____ is the price that is exactly sufficient to get producers to sell a specified quantity. It is the minimum acceptable price for the last unit, just covering its cost of production.

5. The difference between demand and quantity demanded and supply and quantity supplied should be noted. Demand shows the various quantities that will be demanded at various prices while _____ shows what will be demanded at one specific price. Supply shows the various quantities that will be supplied at various prices while _____ shows the quantity that will be supplied at one specific price.

6. Economic theory shows the demand curve to be negatively sloped. This negative slope reflects the _____ which states that as price increases quantity demanded will fall. The supply curve, on the other hand, is positively sloped. It reflects the _____ . According to the law of supply, as price increases, quantity supplied will increase.

7. If there is an increase in supply, there will initially be an _____ of the product. In this case, there will be a tendency for the price of the good to fall. On the other hand, when quantity demanded exceeds quantity supplied, _____ will exist. The price of the good will tend to rise.

8. It should be noted that _____ is different than excess demand. Scarcity is common to all societies. It means that in the aggregate wants exceed the ability to meet them. Excess demand is eliminated as price adjusts to _____ a limited supply of goods and services to people. Scarcity persists even in the face of price adjustments.

9. _____ initially occur if there is an increase in demand. In this case, the market price exceeds suppliers' opportunity cost of providing the good. This provides incentives for suppliers to increase production of the good.

10. In order to function effectively, market economic systems must have well-established _____ and the ability to enforce the validity of _____ In addition, stable yet flexible _____ are required to increase certainty in markets. Those countries that have been most successful in the transition from socialism to _____ , such as _____ and _____ , have been best able to adopt these reforms.

Problems Applying Economic Concepts

Use the information in the following table to answer questions 1 - 4.

Price per Unit	Quantity Demand Per Week	Quantity Supplied per Week
$1	12	2
2	10	4
3	8	6
4	6	8
5	4	10
6	3	12

1. Use the following diagram to plot the demand for and the supply of pizza.

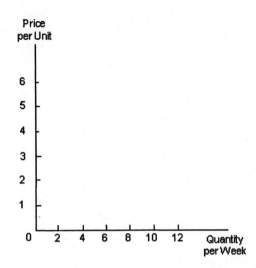

2. The equilibrium price is _____ per unit. The equilibrium quantity is _____ pizzas per week.

3. If the price is pizza is currently $5 per unit, an _____ of _____ pizzas exists and there will be a tendency for price to _____.

4. If 10 pizzas are currently on the market, the demand price of the tenth pizza will be $2 while the supply price the tenth pizza will be _____. Because the demand price is less than producers' supply price, there will be a tendency for quantity of pizzas on the market to _____.

5. Suppose you are given the following information on the market for chocolate milk in New York State per day:

   demand: $P = 180 - 2Q$
   supply: $P = 30 + Q$
   where quantity is measured in thousands of gallons and price in cents per gallon.

   a. Show the demand and supply curves on a graph. What is the equilibrium price and quantity? Show on your graph.

   b. Suppose that cows across New York State go on strike, so that the price of milk increases. The new supply curve becomes:

      supply': $P = 60 + Q$
      Does this represent an increase or decrease in supply? At the old price, is there a shortage or a surplus? Of how much?

   c. Find the new equilibrium price and quantity. Show graphically on your graph from a).

6. Assume that France and Britain each produce two goods, champagne and muffins. The amounts of champagne and muffins which can be produced in a day (if they devote all resources to that good) are shown by the following table:

	FRANCE	BRITAIN
CHAMPAGNE PER DAY	4,000	8,000
MUFFINS PER DAY	1,000	4,000

where champagne is measured in litre bottles and muffins are measured in units.

a. Which country is more efficient at producing champagne? Muffins? (Assume that each country has the same quantity of resources.)

b. For France, what is the opportunity cost of champagne? Of muffins?

c. For Britain, what is the opportunity cost of champagne? Of muffins?

d. Should France and Britain specialize and trade? (Assume that transportation costs are zero.) Why or why not? If so, in what direction should trade take place? Show and explain.

e. Assume that France starts off by producing 1000 bottles of champagne and 750 muffins. Britain produces 2000 bottles of champagne and 3000 muffins. Show that specialization and trade makes each country better off.

Problems Applying Economic Concepts Solutions

1.

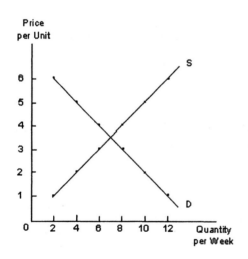

2. $3.50; 7

3. excess supply; 6; decrease

4. $2; $5; decrease

5.

a. For the demand curve, the vertical intercept = 180. The horizontal intercept occurs where P = 0. So

$0 = 180 - 2Q$ and $Q = 90$.

For the supply curve, the vertical intercept = 30. A second point for the supply curve is equilibrium, where it intersects the demand curve. To find equilibrium:

$$180 - 2Q = 30 + Q$$
$$150 = 3Q; \quad Q = 50$$
$$P = 180 - 2(50) = 80; \quad P = 30 + 50 = 80 \ \text{(check)}$$

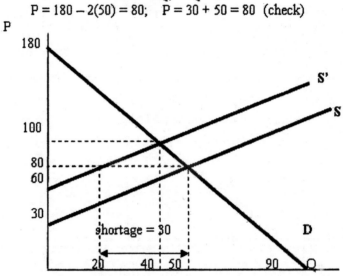

b. This would be a decrease in supply, which results in a shortage at the old price of 80. The quantity demanded is still 50, but the quantity supplied is now given by $80 = 60 + Q$, so the quantity supplied = 20. Shortage = 50 − 20 = 30.

c. $180 - 2Q = 60 + Q$, so $120 = 3Q$ and $Q = 40$; $P = 60 + 40 = 100 = 180 - 2(40)$

6.

a. Britain is more efficient at producing both champagne and muffins, since it can produce more of both goods with the same quantity of resources. Britain has an absolute advantage in the production of both goods.

Next, find the opportunity costs:

b. For France,

$$4000C = 1000M$$
$$1C = (1/4)M$$
$$1M = 4C$$

c. For Britain,

$$8000C = 4000M$$
$$1C = (1/2)M$$
$$1M = 2C$$

b. For France, the opportunity cost of a bottle of champagne is ¼ of a muffin, and the opportunity cost of a muffin is 4 bottles of champagne.

c. For Britain, the opportunity cost of a bottle of champagne is ½ of a muffin, and the opportunity cost of a muffin is 2 bottles of champagne.

d. Yes, France and Britain should specialize and trade. France has a comparative advantage in champagne since it has a lower opportunity cost in producing champagne ((1/4)M vs. (1/2)M). So France should specialize in champagne production. Britain has a comparative advantage in muffins since it has a lower opportunity cost in producing muffins (2C vs. 4C). So Britain should specialize in muffin production.

e. If Britain specialized in muffins, it could produce 4000 muffins. If it traded 1000 muffins for 3000 bottles of champagne from France, it would then have 3000 muffins left, along with 3000 bottles of champagne. This is more than the 3000 muffins and 2000 bottles of champagne that Britain could produce on its own. If France specializes in champagne, it can produce 4000 bottles. If it trades 3000 bottles to Britain for 1000 muffins, it then has 1000 bottles of champagne left along with 1000 muffins. This is more than the 1000 bottles and 750 muffins that France can produce on its own. So both countries are better off by trading 3000 bottles of French champagne for 1000 English muffins.

Internet Exercises

1. Go to Google.com and type in "gasoline prices". Read a recent article concerning changes in gasoline prices. According to the article, is the price change in gasoline due to a change in demand, a change in supply, or both? Use a supply and demand graph to illustrate the changes discussed in the article.

2. Go to the IMF website on country reports at: http://www.imf.org/external/country/index.htm. Examine the web pages for each of the four countries discussed in the text (Hungary, Slovenia, Russia, and the Ukraine). Do the trends mentioned in the text seem to be continuing? Which countries seem to be the most successful?

Solutions

True False Questions

1. F, False, in a command economy, economic decisions are made by government bureaucrats based on a central plan. In a market economy, economic decisions are made by millions of independent producers and consumers, and then the market coordinates these independent decisions to organize production, distribution and consumption.

2. T, Relative price measures the price of one good in terms of another. Relative price measures what must be given up to obtain a good.

3. T, Relative prices tell consumers what must be given up in order to purchase a good. If inflation changes over time and has different impacts on prices in various sectors of the economy, people can no longer rely on experience to judge exchange values. In order to know what must be given up to make a purchase, consumers would have to carefully study all prices. Performing this analysis for every purchase would be quite costly. Thus, if relative prices are to inform consumers, a relatively stable price level is necessary. Similarly, if prices are increasing at different rates, firms will find it more difficult to predict profits.

4. F, False, since we have no information about the price of bananas. If the price of bananas is constant, or increasing less than 100%, then the relative

price of apples will be increasing. But if the price of bananas is increasing by more than 100%, then the relative price of apples will be falling.

5. T, True, property rights and a system of contracts encourage economic transactions by making the terms of the agreements less ambiguous and more binding, so that more transactions are likely to take place. As more transactions take place, a price system can develop.

6. F, False, in his famous butcher, brewer, and baker example, Adam Smith was utilizing the idea of absolute advantage, that each should specialize where resource costs are lowest. It was David Ricardo, writing over 40 years later than Smith, who developed that idea of comparative advantage, that countries should specialize where opportunity costs are lowest.

7. F, False, according to the principle of comparative advantage, Japan should specialize in computers, since it has a lower opportunity cost. Japan gives up less shirts (10) to produce a computer compared to China (15), so Japan should specialize in computers. Similarly, China should specialize in shirts.

8. F, False, a change in quantity supplied is represented as a movement along a given supply curve that results from a change

in the price of that good. A change in supply is a shift of the entire supply curve that results from a change in one of the variables being held constant along a given supply curve, such as resource prices, technology or business expectations.

9. F, At the current market price, quantity supplied will exceed quantity demanded. An excess supply of CDs exists. Only if quantity demanded exceeds quantity supplied will there be an excess demand for CDs. This would occur if market price was below the equilibrium price.

10. T, True, if coffee and tea are substitutes, then an increase in the price of coffee will lead to an increase in the demand for tea, as consumers substitute tea for the relatively more expensive coffee. An increase in the demand for tea leads to an increase in the price and quantity of tea.

11. F, It is very costly for government bureaucracies to change prices. First, it is not feasible to change the price of some products without changing the price of others. In addition, price changes can be traced to a particular government agency. This agency will be blamed for any price increases. This can be costly politically. Thus, prices in a command economy do not change very often.

12. F, Buyers and sellers in competitive markets are small relative to the entire market. A buyer is not concerned that price will increase if they buy more computer paper. Likewise, if only one seller in the market increases production, there will be little or no impact on price. In this case, buyers and sellers are said to be price takers. They take the market price as given to them, and then adjust the quantity they want to buy or sell based on that market price.

13. T, Bankruptcy provides a way for economic resources to be moved from owners who are not using them profitably to other owners who may do a better job. It has been argued that governments in the transition economies have "bought political peace" by allowing inefficient firms to continue to operate. This prevents the economy from moving to a higher level of production.

14. F, Market economies have consistently outperformed command economies by every measure of success. The comparison of East Germany with West Germany is extremely revealing. Before World War II, East Germany probably had a slight edge over West Germany. However, within a few years after the war, the West German economy was providing its citizens with a higher standard of living. By 1990 West Germany per capita income was almost four times as large as in East Germany. A comparison of North and South Korea shows almost the same disparity.

15. F, False, as the text points out, the Ukraine has been among the lowest of the transition economies among many dimensions of social and economic progress. The two economies that have been the most successful are Hungary and Slovenia.

Multiple Choice

1. D	13. D	25. A
2. C	14. B	26. D
3. C	15. C	27. C
4. B	16. A	28. A
5. D	17. C	29. B
6. D	18. A	30. D
7. B	19. C	31. C
8. A	20. C	32. D
9. B	21. D	33. C
10. A	22. D	34. A
11. B	23. B	35. D
12. C	24. B	36. B

Fill-in Questions

1. relative price
2. comparative advantage
3. demand curve; supply curve; equilibrium
4. Demand price; Supply price
5. quantity demanded; quantity supplied
6. law of demand; law of supply
7. excess supply; excess demand

8. scarcity; ration
9. Economic profits
10. property rights; contracts.; prices; capitalism; Hungary; Slovenia

Competitive Markets and Government Policy: Agriculture

Objectives of the Chapter

After you have mastered this chapter you will understand:

1. The distinction between a change in demand and a change in quantity demanded, and the factors that cause the demand curve to change.

2. The distinction between a change in supply and a change in quantity supplied, and the factors that cause the supply curve to change.

3. The effect of changes in demand and supply on equilibrium price and quantity exchanged.

4. The avowed purpose and the actual effects of U.S. agriculture programs.

5. The types of risks faced by farmers and some ways to deal with these risks.

6. The effects of and distinctions among price support programs, target price programs, and output constraint programs.

7. The concept of price gouging, and that allegations of price gouging often arise after natural disasters such as Hurricanes Katrina and Rita.

8. The concepts of economic and political rent-seeking and their importance.

Key Terms

decrease in demand

substitute

complement

competitive markets

increase in demand

normal good

inferior good

increase in supply

decrease in supply

economic profit

price floor

target price

deficiency payments

price gouging

political rent seeking

economic rent seeking

True False Questions

For these statements, indicate whether they are true or false. Defend your answer.

1. In the United States, direct payments from farm programs tend to be focused on the poorest farm families.

    TRUE or FALSE

2. If Spam is an inferior good, then an increase in consumer income will lead to a leftward shift of the demand curve for Spam.

    TRUE or FALSE

3. Suppose government sets a price floor on bread which causes an excess supply to emerge. The excess supply will be a temporary phenomenon because producers will lower the price of bread. This will lead to an increase in quantity demanded and a decrease in quantity supplied, thereby eliminating the excess supply.

    TRUE or FALSE

4. Suppose there is an advance in technology that affects the production of milk. We would expect the equilibrium price and quantity of milk to fall.

    TRUE or FALSE

5. A reduction in demand causes a reduction in supply.

    TRUE or FALSE

6. In competitive markets such as agriculture, the easy entry and exit of firms in the long run forces economic profits to zero.

    TRUE or FALSE

7. Long-term changes in agriculture have caused the income of farmers to increase.

    TRUE or FALSE

8. Suppose that an increase in the price of orange juice causes an increase in the price of apple juice. We may conclude that orange juice and apple juice are complements.

   TRUE or FALSE

9. Price gouging always occurs after natural disasters as firms take advantage of the shortages of goods caused by the disaster by raising their prices.

   TRUE or FALSE

10. In the US agricultural industry, lobbying for price supports and tariffs provide examples of political rent seeking.

    TRUE or FALSE

Multiple Choice

Check yourself. Choose the best answer. Answers are found at the end of the chapter.

1. In the US economy, approximately what percentage of the labor force is devoted to agricultural production?
   a. 50%
   b. 20%
   c. 10%
   d. 2%

2. Suppose consumers hear a report that increasing the consumption of fruit can significantly decrease the risk of heart disease. This would likely cause:
   a. a decrease in the demand for fruit.
   b. an increase in the demand for fruit.
   c. a decrease in the quantity of fruit demanded.
   d. an increase in the quantity of fruit demanded.

3. Which of the following could increase the quantity of milk supplied?
   a. an advance in technology.
   b. a decrease in wages paid to workers in the milk industry.
   c. a decrease in the price of corn.
   d. an increase in the price of milk.

4. According to the law of supply, at a higher price producers will plan to produce and sell:
   a. more.
   b. less.
   c. the same.
   d. it could be either more or less, depending on the profits they will receive.

5. Suppose shrimp is a normal good. As consumer income rises, the demand for shrimp:
   a. increases.
   b. decreases.
   c. does not change.
   d. will first increase, and then fall.

6. Suppose the price of Coca-Cola decreases. There will be:
   a. an increase in the demand for Coca-Cola.
   b. an increase in the demand for Pepsi.
   c. a decrease in the demand for Coca-Cola.
   d. a decrease in the demand for Pepsi.

7. Suppose macaroni and cheese are complements. The price of cheese rises. This will result in:
   a. a decrease in the demand for macaroni.
   b. a decrease in the demand for cheese.
   c. an increase in the equilibrium price of macaroni.
   d. an increase in the equilibrium quantity of macaroni.

8. Suppose tractors and gasoline are complements. A decrease in the price of gasoline will cause:
   a. the equilibrium price and quantity of tractors to increase.
   b. the equilibrium price and quantity of tractors to decrease.
   c. the equilibrium price of tractors to increase and the equilibrium quantity of tractors to decrease.
   d. the equilibrium price of tractors to decrease and the equilibrium quantity of tractors to increase.

9. A decrease in the price of soft drinks would cause:
   a. a movement down the demand curve for soft drinks.
   b. a movement up the demand curve for soft drinks.
   c. a rightward shift of the demand curve for soft drinks.
   d. a leftward shift of the demand curve for soft drinks.

10. Suppose Brooke's income decreases by 5 percent. She reports that she plans to buy more bologna. For Brooke, bologna is:
    a. a normal good.
    b. an inferior good.
    c. a rational good.
    d. an irrational go

11. Which of the following is correct for a normal good?
    a. You want to buy more if the price of the good falls.
    b. You want to buy more if the price of the good rises.
    c. You want to buy more if your income increases.
    d. You want to buy more if your income decreases.

12. An increase in supply is illustrated as:
    a. a rightward shift of the supply curve.
    b. a leftward shift of the supply curve.
    c. a movement up a given supply curve.
    d. a movement down a given supply curve.

13. Which of the following might lead to a decrease in the quantity demanded of corn?
    a. an increase in the price of corn
    b. a decrease in the price of corn
    c. an increase in the price of rice
    d. an increase in income if corn is an inferior good

14. A main ingredient of cola drinks is corn syrup. If the price of corn syrup increases, what is the likely effect on the market for cola drinks?
    a. an increase in demand for cola drinks
    b. an increase in the supply of cola drinks
    c. a decrease in the supply of cola drinks
    d. a decrease in the demand for cola drinks

15. Suppose that both the demand and supply for gasoline decrease at the same time. We know for certain that
    a. the price of gasoline will increase.
    b. the demand for automobile travel will increase.
    c. the demand for oil and tires will increase.
    d. the quantity of gasoline exchanged in the market will decrease.

16. Suppose there is a decrease in the cost of producing asparagus. At the original market price there will now be:
    a. an excess supply of asparagus and equilibrium price will tend to increase.
    b. an excess supply of asparagus and equilibrium price will tend to decrease.
    c. an excess demand for asparagus and equilibrium price will tend to increase.
    d. an excess demand for asparagus and equilibrium price will tend to decrease.

17. If there is an excess demand in the wheat market, it means that:
    a. there is pressure for price to fall.
    b. there is pressure for price to rise.
    c. the market is in equilibrium.
    d. sellers really want to sell wheat.

18. A condition of excess supply means that:
    a. quantity supplied exceeds quantity demanded at a given price.
    b. quantity demanded exceeds quantity supplied at a given price.
    c. sellers could raise the price of the product and still make sales.
    d. the market is in equilibrium.

19.

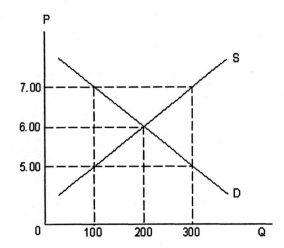

The equilibrium price and quantity exchanged are:
a. $7 and 300, respectively.
b. $6 and 200, respectively.
c. $5 and 100, respectively.
d. $5 and 200, respectively.

20.

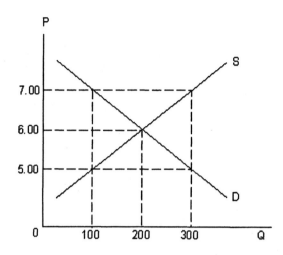

If the current market price is $7, there is:
a. equilibrium in the market.
b. an excess demand of 200 units.
c. an excess supply of 100 units.
d. an excess supply of 200 units.

21. Suppose the current market price of milk is $2.00 per gallon. The equilibrium price of milk is $1.50 per gallon. We would expect:
a. equilibrium price to remain unchanged.
b. equilibrium price could either rise or fall, depending on the action of buyers.
c. market price to rise.
d. market price to fall.

22. Ice cream is a normal good. An increase in consumer income will cause:
a. both the equilibrium price and quantity of ice cream exchanged to rise.
b. both the equilibrium price and quantity of ice cream exchanged to fall.
c. the equilibrium price of ice cream to rise and the equilibrium quantity of ice cream to fall.
d. the equilibrium price of ice cream to fall and the equilibrium quantity of ice cream to rise.

23. Rent seeking occurs when special interest groups like farmers:
a. maximize their property values rather than there self interests.
b. seek political favors that are beneficial to them.
c. seek to maximize their returns by forming cooperatives.
d. buy land and rent it out at the highest possible price.

24. Logrolling refers to:
    a. the exchange of votes between legislators on specific issues favorable to their constituents.
    b. the tendency of voters to free ride on the payment for public goods.
    c. government spending programs that favor the timber industry.
    d. the power of special interest groups to influence their members.

25. The equilibrium price:
    a. provides no incentives to buyers.
    b. is the same as the equitable price.
    c. is the price at which the plans of buyers and sellers are identical.
    d. is the price at which buyers can purchase all they want.

26. Suppose the costs of production increase at the same time that income is declining. What will be the net effect of these two changes on equilibrium price and quantity?
    a. The change in quantity will be indeterminate but the price will increase.
    b. The change in both price and quantity will be indeterminate.
    c. Price will increase but quantity will decline.
    d. The change in price will be indeterminate but quantity will decrease.

27. Price floors on agricultural products generally create political pressures for the government to:
    a. produce the good itself.
    b. reduce the demand for the good by consumers.
    c. buy and store some of the output or use output constraints.
    d. use rationing to control the shortages.

28. Among the predictable results of U.S. agricultural policies have been:
    a. acceleration of farm land into suburban housing communities.
    b. higher food prices for consumers.
    c. shortages of a large number of agricultural commodities.
    d. a decline in the ability of U.S. farmers to produce food.

29. Suppose perfect weather conditions results in a bumper crop of corn. We would expect:
    a. both the equilibrium price and quantity of corn exchanged to rise.
    b. both the equilibrium price and quantity of corn exchanged to fall.
    c. the equilibrium price of corn to rise and the equilibrium quantity of corn to fall.
    d. the equilibrium price of corn to fall and the equilibrium quantity of corn to rise.

30. Suppose corn and wheat are substitutes. If there is a decrease in the price of corn, we would expect:
    a. both the equilibrium price and quantity of wheat exchanged to rise.
    b. both the equilibrium price and quantity of wheat exchanged to fall.
    c. the equilibrium price of wheat to rise and the equilibrium quantity of wheat to fall.
    d. the equilibrium price of wheat to fall and the equilibrium quantity of wheat to rise.

31. Suppose that demand for wheat increases while the supply of wheat decreases. Which of the following will happen in the wheat market?
    a. A decrease in quantity. The change in price of wheat depends on the sizes of the two changes.
    b. An increase in quantity. The change in price of wheat depends on the sizes of the two changes.
    c. A decrease in price. The change in amount of wheat exchanged depends on the sizes of the two changes.
    d. An increase in price. The change in amount of wheat exchanged depends on the sizes of the two changes.

32. Suppose there is a decrease in the wage paid to workers who harvest grapes. There will be:
    a. a decrease in both the equilibrium price and quantity of grapes exchanged.
    b. an increase in both the equilibrium price and quantity of grapes exchanged.
    c. an increase in the equilibrium price of grapes and a decrease in the equilibrium quantity of grapes exchanged.
    d. a decrease in the equilibrium price of grapes and an increase in the equilibrium quantity of grapes exchanged.

33. Government programs affecting agriculture often receive support because:
    a. farmers face individual risk.
    b. farmers face market risk.
    c. farmers face intense competition.
    d. all of these.

34.

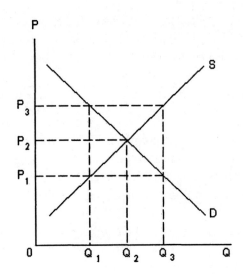

Suppose government sets a target price of P_3. The market price of milk will be:

a. P_1.
b. P_2.
c. P_3.
d. somewhere between P_1 and P_2.

35.

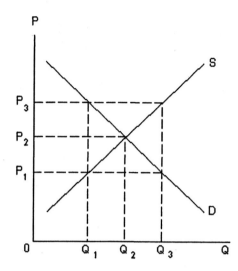

Suppose government sets a target price of P_3. Government will pay farmers a deficiency payment per unit of milk equal to:

a. $P_2 - P_1$.
b. $P_3 - P_2$.
c. $P_3 - P_1$.
d. P_3.

36.

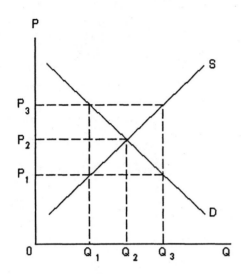

If government sets a price floor of P_3, there will be:
a.   an excess demand for milk.
b.   an excess supply of milk.
c.   a shortage of milk.
d.   equilibrium in the market for milk.

37. Government output restrictions are designed to:
a.   increase the supply of agricultural products.
b.   decrease the supply of agricultural products.
c.   increase the demand for agricultural products.
d.   decrease the demand for agricultural products.

38. Farm income might fall because:
a.   of rapid increases in output per farmer.
b.   of slow increases in the demand for agricultural products.
c.   the demand for farm products is not very sensitive to changes in price.
d.   all of these.

39. Suppose economic profits exist in the market for limes. Over the long run, we would expect:
a.   the economic profits to fall as new firms enter the market.
b.   the economic profits to rise as new firms enter the market.
c.   the economic profits to be unaffected by entry into the market.
d.   the price of limes to rise.

40. When economic profits are zero,
    a. firms will exit the industry because they are not covering their costs.
    b. firms will enter the industry.
    c. the costs of production will decline.
    d. firms are just covering all of their costs, including their opportunity costs.

41. Which of the following is an example of economic rent seeking in the agricultural industry?
    a. New York dairy farmers lobby their state legislature for price controls.
    b. Louisiana sugar cane growers ask the federal government for quotas on imported sugar.
    c. Wisconsin cheese producers develop new milking technology that enables them to lower the costs of production.
    d. all of the above.

42. Price gouging occurred when
    a. gasoline stations increased gasoline prices due to shortages caused by the start of the Iraqi war.
    b. the price of plywood increased after Hurricanes Katrina and Rita.
    c. the price of holiday ornaments was higher before Christmas than after Christmas.
    d. none of the above.

Fill-in Questions

1. According to the _____ , at a higher price consumers would plan to purchase less of a good during a particular time period. According to the _____ , producers of a good would plan to sell more milk per week at a higher price. Within the context of demand and supply, an economy is said to be in

2. _____ when the quantity that people plan to buy at the going price is the same as the quantity that producers plan to sell at that price.

3. If factors other than the price of a good change there will be a change in demand. A change in demand is illustrated as a shift of the demand curve. A(n) _____ is illustrated as a rightward shift of the demand curve. It means that people are willing to buy more of the good at each possible price.

4. If an increase in the price of one good causes demand for another good to increase, the goods are said to be _____ . Substitutes are goods that satisfy similar needs or desires. A(n) _____ is a good which is used with another good. If the price of one complement increases, there will be a _____ for the other complement.

5. If an increase in income causes an increase in demand, the good is said to be a(n) _____ . If, on the other hand, an increase in income causes demand to fall, the good is said to be a(n) _____ .

6. In addition to demand, supply can also change. If producers plan to sell more of their product at each possible price, a(n) _____ has occurred, and the supply curve will shift rightward. On the other hand, if producers plan to sell less of their product at each possible price, a(n) _____ has occurred, and the supply curve will shift leftward.

7. Government has enacted several different farm policies. If a _____ is set, products cannot be sold at a price below this minimum. Price floors create an excess supply of farm products.

8. Under the _____ program, government guarantees farmers a certain price for their product. If market price is less than the guaranteed price, government will pay the producer the difference in the form of a subsidy. This subsidy is also known as a deficiency payment.

9. When unscrupulous suppliers take advantage of natural disasters to unduly raise prices to earn exorbitant profits, then _____ results. However, media claims of such practices are often exaggerated, as an increase in price is the rational response to a decrease in market _____ .

10. Policies like farm programs can result from _____ whereby certain groups or individuals attempt to gain an economic advantage through government activity. Often, farmers hope that government programs will help to maintain _____ . Without government programs, these profits would be competed away as new producers entered the market. _____ can also result in producers earning economic profits. In this case, however, new entrants are able to come into the market. Economic profits are not protected by government actions, and are eventually competed away.

Problems Applying Economic Concepts

1.

    a. Use the following information to graph the demand and supply curves for bagels.

Price	Quantity demanded (dozens per week)	Quantity supplied (dozens per week)
$6.00	2,500	5,500
5.00	3,000	5,000
4.00	3,500	4,500
3.00	4,000	4,000
2.00	4,500	3,500
1.00	5,000	3,000

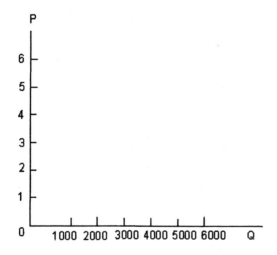

The equilibrium price of bagels is _____ and the equilibrium quantity exchanged is _____.

b. Suppose there is a decrease in the price of flour. As a result of this change, the quantity of bagels producers are willing to supply is given below. Draw in the new supply curve for bagels. There has been a(n) _____ in the supply of bagels. At the original equilibrium price, there is a(n) _____ of bagels. As a result of the change in supply, equilibrium price will _____ and equilibrium quantity exchanged will _____.

Price	Quantity supplied (dozens per week)
$6.00	6,000
5.00	5,500
4.00	5,000
3.00	4,500
2.00	4,000
1.00	3,500

2. The following is data for the corn market:

Corn Market	2001	2004
Price per bushel	$9	$12
Quantity (millions of bushels)	100	150

a. Show the changes in demand and/or supply that could have caused the price-quantity combinations above.

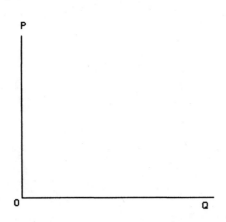

b. Discuss (verbally and graphically) how the changes you described above will affect the market for wheat.

3. The diagram below shows the demand for and supply of sugar. Use this diagram to answer the following questions.

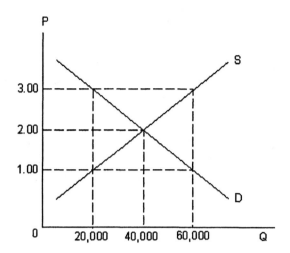

a. In this diagram, the equilibrium price and quantity of sugar exchanged are _____ and _____, respectively.

b. Suppose the government sets a price floor of $3 per pound. Quantity demanded will be _____ pounds while quantity supplied will be _____ pounds. The price floor will cause a(n) _____ of sugar.

c. Suppose that instead of a price floor, the government sets a target price of $3 per bushel. The market price for sugar will be _____ per pound and the government will pay farmers a subsidy of _____ per pound.

4. Suppose that the market for wheat can be described by the following equations:

$$\text{demand: } P = 12 - 0.5\,Q$$
$$\text{supply: } \quad P = 2 + 0.5\,Q$$

where P is the price per ton and Q is the number of tons produced.

5. Assume that the wheat market is unregulated. What is the equilibrium price and quantity? Show graphically.

a. If the government imposes a price floor of $10 per ton, what is the quantity supplied? What is the quantity demanded? What is the cost to taxpayers of the surplus wheat that must be purchased? Show on your graph from a).

b. Assume instead that the government imposes a target price of $10 per ton in the wheat market. What price is received by wheat farmers? What price is paid by consumers? What is the cost of the program to taxpayers? Show on your graph from a).

Problems Applying Economic Concepts Solutions

1. a.

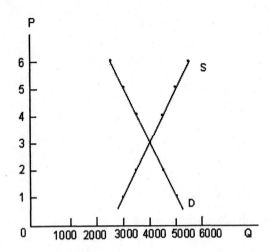

$3.00, 4,000

b.

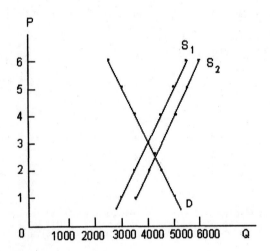

increase, excess supply

decrease, increase

2. a.

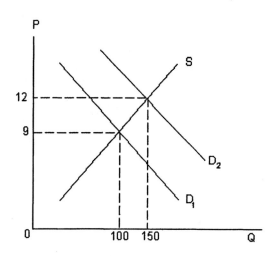

As the table shows, the price of corn increases from $9 to $12 per bushel _____ while the quantity of corn exchanged in the market increases from 100 _____ million to 150 million bushels. As the diagram above illustrates, this type _____ of change in price and quantity exchanged was caused by a increase in _____ the demand for corn from D_1 to D_2.

b. Wheat and corn are substitutes. Thus, an increase in the price of corn will _____ cause an increase in the demand for wheat. As the demand for wheat _____ increases, the equilibrium price and quantity of wheat exchanged will _____ increase as well. These changes are illustrated in the graph below.

3 a. $2.00, 40,000

b. 20,000, 60,000, excess supply

c. $1.00, $2.00

4. a. To find equilibrium, set the supply and demand equations equal to each other:

$$12 - 0.5 Q = 2 + 0.5 Q$$

$$-Q = -10$$

$$Q^* = 10$$

$$P^* = 12 - 0.5(10) = 7$$

$$P^* = 2 + 0.5(10) = 7 \ \text{(check)}$$

graphically,

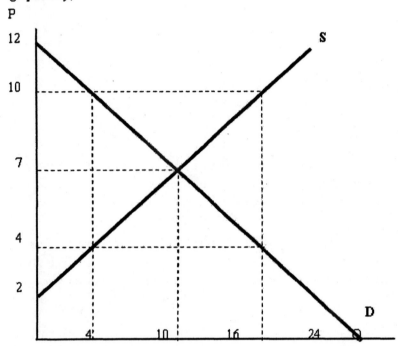

b. If the government imposes a price floor of $10, the quantity demanded becomes

$$10 = 12 - 0.5 Q$$

$$-2 = -0.5 Q$$

$$Q_d = 4$$

The quantity supplied is now

$$10 = 2 + 0.5Q$$

$$8 = 0.5Q$$

$$Q_s = 16$$

Since the quantity supplied is 16 tons but the quantity demanded is 4 tons, there is now a surplus of $(16 - 4 =) 12$ tons. The cost to taxpayers of purchasing this surplus is $10 \times 12 = \$120$.

c. With a target price of $10, farmers receive $10 for each ton of wheat produced. Farmers will still produce 16 tons of wheat, the same as under a price floor In order to convince consumers to purchase 16 tons of wheat, the market price must be

$$P = 12 - 0.5\,(16) = \$4.$$

Since consumers are paying $4 per ton but producers are receiving $10 per ton, the government must make a deficiency payment of (10 − 4 =) $6 per ton. Since farmers produce 16 tons, the total cost to taxpayers is $6 x 16 = $96.

Internet Exercises

1. Visit the American Farm Bureau newsroom at the following web site: www.fb.org/newsroom After browsing through several of the recent articles listed in the newsroom, what are the current issues that are on the minds of the lobbyists for the American Farm Bureau?

2. The United States Department of Agricultural, which sponsors many of the farm support programs, can be found at the following website: www.usda.gov. From the home page, click on "marketing and trade". Then click on "marketing assistance" and "price support" to learn about the various types of farm assistance programs. What types of crops and programs are listed? Does US agricultural policy appear consistent? Is it simple or complex?

Solutions

True False Questions

1. F, False, as the text points out, agricultural subsidies are not focused on poor farm families. The largest benefits go disproportionately to the largest and wealthiest farmers.

2. T, True, if Spam is an inferior good, then demand moves in the opposite direction of changes in income. If income increases, then the demand for Spam will decline (shift to the left), as consumers can afford to purchase more real ham and less artificial ham spread.

3. F, Generally, the market would correct a situation of excess supply in the manner described. In this instance, however, government prevents the price from falling below the price floor. Hence, the excess supply is permanent.

4. F, The advance in technology will cause an increase in the supply of milk. As supply increases, the equilibrium price of milk will fall, but the equilibrium quantity of milk will increase.

5. F, False, a reduction in supply implies a leftward shift of the supply curve. If there is a shift to the left of the demand curve (a reduction in demand), then the price will decrease, leading to a decline in the quantity supplied. This is represented as a movement along the given supply curve, not as a leftward shift of the entire supply curve.

6. T, True, if there are economic profits, then firms will enter the industry, and if there are economic losses, some firms will exit the industry. This will continue until economic profits are zero, or there is no longer any incentive for firms to enter or exit the industry. The existence of zero economic profits means that firms are just covering all of the costs of production, including the opportunity costs of resources devoted to the firm.

7. T, Technical change and opportunities in the non-agriculture sector have led to relatively large decreases in the supply of workers in the agriculture industry. This has put upward pressure on wages paid to workers in this industry. At the same time, the technical change and falling prices for agriculture products has led to a decrease in the demand for workers in the agriculture industry. This has put downward pressure on wages paid to workers in this industry. The decrease in supply has been relatively larger than the decrease in demand. This means that the increase in farm wages has more than offset the decrease in farm wages. On balance, then, the wages (income) of farmers has increased.

8. F, Complements are goods that are used or consumed jointly. If the price of one good increases, people will decrease their demand for its complement, and its price will fall. The increase in the price of orange juice caused the demand for apple juice to increase. This, in turn, increased the price of apple juice. In this case, orange juice and apple juice are substitutes, not complements.

9. F, False, when shortages occur in markets, the rational, natural response is to raise prices so that the market can effectively ration the shortage. While natural disasters often provoke cries of price gouging by the media, the resulting increase in prices is exactly how markets are supposed to respond to shortages that are created by such negative climatic events.

10. T, True, agricultural interest groups often lobby the federal government for price supports, protectionism, and subsidies. They achieve profit advantages through their ties to government rather than through economic rent-seeking such as reducing costs or promoting demand. Since the benefits of agricultural policies are concentrated among a few with political connections, while the costs of such policies are spread among millions of agricultural consumers, the government tends to favor the interests of farmers over farm product consumers.

Multiple Choice

1. D	15. D	29. D
2. B	16. B	30. B
3. D	17. B	31. D
4. A	18. A	32. D
5. A	19. B	33. D
6. D	20. D	34. A
7. A	21. D	35. C
8. A	22. A	36. B
9. A	23. B	37. B
10. B	24. A	38. D
11. C	25. C	39. A
12. A	26. D	40. D
13. A	27. C	41. D
14. C	28. B	42. D

Fill-in Questions

1. law of demand; law of supply
2. Equilibrium
3. increase in demand
4. substitutes; complement; decrease in demand
5. normal good; inferior good
6. increase in supply; decrease in supply
7. price floor
8. target price
9. price gouging; supply
10. political rent seeking; economic profits; Economic rent seeking

CHAPTER 4

Efficiency in Resource Allocation: How Much Do We Have? How Much Do We Want?

Objectives of the Chapter

After you have mastered this chapter you will understand:

1. How the competitive market works to achieve efficiency.

2. That efficiency is a desirable goal, but achieving efficiency in itself will have other costs such as reduced equity.

3. Why monopoly power leads to inefficiencies.

4. How external benefits and external costs create problems for the market system.

5. Why public goods create free-rider problems.

6. The impact of government intervention in the case of rent controls, agricultural price supports, and medical care subsidization.

7. The deadweight loss associated with taxation.

8. The tradeoffs that exist between efficiency and equity.

Key Terms

efficiency in resource allocation (allocative efficiency).

static allocative efficiency

dynamic allocative efficiency

marginal benefit curve (demand curve)

marginal cost curve (supply curve)

total benefit

total cost

total net benefit

market failure

profit

total revenue

efficiency loss

deadweight loss

external benefits

marginal external benefits

marginal social benefits

public goods

external costs

marginal external costs

marginal social costs

moral hazard

adverse selection

excess burden of taxation (deadweight loss)

capital gains

True False Questions

For these statements, indicate whether they are true or false. Defend your answer.

1. Static allocative efficiency assures that the right amount of goods and services are produced in the long run.

    TRUE or FALSE

2. A competitive market at equilibrium exhibits static allocative efficiency.

    TRUE or FALSE

3. If the market fails, government should undertake some type of corrective policy.

    TRUE or FALSE

4. The existence of monopoly will cause the market to overproduce.

    TRUE or FALSE

5. Rent controls are an excellent example of market failure.

    TRUE or FALSE

6. Adverse selection occurs when self-selection results in an insurance pool of predominately high-risk individuals.

    TRUE or FALSE

7. An effective price floor, such as an agricultural price support, will cause a surplus to exist in the market, so inefficiency results.

TRUE or FALSE

Multiple Choice

Choose the best answer. Check yourself. Answers are found at the end of the chapter.

1. Which of the following is most likely to achieve static allocative efficiency?
   a. a monopoly
   b. a market dominated by external costs.
   c. a competitive market.
   d. a market for a public good.

2. The demand curve can also be thought of as a
   a. Marginal cost curve.
   b. Marginal benefit curve.
   c. Marginal external benefit curve.
   d. Production possibilities curve.

3. Which of the following would be an example of market failure?
   a. the absence of inflation.
   b. the Environmental Protection Agency (EPA) over-regulates air pollution.
   c. the production of paper results in pollution.
   d. the economy grows at an annual rate of 4 percent.

4. The rule for efficient resource allocation is that one should
   a. maximize the difference between total benefits and total costs.
   b. equate marginal benefits with marginal costs.
   c. continue an activity as long as the additional benefits exceed the additional costs.
   d. all of the above.

5. Which of the following is the condition for efficiency?
   a. MSB = MSC.
   b. MSB = MPC.
   c. MPB = MSC.
   d. MPB = MPC.

6. An external cost occurs when
   a. MPB > MSB.
   b. MSB = MSC.
   c. MPC > MSC
   d. MSC > MPC

7. Adverse selection occurs when
   a. someone with a rental car drives more recklessly than with her own car.
   b. a person with health insurance visits the doctor more often.
   c. owner-occupied houses are maintained better than rental houses.
   d. risky consumers are the ones more likely to purchase a product.

8. Roger purchases home insurance. He now leaves his doors unlocked because if there is a theft, his insurance will cover any loss. This is an example of:
   a. efficiency.
   b. cost-minimization.
   c. insurance failure.
   d. moral hazard.

9. The laws of supply and demand reflect:
   a. marginal costs and marginal external benefits.
   b. marginal costs and marginal benefits.
   c. marginal external costs and marginal external benefits.
   d. marginal external costs and marginal benefits.

10. Suppose MSB is greater than MPB. In this case we would expect the market to:
    a. produce the efficient quantity.
    b. produce less than the efficient quantity.
    c. produce greater than the efficient quantity.
    d. cause government failure.

11. Hannah has spent the summer landscaping her yard. Her neighbors benefit by having their property values increase slightly. This is an example of:
    a. a marginal private cost.
    b. a marginal external cost.
    c. a marginal private benefit.
    d. a marginal external benefit.

12.

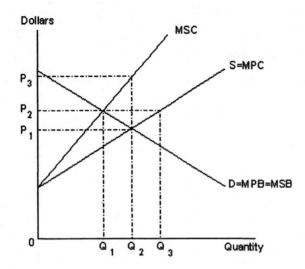

At the efficient level of production, price and quantity are:

a. P_1 and Q_1, respectively.
b. P_2 and Q_2, respectively.
c. P_1 and Q_2, respectively.
d. P_2 and Q_1, respectively.

13.

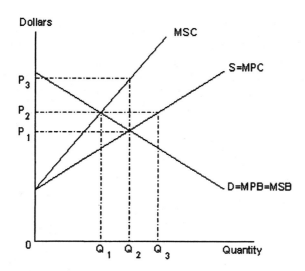

In the absence of government intervention, the market will tend to:

a.   produce quantity Q_1 and charge a price of P_1. (note − this was incorrectly given as the answer)
b.   produce quantity Q_2 and charge a price of P_2.
c.   produce quantity Q_2 and charge a price of P_1.
d.   produce quantity Q_1 and charge a price of P_2.

14.

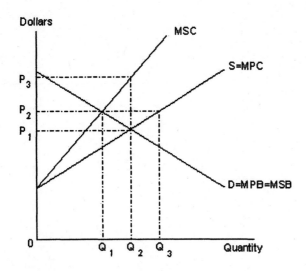

We know that in this market:
a. marginal external costs exist.
b. marginal external benefits exist.
c. marginal social cost and marginal private cost are equal.
d. marginal private cost exceeds marginal social cost.

15.

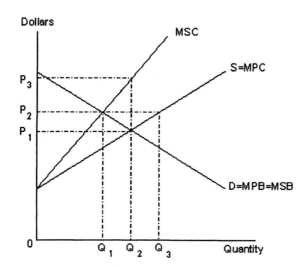

If quantity Q_1 is produced, the marginal social cost is:
a. P_1.
b. P_2.
c. P_3.
d. somewhere between P_1 and P_2.

16. One-of-a-Kind, Inc. is a monopoly. Relative to a competitive market, One-of-a-Kind will:
a. produce the efficient quantity.
b. produce less than the efficient quantity.
c. produce more than the efficient quantity.
d. produce at a point where marginal social cost exceeds marginal social benefit.

17. Market failure can be caused by:
a. external costs.
b. monopoly.
c. public goods.
d. all of the above.

18. Government intervention in the economy is justified:
a. whenever there is market failure.
b. when the distribution of income is unfair.
c. when there is market failure and the intervention will make society better off.
d. when the intervention will result in increases in inflation.

19. Suppose government price supports on cheese result in a surplus of cheese in the market. This is an example of:
    a. government failure.
    b. market failure.
    c. a marginal external cost.
    d. allocative inefficiency.

20. Suppose the government in Gotham City imposes rent controls. If there are no externalities in the market for rental units, this government action will cause:
    a. output to be equal to the efficient quantity.
    b. output to be less than the efficient quantity.
    c. output to be greater than the efficient quantity.
    d. MSC to be greater than MSB.

21. Suppose the equilibrium price of cheese is $2.95 per pound. Government imposes a price support of $3.50 per pound. As a result of this government action:
    a. the MSC of cheese will exceed the MSB of cheese.
    b. the MSB of cheese will exceed the MSC of cheese.
    c. the output of cheese will be the efficient quantity.
    d. the output of cheese will be less than the efficient quantity.

22.

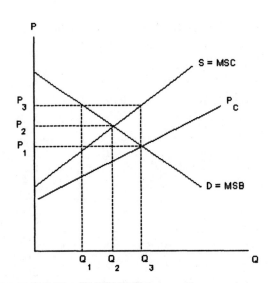

The efficient quantity of health care is:
    a. Q_1.
    b. Q_2.
    c. Q_3.
    d. somewhere between Q_1 and Q_2.

23.

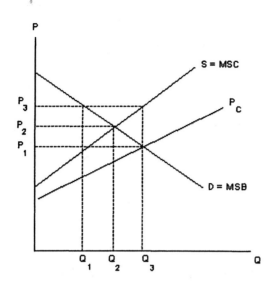

If government subsidizes health care, the quantity consumed will be:

a. Q_1.
b. Q_2.
c. Q_3.
d. somewhere between Q_1 and Q_2.

24.

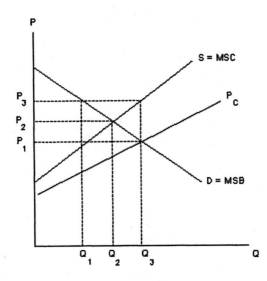

Suppose government subsidizes health care. If consumption is Q_3, the price paid by consumers will be:
a. somewhere between P_3 and P_2.
b. P_3.
c. P_2.
d. P_1.

25. Suppose government provides an excessive amount of pollution control. We know that:
a. the marginal external costs of pollution will disappear.
b. the marginal external benefits of pollution control will disappear.
c. the marginal social benefit of pollution control will exceed the marginal social cost of pollution control.
d. the marginal social cost of pollution control will exceed the marginal social benefit of pollution control.

26. Which of the following is most likely to involve a marginal external cost?
a. Using a personal computer.
b. Consuming a beer and pizza.
c. Smoking in a crowded room.
d. Being immunized against measles.

27. While it is true that a market system generally yields an efficient outcome, it is also true that it:
a. is likely to generate an unequal distribution of income.
b. contains no incentives to bring about this result.
c. is a highly centralized and controlled economic system.
d. places too little importance on private decision making.

28. One of the characteristics of a public good is that the:
    a. costs are imposed on individual consumers.
    b. all benefits accrue only to those who pay for the good.
    c. payers cannot be excluded.
    d. Non-payers cannot be excluded.

29. The free rider problem of public goods refers to:
    a. the ease with which payers can be excluded from the benefits of a good.
    b. the relatively low cost associated with consuming goods produced by public utilities.
    c. the difficulty of excluding non-payers.
    d. the benefits that accrue to government as a result of intervening in the market.

30. Taxes can impose costs on the economy because they can:
    a. increase output.
    b. decrease output.
    c. increase saving.
    d. increase investment.

31. A capital gains tax refers to:
    a. a tax on the difference between the market value of an asset and the purchase price.
    b. capital which the government gains through a tax.
    c. gains within the financial capital market.
    d. increase in taxes which occurs because of increases in the capital stock.

32. The height of the demand curve indicates the:
    a. minimum amount that buyers are willing to pay for the last unit purchased.
    b. maximum amount that buyers are willing to pay for the last unit purchased.
    c. difference between the value that consumers place on the good and the amount that sellers must receive.
    d. difference between the value that consumers and producers place on the last unit purchased and sold.

33. Taxes on earnings of individuals and corporations are referred to as:
    a. value added taxes.
    b. income taxes.
    c. benefit taxes.
    d. sin taxes.

Fill-in Questions

1. If the market system fails to generate economic efficiency, _____ occurs. Efficiency means achieving an objective at the lowest possible cost. When resources allocated to an activity produce the highest value to all of the individuals affected by that activity, _____ is achieved. An economy

that allocates resources efficiently in the short run is said to achieve _____ . Dynamic efficiency refers to achieving allocative efficiency in the long _____ .

2. There are several reasons markets may fail to achieve economic efficiency. _____ will not be produced efficiently by the market. Because no one can be excluded from consuming public goods once they are provided, the market will not provide them. In this case, we say there is a _____ . In other markets there may be *external costs* so that unregulated firms will supply too much of the good since they don't have to bear the full costs of their actions.

3. Insurance may make individuals less careful about their choices. This is referred to as _____ . When moral hazard exists, there will be _____ . The pool of policy holders will be dominated by high-risk individuals. This may cause insurance companies to not insure certain groups. _____ refers to the possibility that the cost of taxation may exceed the amount of the taxes collected.

Problems Applying Economic Concepts

1. Suppose we are interested in the market for magazines. Using the diagram below, show and explain that the market outcome will result in economic efficiency. (Be certain to correctly label the diagram.)

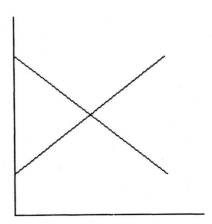

2. Suppose that each summer Open Skies Theater puts on a series of outdoor concerts. The noise and traffic congestion associated with the concert impose a cost on residents who live around the amphitheater. Use the following diagram to show:

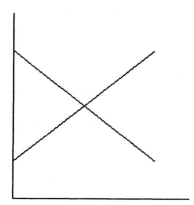

a. The impact of the externality on the graph.

b. The efficient quantity of concerts.

c. The quantity of concerts that will be played in the absence of government intervention in the market.

d. Does the market over- or under-produce (relative to the efficient amount) in the presence of the externality?

3. Suppose we are interested in the market for rental units in College Town, U.S.A. Suppose local officials believe rent is too high and impose a rent ceiling less than the equilibrium level of rent. Use the diagram to show:

a. The initial equilibrium price and quantity of rental units.

b. The efficient quantity of rental units.

c. A possible rent ceiling that local officials might impose.

d. The quantity supplied with the rent ceiling.

e. Why the market is no longer efficient when the price ceiling is imposed.

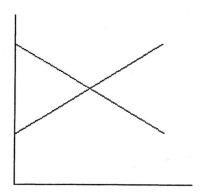

4. Suppose that we are interested in the market for medical care in Zircon. In order to ensure that health care is available to all citizens, the national government decides to subsidize health care. Use the following diagram to show:

   a. The impact of subsidizing health care on the graph.

   b. The efficient quantity of health care.

   c. The quantity of health care that will be provided in the absence of the government subsidy.

   d. Does the market over- or under-produce in the presence of the subsidy?

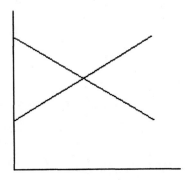

5. Assume that the market for unskilled fast food workers is given by the following equations:

   demand: $P = 8.00 - .002Q$
   supply: $P = 2.00 + .001Q$

   where P is the price of labor (wage rate per hour) and Q is the quantity of labor hours per day.

5. Find the equilibrium price and quantity. Show graphically.

6. Suppose that the government imposes a minimum wage of $6.00 per hour. What is the result in the market? Is there a shortage or surplus? Of how much?

Problems Applying Economic Concepts Solutions

1.

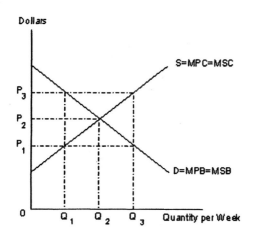

The demand curve shows the maximum amount that someone is willing to pay for each unit. Thus, it has been labeled marginal private benefit (MPB). It has also been labeled marginal social benefit (MSB) due to the assumption of no externalities. The supply curve shows the price the supplier must have to cover costs. It has been labeled marginal private cost (MPC). Because of the assumption of no externalities, it has also been labeled marginal social cost (MSC). The market will tend to move to equilibrium where Q_2 units are produced and a price of P_2 is charged. Note that at this quantity MPB = MPC and MSB = MSC.

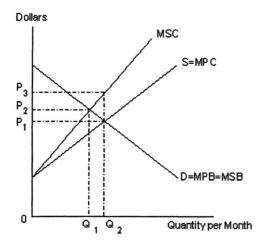

1. The existence of the marginal external cost (MEC) will cause a divergence between marginal social and marginal private cost. Thus, the MSC curve (which includes both marginal private and marginal external costs) is drawn above the MPC curve.

    a. The efficient quantity of concerts occurs at the point where MSB = MSC. Thus, quantity Q_1 is the efficient quantity.

b. The market will produce at the point where MPB = MPC. Thus, the quantity provided by the market will be quantity Q_2. Note that at this quantity MSC (given by P_3) exceeds MSB (given by P_1).

c. The existence of the MEC causes the market to produce a quantity greater than the efficient quantity.

2.

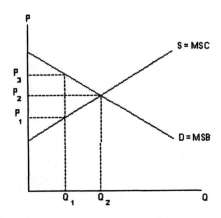

a. P_2 and Q_2 are the equilibrium price and quantity, respectively.

b. Q_2. At this quantity, MSB = MSC.

c. P_1.

d. Q_1.

e. Q_1 is not efficient. At this quantity, MSC = P_1 while MSB = P_3. Thus, MSB is greater than MSC at Q_1.

3.

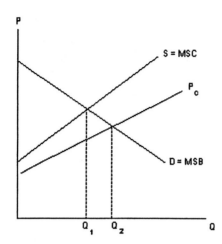

a. The subsidy causes a divergence between the cost of health care and what consumers are willing to pay for health care. MSC represents the marginal social cost of producing an additional unit of health care. PC represents the amount consumers pay for an additional unit of health care. The vertical distance between MSC and PC represents the subsidy paid by the government.

b. The efficient quantity is the quantity at which MSC = MSB. Q_1 is the efficient quantity.

c. Consumers buy up to the point at which the price they pay for the last unit of health care is equal to the benefit they receive for the last unit of health care. In the absence of the subsidy, this occurs at Q_1.

d. With the subsidy, consumers' cost of health care is PC. Consumers now consume Q_2 of health care. The subsidy results in overproduction.

4.

a. To find equilibrium, set the equations equal to each other and solve for Q:

$$8.00 - .002Q = 2.00 + .001Q \qquad P^* = 8.00 - .002(2000) = 4.00$$
$$-.003Q = -6.00 \qquad\qquad P^* = 2.00 + .001(2000) = 4.00$$
$$Q^* = 2000 \qquad\qquad\qquad\text{(check)}$$

P

8.00

surplus = 3000

6.00 .... S

4.00 ....

2.00

D

1000   2000   4000   Q

Internet Exercises

1. Go to the American Petroleum Institute's web site, www.api.org. From the home page, click on "industry statistics", and then click on "Monthly Statistical Report News Release." After reading the report, do the energy markets appear to be efficient? Why or why not? What factors contribute to changes in supply or demand? How does the market respond?

2. Go to the EPA web page at www.epa.gov. What are some examples of external costs that are discussed on the home page?

Solutions

True False Questions

1. F, False, static allocative efficiency means the marginal benefits are equal to marginal costs in the short run, not the long run. Dynamic allocative efficiency deals with the long run.

2. T, In equilibrium, where the supply and demand curves intersect, the marginal benefit is equal to the marginal cost, and static allocative efficiency is achieved.

3. F, Market failure does not necessarily imply that government should intervene in the market. We need to also ask if the economy will be made better off as a result of the government action. It is possible that a government policy might put the economy in a worse position than would market failure. Thus, both questions, (that of market failure and that of improvement as a result of government action) should be answered before government policies are enacted.

4. F, A monopoly will cause inefficiencies, but these inefficiencies are not due to overproduction. Compared to a competitive market, a market characterized by monopoly will restrict output. Thus, the problem is one of underproduction.

5. F, Rent controls are an example of government, not market failure. Rent controls cause too few rental units to be provided relative to the allocatively efficient quantity. As a result of the government action, production occurs at a point where MSB > MSC.

6. T, Moral hazard flourishes when individual policyholders can shift the increased costs of their actions onto others who are insured. When this occurs healthy individuals will avoid buying insurance with the result that the insurance pool will be dominated by relatively high-risk individuals.

7. T, Since an effective price floor is a price above the equilibrium price, a surplus results in a market. Due to the higher prices, suppliers will produce an inefficiently large quantity of output.

Multiple Choice

1. C
2. B
3. C
4. D
5. A
6. D
7. D
8. D
9. B
10. B
11. D
12. D
13. A
14. A
15. B
16. B
17. D
18. C
19. A
20. B
21. B
22. B
23. C
24. D
25. D
26. C
27. A
28. D
29. C
30. B
31. A
32. B
33. B

Fill-in Questions

1. market failure; allocative efficiency; static allocative efficiency; run

2. Public goods; free rider problem

3. moral hazard; adverse selection; Deadweight loss of taxation

Market Power: Does It Help or Hurt the Economy?

Objectives of the Chapter

After you have mastered this chapter you will understand:

1. The relationship between the demand curve and the marginal revenue curve.

2. The basic monopoly analysis, including a basic comparison of monopoly equilibrium with competitive equilibrium.

3. Elementary conclusions about competition and economic efficiency.

4. The sources and extent of monopoly in the U.S. economy.

5. The conditions under which a cartel might succeed.

6. OPEC's history in light of cartel analysis.

7. The relationship between market power and economic growth.

Key Terms

market power

monopoly

oligopoly

cartel

marginal revenue

marginal principle

competitive industry

efficient output

barrier to entry

natural monopoly

product differentiation

patents

tariffs

quotas

True False Questions

For these statements, indicate whether they are true or false. Defend your answer.

1. If the demand curve is downward-sloping, than price is greater than marginal revenue.

    TRUE or FALSE

2. In order to maximize profit, a monopolist should always produce where marginal revenue exceeds marginal cost. This way it will always be adding more to revenue than to cost, and profit will increase.

    TRUE or FALSE

3. Unlike a competitive industry, a monopolist does not produce the efficient output.

    TRUE or FALSE

4. The fewer the number of firms, the greater the likelihood that cheating will occur in a cartel.

    TRUE or FALSE

5. The pharmaceutical industry often reaps tremendous profits at the expense of individuals whose very lives depend on their product. Because of this "profiting from disease," government should work to lower prices (and hence profits) in this industry.

    TRUE or FALSE

6. The primary explanation for the record increase in oil prices in the fall of 2005 was the power of the OPEC oil cartel.

    TRUE or FALSE

Multiple Choice

Check yourself. Choose the best answer. Answers are found at end of chapter.

1. Market power exists when:
    a. economic profits exist for long periods without attracting new competitors.
    b. economic profits become negative for only short periods of time.
    c. economic profits exist for only a short period because competitors are attracted to the market.
    d. accounting profits exist for long periods without attracting new competitors.

2. If price is greater than marginal revenue, then
   a. the demand curve is horizontal.
   b. the demand curve is downward-sloping
   c. the firm is operating in a competitive market.
   d. the firm must be a monopoly.

3. Monopoly firms typically:
   a. produce a good for which there are many close substitutes.
   b. are one of many firms in an industry.
   c. are price searchers.
   d. have horizontal demand curves.

4. Suppose a monopolist currently sells its output for $15 per unit. We know that:
   a. marginal revenue is less than $15.
   b. marginal revenue is greater than $15.
   c. marginal revenue is equal to $15.
   d. marginal revenue could either be equal to or greater than $15.

5. Use the following information to answer question 4. The marginal revenue associated with increasing production from 1 to 2 units is:

Price	Quantity
$10	1
8	2
6	3

   a. $10.
   b. $8.
   c. $6.
   d. $2.

6. In order to sell additional units of output, a monopolist:
   a. must increase price.
   b. must decrease price.
   c. can leave price unchanged.
   d. must increase its advertising budget.

7.

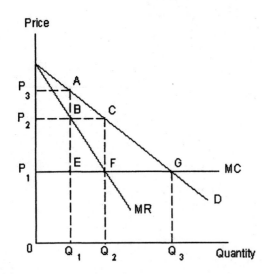

For a monopoly, the profit maximizing price and level of output are:

a. P_3 and Q_1, respectively.

b. P_1 and Q_1, respectively.

c. P_2 and Q_2, respectively.

d. P_1 and Q_3, respectively.

8.

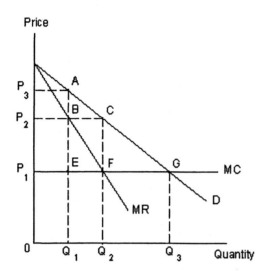

The profits earned by a monopolist would be represented by area:

a. P_1P_2BE.

b. P_1P_2CF.

c. EACF.

d. EBCF.

9.

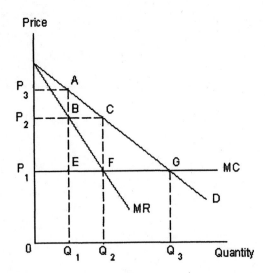

The price and output that would emerge if the industry were competitive are:
a. P_3 and Q_1, respectively.
b. P_1 and Q_1, respectively.
c. P_2 and Q_2, respectively.
d. P_1 and Q_3, respectively.

10. The monopolist's marginal revenue falls as output is increased because:
a. the monopolist must lower price in order sell additional units of output.
b. the monopolist's profits fall as output is increased.
c. the monopolist's costs increase as output increases.
d. the monopolist will face increasing government regulation as it tries to expand in a particular market.

11. The marginal principle states that a monopoly maximizes profit by producing at the point where:
a. marginal revenue and marginal cost are equal.
b. marginal revenue is greater than marginal cost.
c. marginal cost is greater than marginal revenue.
d. price and marginal revenue are equal.

12. Merrimax Industries is currently producing at a point where marginal revenue is $35 and marginal cost is $33. This firm should:
a. leave the level of production unchanged.
b. decrease the level of production.
c. increase the level of production.
d. temporarily increase the level of production in order increase its profits. Once it stops earning a loss, return production to its original level.

13. Which of the following statements is correct?
    a. In order to maximize profits, a monopolist should produce at the point where marginal revenue exceeds marginal cost.
    b. Compared to a competitive industry, a monopolist tends to produce a lower level of output.
    c. Compared to a competitive industry, a monopolist tends to charge a lower price.
    d. Monopolists produce efficiently because at the level of output produced by the firm, marginal benefit exceeds marginal cost.

14. Which of the following would most likely have market power?
    a. Industry A composed of a large number of firms that produce a similar product.
    b. Industry B composed of a small number of firms who face a large number of foreign competitors.
    c. Industry C composed of a small number of firms who control access to vital raw materials.
    d. Industry D composed of a small number of firms with relatively low barriers to entry.

15. Suppose that Soley Ours Incorporated is a monopoly. The firm is currently producing at a point where marginal revenue is $8 and marginal cost is $10. We know that the firm:
    a. is currently maximizing profits.
    b. should not change output.
    c. should increase output.
    d. should decrease output.

16. When a monopolist maximizes its profits:
    a. the marginal benefit to consumers is less than the monopolist's marginal revenue.
    b. the marginal benefit to consumers is greater than the monopolist's marginal revenue.
    c. the marginal benefit to consumers coincides with the monopolist's marginal revenue.
    d. the monopolist's marginal cost is greater than the marginal benefit to consumers.

17. Barriers to entry include:
    a. technical conditions.
    b. cost advantages.
    c. product differentiation.
    d. all of these.

18. If a competitive industry were to form a cartel:
    a. both price and output would increase.
    b. price would increase and output would fall.
    c. both price and output would fall.
    d. price would fall and output would increase.

19. A cartel would be most successful if:
    a. there were a small number of firms producing a similar product.
    b. there were a large number of firms producing a dissimilar product.
    c. there were relatively low barriers to entry into the industry.
    d. there were a small number of dissimilar firms in the industry.

20. Problems occurred with the OPEC cartel because:
    a. the supply of oil did not change much as price changed.
    b. the demand for oil did not change much as price changed.
    c. suppliers increased output as the price of oil increased.
    d. the price of oil increased as output rose.

21. Members of a cartel may be tempted to cheat by:
    a. lowering price and output in order to increase profits.
    b. raising price and output in order to increase profits.
    c. lowering price and increasing output in order to increase profits.
    d. raising price and lowering output in order to increase profits.

22. Competition in the U.S. economy has increased over time. This increased competitiveness can be partially attributed to all of the following except:
    a. decreased foreign competition.
    b. a decrease in government regulations in the economy.
    c. the information revolution.
    d. increased foreign competition.

23. An attempt to gain an economic advantage through government action is known as:
    a. political rent seeking.
    b. economic rent seeking.
    c. patronism.
    d. bureaucratic rent seeking.

24. All of the following exemplify government activity which promotes market power except:
    a. requiring plumbers to be licensed.
    b. imposing import restrictions.
    c. strictly enforcing antitrust legislation.
    d. imposing licensing requirements on interior decorators.

25. The economic profits earned by a monopoly may be beneficial to the economy if such profits:
    a. encourage political rent seeking.
    b. encourage economic rent seeking.
    c. encourage government regulation of industry.
    d. encourage the break-up of monopolies by the government.

26. Some analysts argue that Microsoft is NOT a monopolist that harmed consumers because:
    a. Microsoft sacrificed huge rewards for uncertain future benefits.
    b. compared to a Mac system, DOS was relatively expensive operating system.
    c. early in the computing era, users gained large advantages by using a Mac system.
    d. Windows could not run DOS programs.

27. Marginal revenue measures:
    a. the change in total revenue associated with a one unit change in the output sold.
    b. the change in price associated with increasing sales by one unit.
    c. the benefit accruing to the consumer from purchasing one more unit.
    d. the profits that a monopolist makes because of its market power.

28. Because of a monopolists ability to restrict output and charge a higher price than would a competitive firm:
    a. the value of one more unit is greater than the demand price.
    b. the demand price is less than the supply price.
    c. the value of one more unit exceeds the value of the units of other goods given up to produce it.
    d. the value of one more unit is less than the value of the units of other goods given up to produce it.

29. A natural monopoly is said to occur when:
    a. through government regulation only one firm occurs through the natural workings of the market process.
    b. demand and cost conditions are such that only one firm can survive in the industry.
    c. the state of nature dictates that only one firm can legitimately produce the good.
    d. there is a limited amount of some valuable natural resource.

30. All of the following are general principles that guide public policy toward market power except one. Which one?
    a. Government can limit mergers of firms that produce similar products.
    b. Government can prohibit price fixing.
    c. Government can prohibit the monopolist from making a profit.
    d. Government should avoid becoming a source of market power.

31. Which of the following would not be considered a problem encountered by the OPEC cartel?
    a. There are 11 members of OPEC and 6 to 10 oil producing nonmembers and OPEC accounts for less than one-half of world production.
    b. Demand and supply conditions are different when consumers and producers have time to adjust to any price change by OPEC.
    c. The members of OPEC have different goals.
    d. OPEC countries have the same goals and objectives.

Fill-in Questions

1. _____ exists whenever a firm or a small group of firms can affect the price received for their product and new firms do not enter the industry in response to profit. Market power exists if there is a single producer of a good with no close substitutes. This situation describes a _____ . An _____ exists when there is an industry with only a few sellers of a good. A(n) _____ is an organized group of producers who manage their output and pricing as if they were a monopoly.

When market power exists, there is a tendency for price to be above the competitive price and output to be below the competitive level of output.

2. _____ measures the change in total revenue associated with a one unit change in output sold. It is the private benefit to the monopolist of selling an additional unit of output. In order to maximize profits, a monopolist must follow the _____ _____ . According to this principle, the firm will produce where marginal revenue and marginal cost are equal.

3. When the monopolist maximizes profit, it does not produce the _____ . The efficient output is not produced because when the monopolist maximizes profits by following the marginal principle, there is a wedge between the demand price (the value consumers place on the good) and the supply price (marginal cost). The efficient output occurs when the demand price and the supply price are equal.

4. There are several sources of market power. For example, _____ may prevent new firms from entering an industry with the same cost conditions as existing firms. Another source of market power could be cost conditions which are such that only one firm can survive in an industry. These cost conditions create a _____ .

Problems Applying Economic Concepts

1. Fill in the blanks in the following table. Assume that it costs Show Me DVDs $7.00 to produce each CD.

Quantity	Price	Total Revenue	Total Cost	Profit
0	$50	$_____	$_____	$_____
1	45	_____	_____	_____
2	40	_____	_____	_____
3	35	_____	_____	_____
4	30	_____	_____	_____

2. Fill in the blanks in the following table. Assume that it costs Fright Incorporated $5 to produce each monster mask for Halloween.

Quantity	Price	Total Revenue	Total Cost	Marginal Revenue	Marginal Cost	Profit
0	$20	$_____	$_____		$_____	$_____
1	19	_____	_____	$_____	_____	_____
2	18	_____	_____	_____	_____	_____
3	17	_____	_____	_____	_____	_____
4	16	_____	_____	_____	_____	_____
5	15	_____	_____	_____	_____	_____
6	14	_____	_____	_____	_____	_____
7	13	_____	_____	_____	_____	_____
8	12	_____	_____	_____	_____	_____
9	11	_____	_____	_____	_____	_____
10	10	_____	_____	_____	_____	_____
11	9	_____	_____	_____	_____	_____

a. According to the information given in question 2, a monopolist wishing to maximize profit will produce _____ units of output and charge a price of _____ per unit. Marginal revenue will be _____, and marginal cost will be _____.

b. At this profit maximizing level of output, the monopolist's total revenue will be _____ and its total cost will be _____.

c. The monopolist will earn profit of _____.

3. Use the following diagram to answer parts a - c.

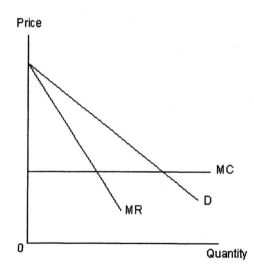

a. Label the total revenue earned by the monopolist at the profit maximizing level of output.

b. Label the total cost incurred by the monopolist at the profit maximizing level of output.

c. Label the profit earned by the monopolist at the profit maximizing level of output.

4. Assume that Motorola is able to gain a patent on the production of videophones, so it has a monopoly over the videophone market for the next seventeen years. Assume that the demand for videophones is given by

$$\text{demand: } P = 60 - 2Q.$$

a. Find the MR curve for videophones. What is the appropriate equation?

b. Assume that average costs are constant at $40 (so MC = $40). What is the profit-maximizing level of output? What price will be charged? What is the firm's profits? Show graphically.

c. What price and quantity would occur under perfect competition? What would be consumer's surplus under perfect competition? How does this compare with consumer's surplus under monopoly? What is the deadweight loss of monopoly? Show graphically.

d. Explain why a perfectly competitive firm is more efficient than a monopoly.

e. What is a monopolist's supply curve?

Problems Applying Economic Concepts Solutions

1.

Quantity	Price	Revenue	Total Cost	Total Profit
0	$50	$0	$0	$0
1	45	45	7	38
2	40	80	14	66
3	35	105	21	84
4	30	120	28	92

2.

Quantity	Total Price	Total Revenue	Total Cost	Marginal Revenue	Marginal Cost	Profit
0	20	$0	$0			$0
1	19	19	5	$19	$5	14
2	18	36	10	17	5	26
3	17	51	15	15	5	36
4	16	64	20	13	5	44
5	15	75	25	11	5	50
6	14	84	30	9	5	54
7	13	91	35	7	5	56
8	12	96	40	5	5	56
9	11	99	45	3	5	54
10	10	100	50	1	5	50
11	9	99	55	-1	5	44

3.

a. 8, $12, $5, $5

b. $96, $40

c. $56

4.

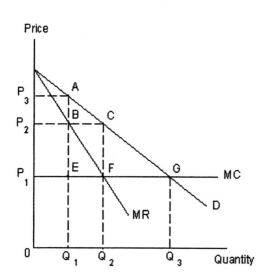

a. Total revenue is equal to price times quantity. The quantity produced by the monopolist is Qm and the price charged is Pm. Thus, total revenue is given by area a + b + c.

b. Total cost is equal to average cost times quantity. The average and marginal cost curves coincide, thus total cost is given by area a.

c. Profits are equal to total revenue minus total cost. Thus, the profits earned by the monopolist are equal to b + c (found by subtracting area a from area a + b + c).

5.

a. If the demand curve is P = 60 - 2Q, then MR = 60 - 4Q.

b. A monopolist maximizes profit where MR = MC, so 60 - 4Q = 40, and Q = 5. To find price, plug into the demand curve -- P = 60 - 2(5) = 50. Profit = (P - ATC)Q = (50 - 40)(5) = 50. (See graph.)

c. Under perfect competition P = MC, so P = 40 and Q can be found by plugging P = 40 into the demand equation. So 40 = 60 - 2Q, and Q = 10. Consumers' surplus is equal to (1/2)(10)(20) = 100 under perfect competition, and (1/2)(5)(10) = 25 under monopoly. The deadweight loss is also 25. (See graph.)

d. Under perfect competition, P = MC so the amount a consumer is willing to pay for the last unit of a good is just equal to the marginal cost of producing the last unit. A monopolist is inefficient since he restricts output in order to charge a higher price, and at the monopolist's output P > MC, so consumers are willing to pay more for additional units than it costs to produce those units.

e. Since a monopolist always chooses points on the demand curve at quantities where

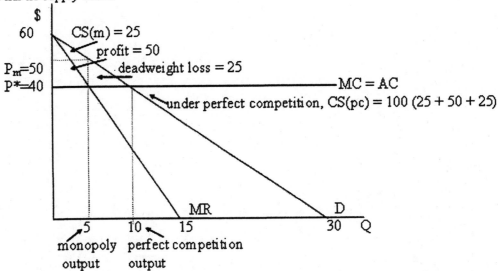

MC, he has no supply curve.

Internet Exercises

1. Visit the Campbell Soup Company website at www.campbellsoupcompany.com. Browse through the "About Us" and "History" sections. What evidence of market power can you find from reading through this website?

2. Go to the following web page of the Antitrust Division of the Department of Justice: http://www.usdoj.gov/atr/overview.html. Briefly, how does the Anti-trust Division attempt to encourage competition and prevent monopolization of markets? What are some current cases?

Solutions

True False Questions

1. T, True, when the demand curve is downward-sloping, then the marginal revenue curve will lie below the demand curve. As the monopolist expands output, it must reduce the price of previously sold units, so the additional revenue received from the next unit will be less than the price received for that unit.

2. F, If profit is at a maximum, then it cannot increase. If a monopolist is producing where marginal revenue is greater than marginal cost, profit is increasing. Since profit is increasing, it is not at a maximum. In order to maximize profit, a monopolist should produce at the point where marginal revenue and marginal cost are equal.

3. T, A monopolist restricts output and charges a higher price. This drives a wedge between the demand price of the good and the supply price (marginal cost) of the good. As a result, the value of producing the last unit exceeds the opportunity cost of producing the last unit. Output is less than the efficient amount.

4. F, The fewer and more similar the firms in a cartel, the easier it is to form and operate a cartel. In this case, cheating is easier to detect. If cheating is easier to detect, it is more likely to retaliate against the cheater. If there are a larger number of firms, overseeing the cartel agreement becomes more difficult, and cheating becomes more difficult to monitor.

5. F, Economic profits provide an incentive for private firms to engage in the risky and expensive research needed to discover new drugs. In the absence of such profits, firms may not undertake the research needed to produce new drugs. Some economists argue that the growth in industrial economies is the result of the economic rent seeking that occurs as firms seek out economic profits.

6. F, False, the primary reasons for the rise in oil prices in the fall of 2005 were the effects of Hurricanes Katrina and Rita.

Multiple Choice

1. A	12. C	22. A
2. D	13. B	23. A
3. C	14. C	24. C
4. A	15. D	25. B
5. C	16. B	26. A
6. B	17. D	27. A
7. C	18. B	28. C
8. B	19. A	29. B
9. D	20. C	30. C
10. A	21. C	31. D
11. A		

Fill-in Questions

1. Market power; monopoly; oligopoly; cartel

2. Marginal revenue; marginal; principle

3. efficient output

4. barriers to entry; natural monopoly

CHAPTER 6

Air Pollution: Balancing Benefits and Costs

Objectives of the Chapter

After you have mastered this chapter you will understand:

1. The causes and consequences of the principal air pollution problems.

2. The rules for determining the efficient levels of production, pollution, and pollution control.

3. Why a competitive market tends to produce too much pollution and a net social loss.

4. The importance and implications of Coase's Theorem for pollution control.

5. The principal features of the Clean Air Act.

6. The effects of the Clean Air Act on air quality in the United States.

7. The costs and benefits attributable to the Clean Air Act.

8. How the costs of environmental regulation can be reduced by using emissions taxes or marketable pollution permits.

9. The implications of the Kyoto protocol and the use of carbon taxes on air quality.

Key Terms

acid rain

greenhouse gas

pollution

external costs

marginal external costs

marginal social costs

efficiency loss from pollution

property right

common property resource

Coase's Theorem

ambient concentrations

criteria pollutants

emissions reduction credit

emissions tax

marginal abatement cost

marketable pollution permit

transactions costs

True False Questions

For these statements, indicate whether they are true or false. Defend your answer.

1. In most instances, government could achieve efficient levels of pollution by assigning property rights rather than by enacting regulations.

   TRUE or FALSE

2. Pig Pen Industries emits pollution as a by-product of its production process. In the absence of government policy, we would expect production at Pig Pen to exceed the efficient quantity.

   TRUE or FALSE

3. The efficient level of pollution will generally not be zero.

   TRUE or FALSE

4. The terms "waste" and "pollution" can be used interchangeably.

   TRUE or FALSE

5. Most studies of the Clean Air Act have shown that the costs of the act have greatly exceeded the benefits.

   TRUE or FALSE

6. Coase's Theorem suggests that, in the absence of transactions costs, bargaining can lead to an efficient level of pollution.

   TRUE or FALSE

7. Two methods of reducing the costs of air pollution are emissions taxes and marketable pollution permits.

   TRUE or FALSE

8. If the marginal social costs of pollution exceed the marginal social benefits, then the current amount of pollution is less than what is optimal from a social standpoint.

   TRUE or FALSE

Multiple Choice

Check yourself. Choose the best answer. Answers are found at end of chapter.

1. Global warming is caused primarily by:
    a. ozone depletion.
    b. the release of carbon dioxide into the atmosphere.
    c. the burning of leaded rather than unleaded gas.
    d. the release of sulfur dioxide into the atmosphere.

2. Emitting sulfur dioxide into the air results in:
    a. ozone depletion.
    b. global warming.
    c. acid rain.
    d. all of these.

3. Carbon dioxide is:
    a. a greenhouse gas.
    b. the primary ingredient in smog.
    c. responsible for desertification.
    d. the gas that protects the planet from ultraviolet radiation from the sun.

4. Which of the following statements is correct?
    a. All waste is pollution.
    b. Pollution is not an inevitable process in a market economy.
    c. The natural environment cannot assimilate waste without harm.
    d. Pollution is a by-product of production and consumption.

5. When production of a good results in waste that cannot be assimilated or recycled, we say there is:
    a. an internal cost.
    b. a societal cost.
    c. a private cost.
    d. an external cost.

6. Suppose the marginal social cost of producing Baby Soft Wipes is currently $12 while the marginal private cost is $9. Then the marginal external cost is:
    a. $3.
    b. $9.
    c. $12.
    d. $21.

7. Suppose the marginal social cost of producing at Big Bob's Novelties is $13, the marginal private cost is $13, and marginal social benefit is $13. In order to produce at the efficient level, Big Bob's should:
    a. increase output.
    b. decrease output.
    c. not change output.
    d. cannot be answered without further information.

8. In a market economy, the amount of pollution is:
    a. likely to be the efficient amount because the price system forces firms to operate at the point at which marginal social cost and marginal social benefit are equal.
    b. likely to be less than the efficient amount due to government regulations.
    c. likely to be more than the efficient amount because firms do not take the marginal external cost of pollution into account.
    d. likely to be more than the efficient amount because firms include only marginal external cost in their production decisions.

9. Suppose Sticky Glue Inc. is currently producing at a point where its marginal private cost is $10.50 and its marginal social cost is $20.25. Suppose that at current consumption levels marginal social benefit is $10.50. The marginal external cost associated with Sticky Glue's level of production is:
    a. $0 because marginal private cost and marginal social benefit are equal.
    b. $9.75.
    c. $15.00.
    d. $22.50.

10. Suppose that Mr. Big's oil refinery is currently producing at a point where marginal social cost is $47 and marginal social benefit is $35. In this instance:
    a. output is not at the efficient level.
    b. Mr. Big's company is imposing a net loss on society.
    c. production should be decreased in order to bring about efficiency.
    d. all of these.

11. According to Ronald Coase, when transactions costs are zero, the efficient level of pollution occurs:
    a. only if property rights are assigned the polluter.
    b. only if property rights are assigned to the non-polluter.
    c. whenever property rights are assigned to either the polluter or the non-polluter.
    d. when government implements uniform emissions standard for all firms.

12. The Clean Air Act does all of the following except:
    a. set emissions standards for carbon dioxide.
    b. set National Ambient Air Quality Standards.
    c. specify technologies that may be used to achieve emissions standards.
    d. use a Pigovian tax to achieve efficient levels of pollution.

13. National Ambient Air Quality Standards (NAAQSs):
    a. set upper limits for permissible concentrations of six common air pollutants.
    b. set lower limits for permissible concentrations of six common air pollutants.
    c. set upper limits for permissible concentrations of all common air pollutants.
    d. set lower limits for permissible concentrations of all common air pollutants.

14. Suppose the government requires automobile manufacturers to decrease carbon monoxide emissions by producing cars that use a combination of gas and electric energy. This is an example of:
    a. technology enforcement.
    b. technology innovation.
    c. technology restrictions.
    d. technology immobility.

15. Analysis shows that:
    a. the costs of the Clean Air Act exceed its benefits.
    b. the benefits of the Clean Air Act exceed its costs.
    c. the costs and benefits of the Clean Air Act are approximately equal.
    d. the Clean Air Act has all but eliminated technology-forcing.

16. The use of marketable pollution permits:
    a. can reduce the cost of controlling pollution.
    b. can encourage firms to reduce pollution beyond the level required by government.
    c. can encourage firms to develop new, less costly means of controlling pollution.
    d. all of these.

17. Market failure refers to:
    a. an inequitable division between private and public sector decision making.
    b. the market process failing to yield any useful outcomes.
    c. a less than efficient use of existing resources.
    d. a situation where market clearing prices fail to clear the market.

18. Government intervention is justified when:
    a. an election indicates that more government is needed.
    b. the public interest of elected officials is preferable to private interests.
    c. the preferences of private interests should be superseded by public interests.
    d. market failure has occurred and government intervention improves upon the use of resources.

19. The extra costs that are not captured by the market process are called:
    a. operating costs.
    b. external costs.
    c. producer surplus.
    d. fixed costs.

20. Whenever there are external costs:
    a. the market price will be too high.
    b. too little of the good is produced.
    c. marginal costs exceed marginal benefits.
    d. too much of the good will be produced.

21. Common property is:
    a. property that all citizens have the right to use.
    b. property that can be purchased by anyone.
    c. a characteristic of all inferior goods.
    d. property that has a large number of good substitutes.

22. The advantage of private property rights is that they:
    a. cannot be bought or sold.
    b. can be used by all citizens and no one can be excluded.
    c. ensure that a profit can be made by the owners.
    d. convey the benefits and costs to the owners.

23. The basic reason why pollution exists is that:
    a. public sector bureaucracies cannot decide what to do about pollution.
    b. consumers are indifferent to the impact of pollution.
    c. there are no defined or enforceable property rights in air and water.
    d. there is no known process for controlling or eliminating pollution.

24. Coase argued that markets could take care of external costs like pollution if:
    a. property rights were assigned exclusively to consumers.
    b. property rights were assigned exclusively to producers.
    c. government intervened in the market process.
    d. property rights were defined and enforced.

25. The major limitation of the Coase theorem is that it:
    a. requires that there be a large number of private and public officials involved in the transaction process.
    b. is most applicable when there are a small number of individuals involved.
    c. requires too much information on the part of government.
    d. is valid only when all property is held in common.

26. The advantage of using emissions taxes to correct for pollution is that it:
    a. involves an all-or-nothing approach.
    b. penalizes producers that are the most successful in controlling pollution.
    c. provides producers with the incentives to reduce pollution.
    d. works when property is held in common.

27. Which of the following is not true of the marketable permits approach to controlling pollution?
    a. It allows the market system with its emphasis on incentives to work.
    b. It involves a one size fits all approach to pollution abatement.
    c. A permit allows the holder to emit a certain amount of pollution.
    d. The owners can sell the marketable permits.

28. Congestion pricing involves:
    a. imposing a fee on vehicles that use the central city.
    b. offering employers who provide free parking to offer a travel allowance to their employees.
    c. increasing the price of each gallon of gasoline by enough to cover the marginal external costs of pollution.
    d. forcing all drivers to car pool.

29. The Clean Air Act has been most successful in reducing which of the following pollutants?
    a. Particles.
    b. Sulfur dioxide.
    c. Lead
    d. Carbon Monoxide.

Fill-in Questions

1. _____ is waste that is not assimilated by the environment or recycled. It is harmful to humans, animals, plants, and structures. It can manifest itself in various forms. For example, _____ , a weak solution of sulfuric acid and precipitation, can impair the ability of lakes and steams to sustain life. Global warming is another by-product of pollution. In this case, _____ such as carbon dioxide accumulate in the atmosphere and cause the Earth's temperature to rise. Whenever _____ is greater than _____ , output will not be at the efficient level. Producers tend to produce output that is greater than the efficient output because they consider only _____ when making production decisions. They do not take _____ into consideration when making their production decisions. Because output is greater than efficient output, a _____ is imposed on society. Decreasing production to the point where marginal social cost and marginal social benefit are equal will result in efficiency.

2. Some argue that problems with pollution arise because the environment is a _____ _____ . In order to deal with the pollution problem, government has relied heavily on regulation.

3. Many think that methods other than regulation could control pollutants at a lower cost. For example, some argue that instead, government should assign _____ . This idea is based on work done by Ronald Coase. Imposition of an emissions tax is another alternative to regulation. _____ require employers who provide free parking to offer a travel allowance worth the value of the parking

space as an alternative. _____ are the upper limits permitted for concentration in the _____ of the six common air pollutants.

4. An _____ regulates the level of pollution by establishing a price the emitters must pay per unit of emissions. The _____ is the cost of not emitting, or eliminating, each successive ton of pollution.

Problems Applying Economic Concepts

1. Suppose you are given the following information about production at Steele, Incorporated. At current levels of production, the marginal private cost of an additional unit is $100, the marginal social cost of an additional unit is $140, and the marginal social benefit of an additional unit is $100. Assume marginal social benefit and marginal private benefit are equal. What are marginal external costs?

2. Suppose that production at Mirage Corporation generates $7,500,000 in total social benefit, $7,000,000 in total private cost and $1,000,000 in total external cost. What is the net benefit or loss imposed on society?

Use the following information to answer questions 3 and 4.

| | Marginal cost of control at | |
Tons per day	Plant X	Plant Y
1	$200	$300
2	400	600
3	600	900
4	800	1,200
5	1,000	1,500

3. Suppose both plants are currently emitting 5 tons of pollution per day. Government enacts regulations that require both plants to control 3 tons of emissions per day. What is the total cost of the emissions reduction?

4. Suppose instead, government requires each plant to control 3 tons of emissions per day and issues each plant 2 pollution permits. Each permit allows it to emit 1 ton of pollution per day. Will these permits be traded? Defend your answer.

5. Assume that the marginal benefits and marginal private costs of driving your car are given by the following equations:

$$\text{marginal benefit (MB):} \quad P = 120 - 2Q$$
$$\text{marginal private cost (MPC):} \quad P = 20 + 2Q$$

where P is the price per mile (in cents) and Q is the number of miles driven per day.

a. How many miles will you drive your car per day? What price are you willing to pay per mile?

b. Assume that your driving imposes costs of 20 cents per mile on others. The marginal social cost is given by the following equation:

marginal social cost (MSC): $P = 40 + 2Q$

What is the socially optimal number of miles to drive each day? What price should you pay? Explain and show graphically.

c. What tax would lead to the social optimum? Explain.

6. Suppose that your roommate Pat is a trumpet major who specializes in Gregorian chants. Since Pat plays the trumpet constantly, and since you want to study (and hate Gregorian chants) you both go to see the Residence Director to settle your problem. There are no empty rooms on campus, and no one is willing to trade rooms with you, so neither one of you can move. Assume that the following table describes Pat's total willingness to pay (total benefits) and your total willingness to accept (total costs) for various hours of trumpet playing per day:

HOURS OF TRUMPET PLAYING	PAT'S TOTAL BENEFIT	YOUR TOTAL COST
0	0	0
1	30	18
2	50	20
3	60	25
4	65	40
5	68	60
6	70	90
7	68	150

a. What is the efficient (socially optimal) hours of trumpet playing?

b. Assume that the Residence Director rules in your favor, so that you must be compensated for any suffering due to your roommate's trumpet playing. If you can costlessly bargain, what agreement will result?

c. Assume instead that the Residence Director rules in Pat's favor, so that she can play the trumpet whenever she wants. Again, if transaction costs are zero, what agreement will you reach?

Problems Applying Economic Concepts Solutions

1. Marginal external cost is the difference between marginal social cost and marginal private cost. In this instance, marginal external cost is $140 - $100 or $40.

2. The net social benefit or loss is equal to total social benefit minus total social cost. Total social cost is equal to total private cost plus total external cost. Thus, total social cost is $7,000,000 + $1,000,000 or $8,000,000. Total social benefit is $7,500,000. Total social benefit minus total social cost is $7,500,000 - $8,000,000 or -$500,000. Society experiences a net loss of $500,000.

3. The cost of decreasing emissions at Plant X by 3 tons per day is $200 + $400 + $600 or $1,200. The cost of decreasing emissions at Plant Y by 3 tons per day is $300 + $600 + $900 or $1,800. Thus, the total cost of the emissions reductions is $1,200 + $1,800 or $3,000.

4. Yes, one of these permits will be traded. Initially, each plant is controlling 3 tons of emissions and releasing two tons. If Plant Y could release an additional ton of emissions (control 1 less ton) it could save $900. Thus, it would be willing to pay up to $900 for one of Plant X's permits. It would cost Plant X $800 to control an additional ton of emissions. Thus, it would be willing to sell one of its permits if it received at least $800. Since Plant Y is willing to pay up to $900 for the permit and Plant X has to receive only $800 for the permit, there is a basis for trade. Note that the second permit would not be traded. The maximum Plant Y would pay for this permit is $600 while Plant X must receive at least $1,000.

5.

   a. As a private individual, you will drive your car until the marginal private benefit is equal to the marginal private cost. To find the number of miles, set the two equations equal to each other:

$$120 - 2Q = 20 + 2Q$$
$$-4Q = -100$$
$$Q_p = 25$$

   With these marginal costs and benefits, you would drive your car 25 miles per day. To find the price you would be willing to pay per mile to drive 25 miles, plug the quantity of 25 into the marginal benefit curve:

$$P = 120 - 2(25) = 70$$

   So you would be willing to pay $0.70 per mile to drive 25 miles per day.

   b. The social optimum occurs when marginal social benefit equals marginal social cost. Assuming that marginal social benefits and marginal private benefits are equivalent, the social optimum can be found by:

$$120 - 2Q = 40 + 2Q$$
$$-4Q = -80$$
$$Q^* = 20.$$

   The socially optimal price is given by $P = MSC$, or
$$P = 40 + 2(20) = 80.$$

   c. The Pigovian tax that would lead to the social optimum would be $0.20 per mile, or the marginal external cost of driving one mile.

Graphically,

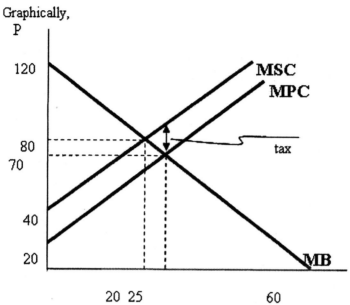

In an unregulated, private market, you would drive your car for 25 miles per day, and be willing to pay $0.70 per mile driven. But since your driving imposes a marginal external cost of $0.20 per mile on others, you drive too much compared to the social optimum. The social optimum is 20 miles per day, at a price of $0.80 per mile. A tax of $0.20 per mile would cause you to internalize the external costs, and drive the optimal number of miles per day.

6. First, it is helpful to determine the net benefits (NB = TB − TC), marginal benefits for Pat, and marginal costs to you:

HOURS	PAT'S TB	PAT'S MB	YOUR TC	YOUR MC	NET BENEFITS
0	0	--	0	--	0
1	30	30	18	18	12
2	50	20	20	2	30
3	60	10	25	5	35
4	65	5	40	15	25
5	68	3	60	20	8
6	70	2	90	30	-20
7	68	-2	150	60	- 82

a. The socially optimal number of hours of trumpet playing is 3, where net benefits are maximized at 35.

b. If the RD rules in your favor so that Pat is liable for any damages caused, then you can insist that she play for 0 hours. From 0 hours, Pat would be willing to pay you $30 to play for the first hour. Your MC is only $18, so you both would agree to some price between $18 and $30 for Pat to play for the first hour. For the second hour, Pat would be willing to pay $20, but you would be willing to accept only $2 for the second hour. (Once you've listened to one hour, the second isn't so bad.) Also, for the third hour, Pat would be willing to pay $10 and you'd be willing to accept $5, so Pat could pay you to play for the third hour. Past three hours Pat's benefits aren't worth the costs to you, so Pat would not be willing to pay for more than three hours of playing. The social optimum results from bargaining.

c. If the RD rules in Pat's favor, he will want to play for 6 hours. From there, you would be willing to pay $30 to get Pat to reduce her playing to 5 hours, and Pat would be willing to accept any price above $2, since that 6th hour of trumpet playing isn't worth that much to her anyway. Similarly, you'd be willing to pay $20 to reduce the playing from 5 to 4 hours, while Pat would be willing to accept any price above $3. At 4 hours, you would be willing to pay $15 and Pat would be willing to accept $5 to reduce her trumpet playing from 4 to 3 hours. At 3 hours, it would not be worth the price for you to pay for any further reductions in trumpet playing. Again, the result is the social optimum of 3 hours. So the moral is known as Coase's Theorem: As long as transactions costs are zero, property rights are well defined, and access to ameliorative technology is absent, then bargaining will result in the social optimum, regardless of who is required to pay. Of course, issues of fairness will be different to the payee and payor in either situation.

Internet Exercises

1. Visit this website of BBC News to read about the Kyoto Protocol: http://news.bbc.co.uk/1/hi/sci/tech/4269921.stm. After reading the article, answer the following questions:

    a. What are the major provisions of the Kyoto Protocol?

    b. When did the Kyoto Protocol go into effect? What event made it legally binding?

    c. Why hasn't the US agreed to ratify the Kyoto Protocol? Do you agree? Why or why not?

2. Go to the following two web sites to learn about President Bush's Clear Skies Initiative: http://www.sierraclub.org/cleanair/clear_skies.asp and http://www.whitehouse.gov/news/releases/2003/09/20030916-2.html. How do the two sites differ in their interpretation of the Clear Skies legislation? Would the Clear Skies Initiative strengthen or weaken the Clean Air Act?

Solutions

True False Questions

1. F, Although it is theoretically possible to achieve the efficient level of pollution by assignment of property rights it is not very practical. This is because parties must be able to bargain with each other in order to achieve efficiency. In most instances, pollution affects numerous people. This means that it is very difficult for the parties to enter into bargains with each other. Thus, it would be difficult for government to achieve efficient pollution levels by assigning property rights.

2. T, When making production decisions, Pig Pen will consider its marginal private costs. It will not consider the marginal external cost the pollution imposes upon third parties. Because of this, production will tend to exceed the efficient amount at which marginal social cost and marginal social benefit are equal.

3. T, The efficient level of pollution is probably not zero in most real world cases. Pollution arises in the production process. However, society is made better off by the goods provided through this process. Hence, in order to achieve the efficient level of pollution, production should be carried out until the marginal social cost of production (which includes the cost of pollution) is equal to the marginal social benefit of production. This will normally be a level of production greater than zero.

4. F, Pollution is residual waste that is harmful to humans, animals, plants, and structures. Not all waste is pollution. Some waste can be assimilated without harm by the natural environment, and some is recycled. Only waste that is not assimilated or recycled constitutes pollution.

5. F, False. As discussed in the text, studies of the Clean Air Act conducted by the EPA have shown that the benefits of the Clean Air Act have been well worth the costs of the regulations.

6. T, True, as long as both parties can bargain costlessly, they each will have an incentive to bargain to an efficient outcome, regardless of where liability is placed.

7. T, True, both are methods that increase the costs of creating air pollution to more closely reflect the marginal social costs of that pollution.

8. F, False, If the marginal social costs of pollution exceed the marginal social benefits, then too much pollution is being produced. If the level of pollution was reduced, then the costs of pollution would fall by more than the benefits fall, so the net benefit to society would increase.

Multiple Choice

1. B
2. C
3. A
4. D
5. D
6. A
7. C
8. C
9. B
10. D
11. C
12. D
13. A
14. A
15. B
16. D
17. C
18. D
19. B
20. D
21. A
22. D
23. C
24. D
25. B
26. C
27. B
28. A
29. C

Fill-in Questions

1. Pollution; acid rain; greenhouse gases; marginal social cost; marginal social benefit; marginal private cost; marginal external cost; net social loss

2. common; property resource

3. property rights; Parking cash outs; Ambient concentrations; atmosphere

4. emissions tax; marginal abatement cost

Health Care: How Much? For Whom?

Objectives of the Chapter

After you have mastered this chapter you will understand:

1. The trends in health care costs in the United States.

2. The reasons for the increasing share of GDP devoted to health care spending.

3. The consequences for the allocation of resources between health and non-health goods if present health care cost trends continue.

4. The effects of third-party payments on the costs of health care.

5. The different techniques and policies that have evolved to limit health care expenditures in the past two decades.

6. The principal reasons why there may be too many resources devoted to health care.

7. How some of the proposals to reduce health care costs would impact the industry.

Key Terms

real NHE per capita

real GDP per capita

Medicare

Medicaid

third-party payment

wasteful spending

physician-induced demand

defensive medicine

managed care

utilization review

value of a life

vouchers

True False Questions

For these statements, indicate whether they are true or false. Defend your answer.

1. Since the 1960's, the share of United States GDP devoted to health care spending has increased.

    TRUE or FALSE

2. Health care is affordable over time if we see the percentage of GDP devoted to National Health Expenditures declining over time.

    TRUE or FALSE

3. In the United States, more than 15 percent of the population is without health insurance.

    TRUE or FALSE

4. Most analysts agree that physician-induced demand is a major contributor to the excessive consumption of health care.

    TRUE or FALSE

5. The typical managed care program reimburses health care providers on the basis of services performed or on the basis of costs of provision.

    TRUE or FALSE

6. Proponents of a voucher system argue that vouchers will put more of the responsibility for health care decisions into the hands of expert boards. As a result, there will be greater efficiency in the health care system.

    TRUE or FALSE

Multiple Choice

Check yourself. Choose the best answer. Answers are found at end of chapter.

1. If real NHE per capita grows at an annual rate one percent faster than the growth of real GDP per capita, then
    a. health care spending will be unsustainable.
    b. health care spending would still be affordable.
    c. health care spending would decline over time.
    d. health care spending as a percentage of real GDP would remain constant.

2. Suppose the market clearing price of hospital days is $1,200 per day. Due to third-party payments, consumers pay $170 per day. At current levels of consumption, we would expect:
   a. the marginal social benefit of hospital days to exceed the marginal social cost of hospital days.
   b. the marginal social cost of hospital days to exceed the marginal social benefit of hospital days.
   c. a quantity less than the efficient quantity of health care days to be consumed.
   d. the efficient quantity of health care days to be consumed.

3. Suppose an economy is currently operating at a point where the marginal social benefit of producing an additional unit of health care is $400. The marginal social cost of this additional unit of health care is $200. This economy should:
   a. increase its production of health care.
   b. decrease its production of health care.
   c. not change its production of health care.
   d. cannot be determined without further information.

4. A payment made for a good or service by a party other than the buyer or seller refers to:
   a. a third-party payment.
   b. the payment made by insurance companies, largely without question, for the costs of services rendered by a doctor or a hospital.
   c. a transfer payment.
   d. cost reimbursement.

5. Which of the following might contribute to an excessive quantity of health care being consumed?
   a. the lack of a federal tax exemption for health insurance.
   b. first-party payments.
   c. physician-induced demand.
   d. marginal external benefits generated by health care.

6. Which of the following is an example of third party payments?
   a. It costs Community Hospital $100 for one person in the emergency room. They only charge a price of $80.
   b. Charles has a blood test that costs $500. He pays the doctor $300 for the test and the lab that performed the test $200.
   c. The city of Astonia gives the community hospital $1,000,000 each year to subsidize the hospital's operations.
   d. Tim has a blood test that costs $500. He pays $100 for the blood test. His insurance company pays the remainder.

7. Limits to physician-induced demand include:
   a. consumers' lack of information about the effectiveness of various health care alternatives.
   b. an increase in potential competition as the supply of doctors has increased.
   c. boards set up by the American Medical Association to review physician practices to ensure that procedures prescribed are of benefit to the patient.
   d. the fact that insurance companies rarely require consumers to seek second opinions before making a choice among various health care alternatives.

8. Kimberly visits her doctor complaining of dizziness. Dr. Smith orders a C-T scan even though she believes Kimberly is suffering from an inner-ear infection. She prescribes the test in order to avoid a potential law suit. This is an example of:
   a. defensive medicine.
   b. offensive medicine.
   c. malpractice.
   d. over-practiced medicine.

9. The federal income tax exemption for health insurance:
   a. ultimately makes workers worse off because they receive lower wages as a result of the deduction.
   b. increases the administrative cost of insurance companies.
   c. increases the quantity of health care demanded because there is an increase in insurance coverage as a result of the deduction.
   d. encourages a greater reliance on high-tech health care.

10. The program that provides health care for individuals 65 and older is known as:
    a. Medicare.
    b. Medicaid.
    c. Supplementary Medical Care.
    d. Temporary Assistance to Needy Families (TANF).

11. As the relative growth in real National Health Expenditures per capita continues to increase, the burden will fall on households because:
    a. they must pay increasingly higher health insurance premiums.
    b. they must pay directly for expenses not covered by insurance, which will continue to increase.
    c. they must pay the taxes required to finance increasing Medicare and Medicaid expenditures.
    d. all of the above.

12. It is likely that the use of vouchers would:
    a. increase competition among health care providers.
    b. decrease competition among health care providers.
    c. increase the third-party payments associated with Medicare.
    d. decrease the cost consumers of health care currently bear.

13. Managed-care organizations can reduce the costs associated with the health care system by:
    a. reducing the amount of ineffective care.
    b. reducing the amount of inappropriate care.
    c. providing physicians with incentives to decrease costs.
    d. all of the above.

14. In 2003, third-parties paid for approximately what percent of national health care expenditures?
    a. 86%.
    b. 15%.
    c. 32%.
    d. 14%.

15. Third-party payments often cause welfare costs to society as a whole because:
    a. the third party payments increase the costs of health care by more then they increase the benefits of health care.
    b. the third party payments discourage the use of medical care by specialists.
    c. the third party payments discourage doctors from ordering unnecessary tests or from practicing defensive medicine.
    d. the third party payments reduce the costs of health care with no change in benefits.

16. The most significant problem with national health insurance is that:
    a. out of pocket costs are higher than in other systems.
    b. not enough health care is provided.
    c. the marginal costs of serving one additional patient is lower than the marginal benefits.
    d. waiting times to obtain needed medical care may be extremely long.

17. With Canada's national health system, the quantity of health care _____ often exceeds the quantity of health care _____ .
    a. supplied, demanded.
    b. demanded, supplied.
    c. purchased, demanded.
    d. supplied, produced.

18. Which of the following factors would NOT tend to limit the impact of the pure exercise of physician-induced demand?
    a. potential competition.
    b. increases in incomes of consumers.
    c. second opinions.
    d. information monitoring by patients.

19. Medical care given to reduce the risk of a malpractice suit is called:
    a. physician-induced demand.
    b. satisfaction maximization.
    c. physician ethics.
    d. defensive medicine.

20. The process that managed care companies use to restrict covered services is called:
    a. defensive medicine.
    b. vouchers.
    c. utilization review.
    d. technological review.

21. One advantage of managed care over traditional insurance systems is that
    a. patients have a wider choice of health care providers.
    b. physicians have more latitude in the types of procedures that can be offered.
    c. the growth in the costs of providing health care increases at a more rapid rate.
    d. the ability to control medical cost increases.

22. Suppose that the job of a policeman carries a risk of death per year that is one in a thousand times more than the risk of death for similar occupations. Also assume that a policeman earns $10,000 more per year than similar occupations with lower levels of risk of death. What is the implicit value of a life from such statistics?
    a. $1 million
    b. $10 million
    c. $10,000
    d. The value of life is infinite.

Fill-in Questions

1. _____ are payments made directly to the provider of a good or service by a party other than the buyer. _____ demand is one of the factors contributing to excessive health care. Consumers lack information about the effectiveness of various health care alternatives. Because of this, they delegate the choice to their physician. The physician, motivated by self-interest, may choose care for which the marginal benefit to the patient is less than the marginal cost.

2. When physicians practice defensive medicine health care costs can rise. _____ medicine occurs because physicians are trying to avoid potential law suits.

3. Proponents of _____ argue that their use can increase competition among health providers. They also state that consumers will make better health care choices because the vouchers will force them to bear a greater share of their health care cost.

4. Some analysts argue that greater reliance on _____ will increase the probability of the health care industry reforming itself. This will reduce the need for government reform of the system.

Problems Applying Economic Concepts

1. Katherine's employer provides her with a health insurance policy. The employer pays a premium of $3,000 annually for this policy. Katherine is in the 28 percent tax bracket.

2. If Katherine is in the 28 percent tax bracket what would she have to earn in order to have the $2,000 after taxes to pay the premium? How would your answer change if Katherine is in the 36 percent tax bracket? (Round your answer to the nearest dollar.) Suppose that the value of the additional life years from improvements in medical care is estimated to be $600,000 and the discount rate is 10%. What is the present value of the value of the additional life years to a 30 year old where the additional life years are delayed until ages 65, 66, and 67?

3. The following graph describes the market for hospital beds per night in the New York metropolitan area. P1 and Q1 represent the equilibrium price and quantity of hospital beds, respectively. Suppose that when health insurance is provided, the price to the patient is reduced to Ps.

   a. What quantity of hospital beds results from the provision of health insurance? What is the cost to hospitals?

   b. What is the total increase in expenditures that results from the provision of health insurance?

   c. What is the welfare cost (deadweight loss) associated with the provision of health insurance?

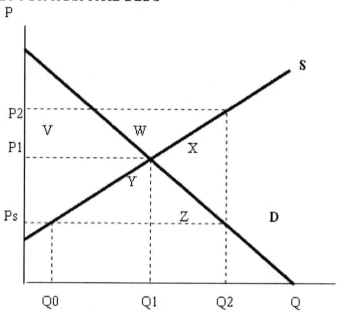

MARKET FOR HOSPITAL BEDS

4. Suppose that the market for health care can be described by the following equations:

   demand: $P = 240 - 4Q$
   supply: $P = 60 + 2Q$

   where Q is the quantity of units of health care (say, doctor visits) and P is the price for a unit of health care, measured in dollars.

   a. What is the equilibrium price and quantity in the health care market? Show graphically.

   b. Suppose that health insurance is provided that reduces the cost to the consumer to $80 per unit of health care. What quantity of health care will result? What is the price paid by patients? What is the price per unit of health care supplied? Show on your graph from a).

   c. What is the wasteful expenditure associated with the health insurance? What is the welfare cost (or deadweight loss) of the health insurance plan?

Problems Applying Economic Concepts Solutions

1. Let X equal the amount Katherine must earn before taxes in order to have the $3,000 needed to pay the insurance premium. Then:

    $3,000 = X - 0.28X$

    $3,000 = 0.72X$

    $3,000/0.72 = X$

    $4,167 = X$

    If Katherine were in the 36 percent tax bracket she would have to earn:

    $3,000 = X - 0.36X$

    $3,000 = 0.64X$

    $3,000/0.64 = X$

    $4,688 = X$

    The amount Katherine must earn increases as she moves into a higher tax bracket.

2.

FVLY	Years Delayed	Discount Factor	PVLY
$200,000	35 years	$(1.05)^{65-30} = 5.516$	$36,258
$200,000	36 years	$(1.05)^{66-30} = 5.792$	$34,530
$200,000	37 years	$(1.05)^{67-30} = 6.081$	$32,889
	Total Present Value		$103,677

3.

   a. The quantity of hospital beds is Q_2, and the cost per bed to hospitals for providing that quantity of beds is given by P_2.

   b. Health insurance would increase expenditures on hospital beds by the sum of the areas V + W + X + Y + Z

   c. The welfare cost is given by the area X.

4.

   a. The equilibrium can be found where the supply and demand curves intersect, or by setting the two equations equal to each other:

   $$240 - 4Q = 60 + 2Q$$
   $$-6Q = -180$$
   $$Q^* = 30$$
   $$P = 240 - 4(30) = 120$$
   $$P = 60 + 2(30) = 120 \text{ (check)}$$

   b. If the price to consumers is reduced to $80, the quantity demanded will be 40:

$$80 = 240 - 4Q$$
$$-160 = -4Q$$
$$Qd = 40$$

The price paid by patients is $80, and the cost to doctors is given by the supply curve at that quantity of 40:

$$P = 60 + 2(40) = 140.$$

Graphically,

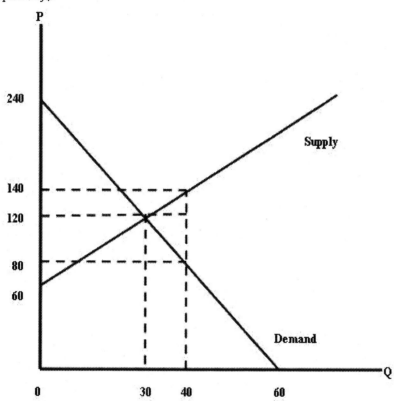

c. The wasteful expenditure associated with health insurance is the amount of extra expenditures when marginal costs exceed marginal benefits (or the supply curve is above the demand curve). This is the difference between the total expenditures with health insurance and the total expenditures at equilibrium:

$$(140 \times 40) - (120 \times 30) = 5600 - 3600 = \$2000.$$

The welfare cost is given by the area of the triangle between the supply and demand curves between the quantities of 30 and 40. This is given by the area of two right triangles, as shown in the graph:

$$\tfrac{1}{2} b \times h = \tfrac{1}{2}(40 - 30)(120 - 80) = \tfrac{1}{2} \times 10 \times 40 = 200.$$
$$\tfrac{1}{2} b \times h = \tfrac{1}{2}(40 - 30)(140 - 120) = \tfrac{1}{2} \times 10 \times 20 = 100.$$

So the welfare cost is equal to 200 = 100 = $300. In other words, the extra costs of providing the extra 10 doctor visits generated through insurance exceed the extra benefits by $300.

Internet Exercises

1. To find country rankings based on the World Health Organization statistics, co to the following website: http://www.photius.com/rankings/healthranks.html. How does the US rank in terms of the WHO health index? For a more detailed look at international health data, go to http://www.photius.com/rankings/world_health_systems.html. How does the US rank in terms of health care expenditures as a percentage of GDP compared to other countries?? How do we rank in terms of the quality of health care? Are we getting our money's worth?

2. For examples of social indicators of the quality of health care, go to http://www3.who.int/statistics/indicatormetadata.htm. Choose several indicators, and see how the United States compares to other industrialized countries.

3. Visit the National Institutes of Health web page of current events at http://www.nih.gov/news/. What current issues in health care seem to be of concern to the NIH?

Solutions

True False Questions

1. T, True, National Health Expenditures as a percentage of GDP has increased from 5.7% in 1965 to 15.3% in 2003.

2. F, False, the test of affordability does not depend on health care expenditures as a percentage of GDP declining over time. Rather, health care is affordable as long as we do not have to reduce the amounts of other goods and services that are consumed as a result in increases in health care costs.

3. T, True, over 46 million Americans, or more than 15 percent of the population, are not covered by health insurance plans.

4. F, Much of the variation in physician practices could be caused by the uncertainty of diagnostic medicine and variations in the training and skill of physicians. In addition, there are several potential limits to the exercise of physician-induced demand. These include: 1) the inability of physicians to close the market to competitors, 2) patients' a priori expectations concerning treatment, 3) the growing practice of third-party payers requiring second opinions, 4) limits on the amount of work a physician would wish to create for themselves, and 5) physicians' views concerning ethical behavior.

5. F, False, typical health insurance plans reimburse on the basis of fee-for service or the costs of provision, so medical service providers often had an incentive to inflate their costs in order to increase their revenues.

Managed care plans attempt to reduce costs through negotiations and selective contracting with physicians.

6. F, Proponents of a voucher system do argue that a system of vouchers will increase efficiency in the market for health care. However, this increased efficiency will come about because recipients of health care will bear a greater share of their own costs. As a result, proponents argue that consumers will make better health care choices. In addition, vouchers would increase the scope of consumer choice and enhance the competition by health care providers for Medicaid/Medicare patients. This will result in cost savings.

Multiple Choice

1. B	9. C	17. B
2. B	10. A	18. B
3. A	11. D	19. D
4. A	12. A	20. C
5. C	13. B	21. D
6. D	14. A	22. B
7. B	15. A	
8. A	16. D	

Fill-in Questions

1. Third-party payments; Physician-induced

2. Defensive

3. Vouchers

4. managed-care

Crime and Drugs: A Modern Dilemma

Objectives of the Chapter

After you have mastered this chapter you will understand

1. What a public good is and why the existence of public goods leads to a role for government.

2. Why the establishment and enforcement of a system of property rights is important.

3. That property rights provision is a public good.

4. Why the efficient level of crime is not zero.

5. The morality arguments for and against drug legalization.

6. The consequences of drug prohibition.

7. The consequences of drug legalization.

Key Terms

public good

nonexcludable good

nonrival good

free rider

hawks, doves and owls

equimarginal principle

True False Questions

For these statements, indicate whether they are true or false. Defend your answer.

1. In a recent news interview a woman stated that, "No risk is acceptable. Crime should be eliminated." Such a stance would increase efficiency in the economy.

    TRUE or FALSE

2. Since public goods are non-rival and non-excludable, the costs of private provision would be high.

   TRUE or FALSE

3. According to the economic approach to crime, an increase in the perceived costs of armed robbery, through increased penalties or greater enforcement, will lead to a reduction in armed robberies.

   TRUE or FALSE

4. The existence of white collar crime proves that those with good job skills and high incomes are more likely to commit crimes, since they have the skills and talents to do so effectively.

   TRUE or FALSE

5. Crime rates in the United States have continued to increase relative to crime rates in England.

   TRUE or FALSE

6. Libertarians argue that government should have the liberty to regulate drug use in any way that legislators see fit.

   TRUE or FALSE

7. Drug prohibition increases criminal activity.

   TRUE or FALSE

8. The increased enforcement of drug laws may have increased the relative supply of cocaine compared to marijuana.

   TRUE or FALSE

Multiple Choice

Check yourself. Choose the best answer. Answers are found at the end of the chapter.

1. If a good is a public good, then:
   a. consumption of the good by one individual decreases the amount of the good available for other individuals to consume.
   b. it is difficult to exclude nonpayers from consuming the good.
   c. the good is a rival good.
   d. all of these.

2. Which of the following is the best example of a public good?
   a. a hamburger.
   b. an automobile.
   c. a national highway system.
   d. a house.

3. Suppose it costs a local government $5,000,000 per year to hire an additional police officer. The marginal cost to an additional user of the security provided by the police department is:
   a. equal to the total cost of security divided by the number of users.
   b. equal to highest valued alternative that had to be given up.
   c. approximately equal to the average cost of construction.
   d. zero.

4. Government provision of public goods will be more efficient than private provision because:
   a. it is costly to exclude people from the benefits of the public good.
   b. there may be privacy costs in monitoring the use of some public goods.
   c. private provision can result in a free rider problem.
   d. all of these.

5. In general, if the private market provides a public good:
   a. the quantity will be greater than the efficient quantity because of firms' desire to maximize profits.
   b. the quantity will be greater than the efficient quantity because the market will charge a price for providing the good.
   c. the quantity will be less than the efficient quantity because of free riders.
   d. the quantity will be greater than the efficient quantity because consumers will be unwilling to purchase all that is produced.

6. Which of the following best exemplifies the free rider concept?
   a. Jack pays for six months of cable and gets the seventh month free.
   b. Your neighborhood association votes to undertake landscaping projects that raise property values in the neighborhood, but you refuse to participate.
   c. You and a friend go to dinner. Your friend pays for both meals.
   d. Jennifer goes to the store and purchases a gallon of Ben and Jerry's ice cream and receives a second gallon free because she has a "buy one, get one free" coupon.

7. The efficient quantity of crime control is:

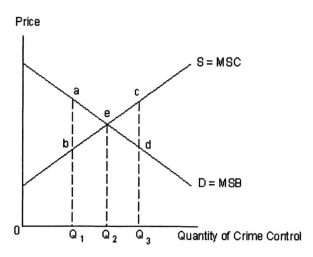

a. Q_1.
b. Q_2.
c. Q_3.
d. zero.

8. If the level of crime control is Q_1:

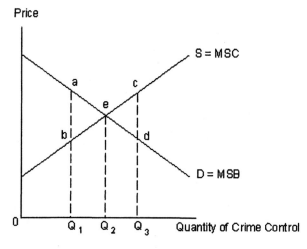

a. marginal social benefit is given by Q_1-a.
b. marginal social benefit is given by a-b.
c. marginal social cost is given by Q_1-a.
d. marginal social cost is given by Q_1-d.

9. If the level of crime control is currently Q_3:

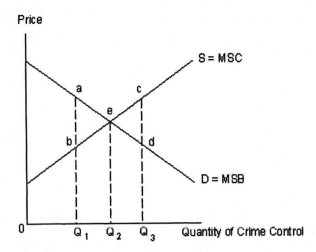

a. marginal social cost exceeds marginal social benefit, and the level of crime control should decrease.
b. marginal social cost is equal to marginal social benefit, and the level of crime control should increase.
c. marginal social cost is less than marginal social benefit, and the level of crime control should increase.
d. marginal social cost is less than marginal social benefit, and the level of crime control should decrease.

10. Suppose the level of crime control is currently Q_2. In this case:

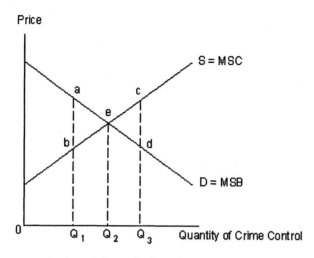

a. marginal social cost is less than marginal social benefit, and the level of crime control should decrease.
b. marginal social cost exceeds marginal social benefit, and the level of crime control should decrease.
c. marginal social cost is less than marginal social benefit, and the level of crime control should increase.
d. marginal social cost is equal to marginal social benefit, and the level of crime control should not change.

11. If government supplies the efficient level of crime control then:
a. the marginal social benefit of crime control will be equal to the marginal social cost of crime control.
b. the marginal social benefit of crime control will exceed the marginal social cost of crime control.
c. the crime rate will be zero.
d. the opportunity cost of crime control to an additional user will be zero.

12. Suppose government were to legalize the use of cocaine. The most likely result would be:
a. an increase in organized criminal activity related to drugs.
b. an decrease in the price of cocaine due to a relatively large increase in the supply of the drug.
c. an increase in property crimes.
d. a decrease in the price of cocaine due to a relatively large decrease in demand for the drug.

13. Suppose the marginal social cost of employing an additional police officer is $45,000 per year while the marginal social benefit of employing an additional police officer is $40,000 per year. In this instance government should:
a. probably not hire the officer as the public will incur a net loss of $5,000 per year.
b. probably not hire the officer as the public will incur costs of $40,000 per year.
c. probably hire the additional officer as the public will gain $40,000 in benefits.
d. probably hire the officer as the public will gain $5,000 per year in net benefits.

14. Suppose government prohibited the production, sale, and use of tobacco. The most likely result would be:
    a. a decrease in the price of tobacco because people would purchase less of the illegal substance.
    b. an increase in the quantity of tobacco bought because some individuals enjoy the thrill of breaking the law.
    c. an increase in the price of tobacco because some producers will cease production as the risk associated with growing the illegal substance rises.
    d. an increase in the supply of tobacco because producers will be enticed to increase production as the price of the illegal substance rises.

15. Suppose the demand and supply of marijuana are currently D_1 and S_2, respectively. The equilibrium price and quantity are:

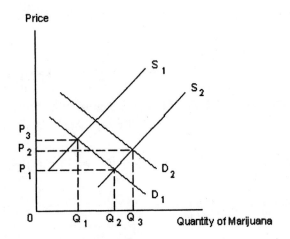

    a. P_1 and Q_1, respectively.
    b. P_3 and Q_1, respectively.
    c. P_2 and Q_3, respectively.
    d. P_1 and Q_2, respectively.

16. Suppose the demand and supply of marijuana, an illegal substance, are currently D_1 and S_1, respectively. Government legalizes the use of marijuana. This would cause:

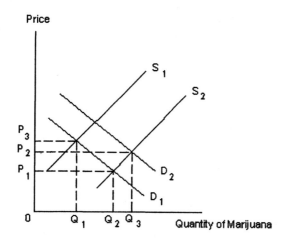

a. an increase in supply from S_1 to S_2.
b. an increase in supply from S_2 to S_1.
c. a decrease in demand from D_1 to D_2.
d. a decrease in demand from D_2 to D_1.

17. One reason for the decrease in supply that occurs if a drug is made illegal is that:
a. property rights deteriorate.
b. organized crime strictly enforces property rights.
c. buyers face a decrease in the risk of punishment.
d. there is increased competition among illegal suppliers.

18. In general, drug prohibition tends to:
a. decrease drug use.
b. cause drug prices to increase due to large decreases in the supply of drugs.
c. cause drug pushers to entice use by providing free drugs to first time users.
d. cause increased supply as organized crime moves in and takes advantage of profitable opportunities.

19. The addicted user's demand for cocaine is represented by:

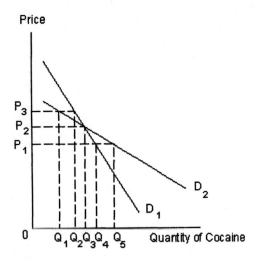

a. D_1.
b. D_2.
c. Q_1.
d. Q_3.

20. Suppose the price of cocaine is initially P_2. Increased enforcement causes the price of cocaine to increase to P_3. The quantity of cocaine demanded by the recreational user will:

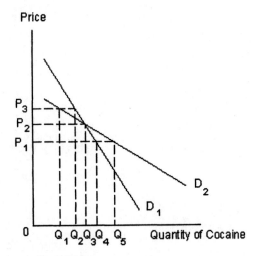

a. decrease from Q_3 to Q_2.
b. decrease from Q_3 to Q_1.
c. increase from Q_3 to Q_4.
d. increase from Q_3 to Q_5.

21. Suppose Jane is a recreational user of marijuana. If the price of marijuana increases due to more strict enforcement, we would expect:
    a. Jane's expenditures on marijuana to be unchanged.
    b. Jane's expenditures on marijuana to increase.
    c. Jane's expenditures on marijuana to decrease.
    d. Jane's expenditures on marijuana to first increase and then fall back to their original level as her demand for the drug stabilizes.

22. One consequence of increased enforcement of drug laws is:
    a. an increase in property crimes.
    b. contamination of the illegal substance.
    c. the creation of criminals.
    d. all of these.

23. Which of the following would favor the legalization of drugs?
    a. Hawks.
    b. Owls.
    c. Doves.
    d. Eagles.

24. According to the owls:
    a. a tradeoff between increased drug use and achieving other social goals may be desirable.
    b. drugs have no socially redeeming value.
    c. strict enforcement of drug laws should be maintained.
    d. informed adults should be able to make their own decisions concerning drug use.

25. A good that is impossible or extremely difficult to exclude nonpayers from consuming is called a(n):
    a. nonexcludable good.
    b. nonrival good.
    c. private good.
    d. non-scarce good.

26. An individual who uses goods or services provided by others without paying for them is called a:
    a. public servant.
    b. bureaucrat.
    c. free rider.
    d. non-rival consumer.

27. The intersection of the marginal social benefit and marginal social cost curves simultaneously yields:
    a. the individual costs and benefits associated with criminal activity.
    b. the free rider cost of criminal activity.
    c. the efficient level of crime control and crime.
    d. a zero crime level.

28. Using an economic analysis of crime control, the September 11 terrorist attacks have had all of the following effects except one. Which one?
    a. The marginal social benefit of crime control has increased because many believe that the world is a more dangerous place.
    b. At the new equilibrium quantity of crime control, the marginal social benefit is greater than it was before.
    c. Given the available techniques it may be too costly or impossible to achieve the previous level of security.
    d. The optimum level of crime control has declined because of the terrorist attacks.

29. In the debate over drug policy, "hawks" are those who
    a. advocate for the legalization of marijuana.
    b. believe in the liberalization of drug laws.
    c. favor increased penalties for the production, distribution, and consumption of illicit drugs.
    d. believe that predatory birds should be used in the war on drugs.

30. In drug policy, the equimarginal principle implies that
    a. the same amount of public funds should be spent enforcing laws against marijuana as cocaine.
    b. the punishments for possession of one ounce of marijuana should be the same as that for an ounce of cocaine.
    c. more should be spent on marijuana enforcement.
    d. enforcement dollars should be allocated among different drugs so that the marginal benefit of the last dollar spent on fighting each drug is the same.

Fill-in Questions

1. A _____ is a good with two characteristics. First, they are said to be _____ goods. This means that it is impossible or extremely difficult to exclude nonpayers from consuming a good. Second, public goods are said to be _____ goods. This means that one person's consumption of a public good does not affect the quantity of the good available for others to consume. Generally, government must provide public goods. This is because the characteristics of these goods lead to the _____ problem.

2. In drug policy, we can characterize different positions with aviary allegories. _____ are those who are strongly opposed to drug use _____ tend to favor liberalization of drug laws, while _____ often take a middle ground.

3. In enforcing drug laws, the _____ implies that drug enforcement dollars should be allocated so as to equate the marginal benefits of the last dollar spent on each enforcement activity.

Problems Applying Economic Concepts

Use the following diagram to answer question 1.

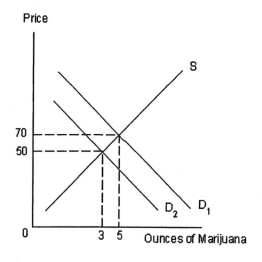

1. Suppose government enacts educational programs designed to decrease marijuana use. As a result, demand for marijuana falls from D_1 to D_2 in the graph below. How much do total expenditures on marijuana change as a result of this program?

2. Suppose the supply of ecstasy increases. As a result, the price of ecstasy falls from $30 per pill to $25 per pill. Purchases of ecstasy increase from 4,000 pills per week to 6,500 pills per week. What happens to expenditures on ecstasy?

3. Fill in the blanks in the following table.

| Total Social Benefit of | | Marginal Social Benefit of | |
Patrol Cars	Drug Dogs	Patrol Cars	Drug Dogs
$2,500,000	$1,750,000		
3,200,000	2,350,000	$_____	$_____
3,600,000	2,850,000	_____	_____
3,850,000	3,250,000	_____	_____
4,050,000	3,550,000	_____	_____
4,200,000	3,750,000	_____	_____
4,300,000	3,850,000	_____	_____

4. Suppose it costs the government $20,000 for either an additional unit of cocaine deterrence or an additional unit of marijuana deterrence. Fill in the blanks in the table.

| Units | Marginal Benefit of | | Marginal Benefit per Dollar of | |
	Cocaine Deterrence	Marijuana Deterrence	Cocaine Deterrence	Marijuana Deterrence
1	$300,000	$125,000	$_____	$_____
2	290,000	120,000	_____	_____
3	270,000	110,000	_____	_____
4	240,000	95,000	_____	_____
5	200,000	75,000	_____	_____
6	150,000	50,000	_____	_____
7	50,000	20,000	_____	_____

5. Suppose you are an economist working for the city government and you are given the information in question 4. If the government has $260,000 to allocate between cocaine and marijuana deterrence, how would you recommend apportioning this budget between the two activities?

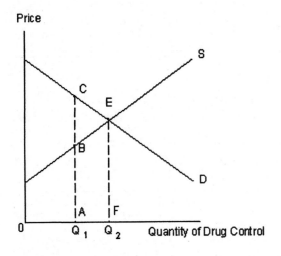

6. Suppose government is currently providing Q_1 of drug control. Identify the marginal social benefit of this quantity of drug control.

7. Suppose government is currently providing Q_1 of drug control. Identify the marginal social cost of this quantity of drug control.

8. Based on your answers to questions 6 and 7, should government increase the quantity of drug control to Q_2?

9. Suppose that the average expected return from a bank robbery is $10,000. Twp of every ten bank robbers are caught, and once caught, there is an 80% chance of conviction that leads to a year in jail. There are two women:

a. An unemployed single woman would be willing to pay $50,000 per year to avoid staying out of jail. She has little job prospects for next year.

b. A lawyer super-mom would also be willing to pay $50,000 per year to avoid staying out of jail, but in addition, she would earn $100,000 during the year. What is the expected cost to each of them of robbing a bank? Who is more likely to rob a bank? Why?

Problems Applying Economic Concepts Solutions

1. Before the program, expenditures were $70 x 5 or $350. After the program, expenditures fell to $50 x 3 or $150. Thus, expenditures on marijuana fell by $200 as a result of the program.

2. At a price of $30 per pill, expenditures on ecstasy are $30 x 4,000 or $120,000. At a price of $25 per pill, total expenditures on ecstasy are $25 x 6,500 or $162,500. The lower price causes expenditures on ecstasy to increase by $42,500.

3. Fill in the blanks in the following table.

| | Total Social Benefit of | | Marginal Social Benefit of | |
Quantity	Patrol Cars	Drug Dogs	Patrol Cars	Drug Dogs
10	$2,500,000	$1,750,000		
20	3,200,000	2,350,000	$70,000	$60,000
30	3,600,000	2,850,000	40,000	50,000
40	3,850,000	3,250,000	25,000	40,000
50	4,050,000	3,550,000	20,000	30,000
60	4,200,000	3,750,000	15,000	20,000
70	4,300,000	3,850,000	10,000	10,000

4. Fill in the blanks in the following table.

| | Marginal Benefit of | | Marginal Benefit per Dollar of | |
Units	Cocaine Deterrence	Marijuana Deterrence	Cocaine Deterrence	Marijuana Deterrence
1	$300,000	$125,000	$15.00	$6.25
2	290,000	120,000	14.50	6.00
3	270,000	110,000	13.50	5.50
4	240,000	95,000	12.00	4.75
5	200,000	75,000	10.00	3.75
6	150,000	50,000	7.50	2.50
7	50,000	20,000	2.50	1.00

5. The first unit of cocaine deterrence gives the city a marginal benefit of $15 per dollar while the first unit of marijuana deterrence gives a marginal benefit of only $6.25 per dollar. Thus, the first $10,000 should be spent on cocaine deterrence. The second unit of cocaine deterrence gives a marginal benefit of $14.50 per dollar while the first unit of marijuana deterrence gives a marginal benefit of only $6.25 per dollar. Thus, the second $10,000 should also be spent on a unit of cocaine deterrence. Continuing in this manner until the entire $260,000 is spent results in the purchase of 7 units of cocaine deterrence and 6 units of marijuana deterrence.

6. Marginal social benefit is represented by the demand curve which gives the maximum price that will be paid for the marginal unit. If the amount of drug control is Q_1, then marginal social benefit is AC.

7. Marginal social cost is represented by the supply curve which gives the minimum acceptable price for the marginal unit. If the amount of drug control is Q_1, then marginal social cost is AB.

8. The marginal social benefit, AC, exceeds the marginal social cost, AB. Since marginal benefit exceed marginal cost, the expansion should be undertaken. Note that at quantity Q_2, marginal social benefit, EF, is equal to marginal social cost, EF. Thus, Q_2 is the efficient quantity.

9. Here, the expected cost of a bank robbery = probability of detection x probability of conviction x total cost. So for a), the expected cost is

$$0.2 \times 0.8 \times 50,000 = 8,000.$$

Since the expected cost is $8,000 but the expected return is $10,000, expected net benefits will increase by robbing a bank. For b), the expected cost is
$$0.2 \times 0.8 \times 150,000 = 24,000.$$
For the lawyer, the expected costs of $24,000 are not worth the expected benefits of $10,000. So the unemployed single woman in b) is more likely to rob a bank, at least according to pure economic calculations, since she has a positive expected net benefit.

Internet Exercises

1. The two major federal agencies that report crime statistics are the FBI and the Department of Justice. The FBI crime statistics page can be found at: http://www.fbi.gov/ucr/2005prelim/table1report.htm. This is the site for the 2005 data. For later years, just click on "Uniform Crime Reports" at www.fbi.gov/ucr. The Department of Justice crime statistics page is located at: http://www.ojp.usdoj.gov/bjs/glance.htm#Crime. What types of crimes are recorded by the FBI? What are the trends in violent crimes? Property crimes? How is the crime rate measured by each agency? Do you detect any differences in the trends discussed by each agency? What differences might the method of measurement make?

2. Let's compare views on marijuana use. First, go to the Office of National Drug Control Policy fact sheet on marijuana at: http://www.ondcp.gov/publications/factsht/marijuana/index.html. Next, visit the National Organization for the Reform of Marijuana Laws website at: http://www.norml.org/index.cfm?Group_ID=3418#question5. How do the views of marijuana as portrayed by the two websites compare? Which seems more realistic to you? Why?

Solutions

True False Questions

1. F, In order to operate efficiently, the marginal social benefit of crime control needs to be equal to the marginal social cost of crime control. Because marginal social cost increases as the quantity of crime control increases and marginal social benefit declines as the quantity of crime control increases, the efficient level of crime control will probably be reached before the crime rate falls to zero. If crime were totally eliminated, society would most likely be operating at a point where the marginal social cost of crime control exceeded the marginal social benefit.

2. T, True, since consumption of a public good is nonrival, one person's consumption doesn't detract from another's consumption. Since public goods are nonexcludable, once the good is consumed by one, it can be consumed by all. Individuals have an incentive to free-ride on the consumption of others, and private firms could not force payment since exclusion is impossible.

3. T, True, according to the economic approach to crime, criminals make rational calculations concerning the costs and benefits of committing a crime. An increase in penalties or a greater probability of apprehension will increase the perceived costs of armed robbery, and that will cause criminals to rationally change their behavior by committing less armed robberies.

4. F, False, those with more job skills and higher incomes face higher opportunity costs from committing a crime. Crimes are more likely to be committed by those with low opportunity costs, such as low skilled workers or those with poor job prospects.

5. F, With the exception of murder and rape, crime rates are lower in the United States than in England. In fact, English crime rates have remained stable or increased since 1981 while almost all types of U.S. crime rates have fallen. On reason for this may be because of differences in punishment between the two countries. The United States increased the severity of punishment while England reduced it.

6. F, False, libertarians argue that individuals should have the liberty to use their bodies in any way they please, as long as the activity doesn't cause any significant harm to others.

7. T, Drug prohibition creates criminals where there were none before. Simply using illegal drugs makes the user a criminal. In addition, some users commit numerous property crimes in order to obtain money for drug purchases. Drug prohibition has also created opportunities for people to earn large income as dealers. Finally, corruption of public officials can also result from prohibition.

8. T, True, since the value per volume of cocaine is much higher than the value per volume of marijuana, increased penalties may have increased the attractiveness of supplying cocaine relative to Marijuana. A thousand dollars worth of cocaine is easier to hide than a thousand dollars of marijuana.

Multiple Choice

1. B
2. C
3. D
4. D
5. C
6. B
7. B
8. C
9. A
10. D
11. A
12. B
13. A
14. C
15. D
16. A
17. A
18. B
19. A
20. B
21. C

22. D	25. A	28. D
23. C	26. C	29. C
24. A	27. C	30. D

Fill-in Questions

1. public good; nonexcludable; nonrival; free rider

2. Hawks; Doves; owls

3. equimarginal principle

College Education: Is It Worth the Cost?

Objectives of the Chapter

After you have mastered this chapter you will understand:

1. The principal benefits and costs of a college education, from both individual and social perspectives.

2. How to determine the present value of a future payment.

3. How the rate of return from investing in a college education is determined.

4. That two ways of evaluating an investment are the present value decision rule and the rate of return decision rule.

5. Why private rates of return exceed social rates of return.

6. The various rationales used to justify government subsidies to college students.

7. That while government subsidies are meant to increase the enrollment of lower-income students, in reality the enrollment increases due to subsidies are likely to be concentrated among middle and upper income students.

Key Terms

present value

future value

discount factor

present value decision rule

rate of return decision rule

rate of return

monetary benefits and costs

nonmonetary benefits and costs

social benefits

social costs

student benefits

non-student benefits

student costs

non-student costs

student rate of return

social rate of return

student rate of return without government support

True False Questions

For these statements, indicate whether they are true or false. Defend your answer.

1. The opportunity costs of college tend to increase as a person becomes older.

   TRUE or FALSE

2. To determine the present value of a future payment, that future payment must be multiplied by the discount factor $(1 + i)^t$.

   TRUE or FALSE

3. For most students at most income levels, the real rate of return for investing in a bachelor's degree is higher than the equivalent investments in stock or bond markets.

   TRUE or FALSE

4. The social benefits of a higher education are greater than the private benefits of a higher education. Because of this government should encourage people to invest in a higher education by subsidizing this activity.

   TRUE or FALSE

5. Because capital markets are imperfect, government should provide loans to students. However, the interest rates on these loans should not be below the market rate of interest.

   TRUE or FALSE

6. Many economic studies have shown that where you go to college makes a significant difference to future earnings.

   TRUE or FALSE

7. A college education may have a negative impact on society.

   TRUE or FALSE

8. Tuition subsidies provide relatively more benefits to higher-income families than to lower-income families.

   TRUE or FALSE

9. The returns to education tend to be higher in high-income countries compared to low-income countries.
    TRUE or FALSE

Multiple Choice

Check yourself. Choose the best answer. Answers are found at the end of the chapter.

1.

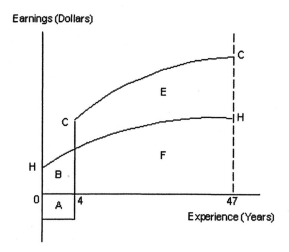

In the figure above, line HH represents the earnings of a high school graduate, and the line containing CC represents the earnings of a college graduate. The earnings foregone as a result of obtaining a college education is represented by area:

a. A.

b. B.

c. A + B.

d. E + F.

2.

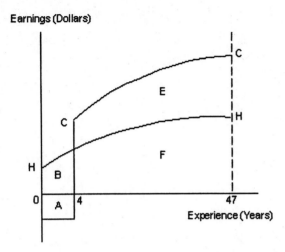

In the figure above, line HH represents the earnings of a high school graduate, and the line containing CC represents the earnings of a college graduate. The additional earnings associated with a college education are represented by area:

a. A.
b. F.
c. E.
d. B + F.

3.

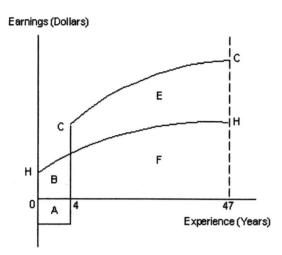

In the figure above, line HH represents the earnings of a high school graduate, and the line containing CC represents the earnings of a college graduate. The life-time earnings of a high school graduate are represented by area:

a. B.
b. B + F.
c. F + E.
d. B + F + E.

4.

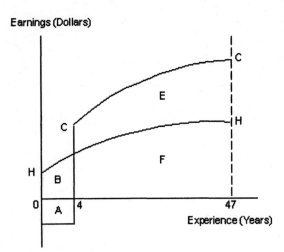

In the figure above, line HH represents the earnings of a high school graduate, and the line containing CC represents the earnings of a college graduate. In order for the individual to consider investing in a college education:

a. area E must exceed area A + B.

b. area A + B must exceed area E.

c. area E must exceed area B.

d. area B must exceed area E.

5.

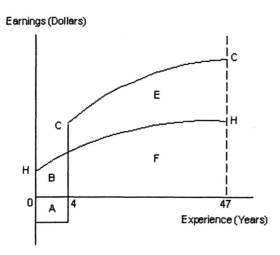

In the figure above, line HH represents the earnings of a high school graduate, and the line containing CC represents the earnings of a college graduate. If the nonmonetary benefits of an education were taken into consideration, then:

a. areas A and B would increase.

b. areas A, B, and E would increase.

c. areas A, B, and E would decrease.

d. area E would increase.

6.

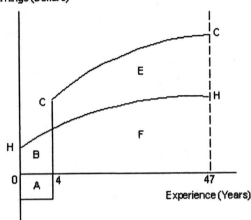

In the figure above, line HH represents the earnings of a high school graduate, and the line containing CC represents the earnings of a college graduate. The cost of tuition, books, and fees incurred during a college education is represented by area:

a. A.

b. B.

c. E.

d. A + B.

7. In order to determine if investment in a college education is a viable alternative, an individual should consider:

a. only the increased earnings associated with the college education.

b. only the explicit costs associated with the college education.

c. only the increased earnings associated with the college education and the explicit costs associated with the college education.

d. the rate of return that could have been earned on the money used to pay the college tuition.

8. When considering investment in college education from a social perspective:

a. after-tax earnings are used in calculating benefits.

b. only tuition costs are used in calculating benefits.

c. before-tax earnings are used in calculating benefits.

d. only room and board are used in calculating costs.

9.

t	PVB$_t$	PVC$_t$
0	$10,000	$30,000
1	9,000	10,000
2	8,000	0
3	7,000	0

The total present value of benefits is:

a. $34,000.

b. $27,000.

c. $19,000.

d. $10,000.

10.

t	PVB$_t$	PVC$_t$
0	$10,000	$30,000
1	9,000	10,000
2	8,000	0
3	7,000	0

The total present value of costs is:

a. $30,000.

b. $10,000.

c. $20,000.

d. $40,000.

11.

t	PVB$_t$	PVC$_t$
0	$10,000	$30,000
1	9,000	10,000
2	8,000	0
3	7,000	0

Based on the information given, should the investment be undertaken?
a. Yes, the investment generates net benefits of $6,000.
b. Yes, the investment generates net benefits of $3,000.
c. No, the investment generates a net loss of $6,000.
d. No, the investment generates a net loss of $3,000.

12. Albert is considering an investment that generates a rate of return equal to 7 percent. The market rate of interest is 5 percent. Should Albert make the investment?
a. No, the market rate of interest is not high enough.
b. Yes, the rate of return will exceed what Albert could earn if he invested his money elsewhere.
c. No, the present value of net benefits will be negative.
d. No, the rate of return will not exceed what Albert could earn if he invested his money elsewhere.

13. What is the present value of a loan that pays $251.94 in three years, if the interest rate is eight percent?
a. $272.10
b. $200
c. $317.37
d. $100
e. $221.32

14. It may be difficult to place a dollar value on:
a. the increased earnings an individual receives as a result of a college education.
b. the enhanced value of leisure that an individual receives as a result of a college education.
c. the foregone earnings an individual gives up in order to receive a college education.
d. the cost of tuition, books, and fees incurred while getting a college education.

15. Which of the following statements is correct?
a. You should undertake an investment if the present value of benefits is positive.
b. Economists argue that the benefits of a college education should be adjusted for unemployment.
c. The private benefits of a college education exceed the social benefits.
d. The social costs of a college education exceed the private costs.

16. All of the following may be external benefits of education except:
    a. reductions in criminal activity.
    b. increased social cohesion.
    c. higher income for the individual who receives the education.
    d. technological change.

17. The social rate of return of an education is:
    a. the rate of return realized by students and nonstudents from investing in an education.
    b. the rate of return realized by students from investing in an education.
    c. the rate of return realized from investing in a college education when government pays none of the cost.
    d. the rate of return realized by nonstudents from investing in an education.

18. Government subsidization of education can be justified:
    a. in order to increase access for lower-income students.
    b. if there are few external benefits associated with education.
    c. if education enhances the earnings of individuals.
    d. if individuals can easily borrow to finance their education.

19. As a result of scientific research undertaken at Polytech University, a new fuel is discovered that reduces the amount of air pollution. This would be an example of:
    a. screening.
    b. a research spillover.
    c. a direct benefit of education.
    d. an external benefit of education.

20. Studies indicate that the subsidies received by college students tend to be distributed:
    a. disproportionately to high-income students.
    b. disproportionately to low-income students.
    c. equally between high- and low-income students.
    d. equally between middle and low-income students.

21. Suppose private lenders are unwilling to lend money for purposes of paying for a higher education. As a result of this capital market failure, government should:
    a. subsidize loans.
    b. provide grants.
    c. guarantee loans at a rate somewhat below the market rate of interest.
    d. guarantee loans at the market rate of interest.

22. The major subsidy to college students is:
    a. Pell grants.
    b. guaranteed student loans.
    c. state appropriations.
    d. savings on interest that accrue as a result of interest-free periods before repayment of student loans.

23. The largest federal government providing support directly to students is:
    a. Pell grants.
    b. guaranteed student loans.
    c. state appropriations for instructional purposes.
    d. interest savings that accrue as a result of interest-free periods before repayment of student loans.

24. An investment is worthwhile if the rate of return on the investment is greater than the rate of return on a person's best alternative. This statement best describes which of the following concepts?
    a. present value decision rule.
    b. marginal social cost decision rule.
    c. rate of return decision rule.
    d. future value decision rule.

25. The principal monetary student benefit from a college education is:
    a. increase in lifetime earnings after taxes.
    b. the additional knowledge gained from obtaining a college degree.
    c. the benefit which accrues to the government in the form of increased tax revenues.
    d. equal to the social benefit from obtaining the college degree.

26. The largest source of support to college students is:
    a. AFDC and TANF.
    b. Pell grants.
    c. Federal tax rebates for education.
    d. state appropriations to colleges and universities.

Fill-in Questions

1. The investment decision requires that an individual compare the costs of acquiring a college education with the benefits. Because these costs and benefits occur in different time periods, their values must be adjusted. For example, the _____ , the value at a future date of a sum of money now is different than the value now of a future sum of money, _____ . Specifically, the future value of a dollar is greater than its present value. The _____ is used to calculate both future value and present value. It is the value of $(1 + i)^t$.

2. In order to determine if an investment should be made either the present value decision rule or the rate of return decision rule can be used. The _____ says that an investment should be made if the sum of the present value of benefits is equal to or greater than the sum of the present value of costs. The _____ _____ says that an investment should be made if the rate of return on the investment is greater than the rate of return on the best alternative use of funds. The

_____ is the discount rate at which the sum of the present value of costs is equal to the sum of the present value of benefits.

3. Benefits and costs typically are classified as _____ or _____ . Monetary benefits and costs are benefits and costs valued in dollars while nonmonetary benefits and costs are not valued in dollars.

4. In the context of education _____ are benefits that accrue to both students and nonstudents. _____ are costs paid by both students and nonstudents. The benefits accruing to nonstudents are _____ . _____ are the costs paid by nonstudents. _____ are the benefits going to students. The rate of return realized by students when they invest in a college education is the _____ . The rate of return realized by students and nonstudents is the _____ .

5. Without government support, it is unlikely that the _____ in education would occur. This is because the _____ would be less than social rate of return.

Problems Applying Economic Concepts

1. Suppose Amy can invest $1000 today. Next year she will earn $500 on her investment. The following year she will earn $600 on her investment. The interest rate is 6 percent. Should Amy invest in the $1,000?

2. How would the lifetime earnings profile of a high school graduate be represented in the diagram?

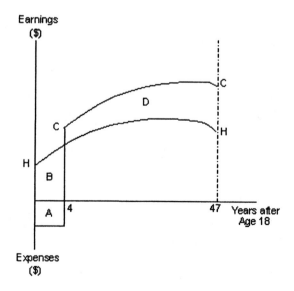

155

3. How would the lifetime earnings profile of a college graduate be represented in the diagram?

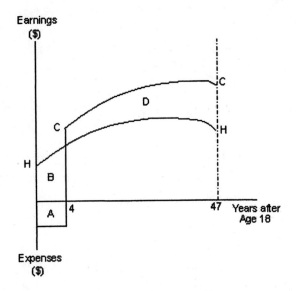

4. What area would represent the earnings foregone as a result of attending college?

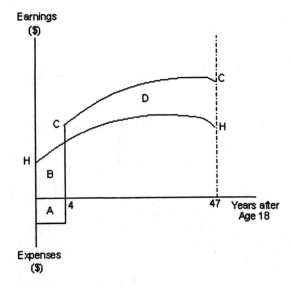

5. What area would represent the cost of tuition, books, and fees while attending college?

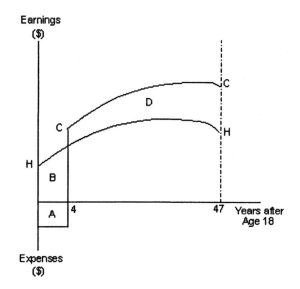

6. What area would represent the difference in earnings between a high school and a college graduate?

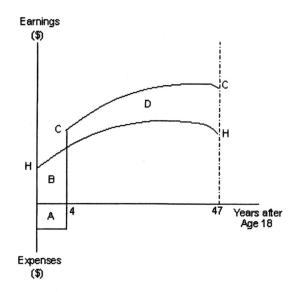

7. What areas should be compared in order to determine if a college investment should be undertaken?

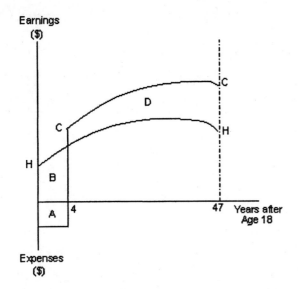

8. Suppose that a friend offers the following investment opportunity. For a loan of $10,000 today, she will pay you $3,000 each year for the next four years. The payment stream would look like this:

year	0	1	2	3	4
costs	10,000	0	0	0	0
benefits	0	3000	3000	3000	3000

a. If interest rates are 2%, should you make this loan?

b. If interest rates are 10%, should you make this loan?

9. Suppose that in the market for college education, the student demand is given by

$$D_{stud} = 8000 - 1000Q.$$

Where P is the tuition per year and Q is the average number of years of college attendance.
The cost to society of providing a college education, the social supply, is given by
$$S_{soc} = 4000 + 1000Q$$

a. In a private market, what would be the quantity of education consumed? What is the equilibrium price of tuition? Show graphically.

b. Suppose that each year of college provides external benefits equal to $4,000. The social demand would be

$$D_{soc} = 12000 - 1000Q$$

What is the socially optimal average number of years of college? What tuition must be charged to supply that quantity? Show on your graph from a).

c. What subsidy will lead to the social optimum? Show on your graph from a).

Problems Applying Economic Concepts Solutions

1. In order to determine if Amy should invest, the present value of costs and benefits must be compared. Since all the cost are incurred in the present, the present value of cost is $1,000. The present value of benefits in the first year is $471.70 ($500/1.06). The present value of benefits in the second year is $534.00 ($600/1.1236). The total present value of benefits is $1,005.70 ($471.70 + $534.00). The total present value of cost is $1,000. Amy would have a net benefit of $5.70 ($1005.70 - $1000.00). Since there is a positive net benefit, she should invest the $1,000.

2. Line HH represents the lifetime earnings profile of a high school graduate.

3. Line CC represents the lifetime earnings profile of a college graduate.

4. Area B represents the foregone earnings.

5. Area A represents the cost of tuition, books, and fees.

6. Area D represents the earnings differential.

7. Area D must be compared with areas A + B. Area D must exceed A + B by enough to yield a rate of return at least as large as the best alternative investment in order to make the investment in college worthwhile. (Note: the present value of these areas should be compared.)

8.

   a. If interest rates are 2%, you should make the loan. The sum of the present value of payments, $11,423.20, is greater than the loan of $10,000.

   b. If interest rates are 10%, you should not make the loan. The sum of the present value of payments, $9509.59, is less than the loan of $10,000. You would be better off leaving the money in the bank. Please consult the following table:

year	0	1	2	3	4	total
costs	10,000	0	0	0	0	$10,000
benefits	0	3,000	3,000	3,000	3,000	$12,000
discount factor i = .02	1	1.02	1.04	1.06	1.08	
discount factor i = .10	1	1.1	1.21	1.33	1.46	
present value i = .02	-	2,941.18	2,883.57	2826.97	2771.54	$11,423.20
present value i = .10	-	2,727.27	2479.34	2283.94	2049.04	$9,509.59

9.

   a. In a private market, the equilibrium would be where student demand is equal to the social supply. This is where:

$$8000 - 1000Q = 4000 + 1000Q$$
$$4000 = 2000Q$$
$$Q = 2$$
$$P = 8000 - 1000(2) = 6000$$
$$P = 4000 + 1000(2) = 6000$$

   See graph below.

b. The social optimum is where the social demand is equal to the social supply. This is given by:

$$12000 - 1000Q = 4000 + 1000Q$$
$$8000 = 2000Q$$
$$Q = 4$$
$$P = 12000 - 1000(4) = 8000$$
$$P = 4000 + 1000(4) = 8000$$

c. In order to convince colleges to supply the socially optimal amount of 4 years, a price of $8000 is required. The problem is, that at a price of $8000, the student demand curve shows that 0 units will be demanded. So to achieve the social optimum, a subsidy of $4000 is necessary. Graphically:

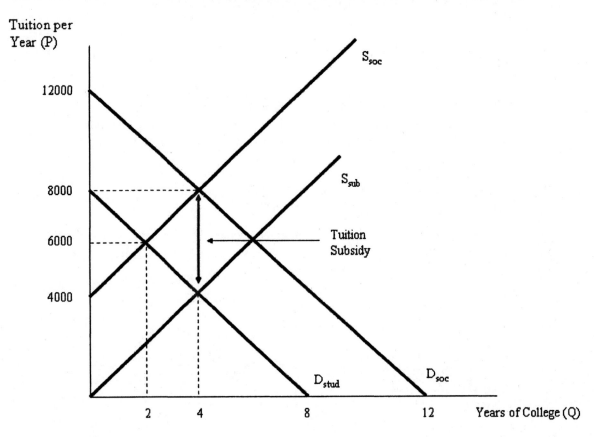

Internet Exercises

1. To find the current costs of a college education, go to the College Board web site at http://www.collegeboard.com/student/pay/add-it-up/index.html. Click on the most recent year under "college costs". What is the current average cost of a four-year private college? A four-year public college? What is the difference? Is the rate of increase in the price of college greater or less than the average inflation rate during the same period?

2. To discover what issues professors are concerned about in higher education, go to the web site for the Chronicle of Higher Education at http://chronicle.com/chronicle/. What current issues are discussed on the website? Are any of these issues important on your campus?

Solutions

True False Questions

1. T, True, as a person becomes older, the opportunity costs of foregone wages will increase. As an individual gains more experience in the workforce, she is likely to earn higher wages even without a college education. Also, as individuals age, the value of time spent with family and friends may become more important. So it is economically rational to attend college while young, when the opportunity costs are lower.

2. F,

    False, to determine the present value of a future payment, the future payment must be divided by the discount factor $(1 + i)^t$. The future value is equal to the present value divided by the discount factor. The relevant equations are: $FV_t - PV_0 \times (1 + 1)^t$. $PV_0 = FV_t/ (1 + 1)^t$.

3. T, True, as pointed out in the text, the real rate of return for a student from a bachelor's degree is 9.51%, while the returns to stocks and bonds average 7.5% and 3%, respectively. From a purely individual financial standpoint, a college education is a good investment.

4. F, First, although the social benefits of higher education are larger than private benefits (due partly to the fact that they are based on before-tax earnings) it is also true that the social costs of a higher education are larger than the private costs. This is due to the fact that social costs include all the costs of operating an institution of higher learning. In general, a student's payments for books and tuition cover only a portion of these costs. Arguing for subsidies on the basis of social benefits exceeding private benefits is faulty. It is net benefits that should be considered.

5. F, False, since the social rate of default on student loans is less than the private rate of default for any individual student, lenders will be unwilling to charge the socially efficient rate of interest reflecting the social risk of default. Since students cannot serve as collateral, lenders will require a higher rate of interest that may discourage some students from attending college. By subsidizing student loans, the interest rate charged can more closely reflect the social rate of default.

6. F, False. Fortunately, most studies have shown that the choice of major, the number of math classes, and what you do while in college, are much more important in determining future earnings than where a student goes to college.

7. T, Overeducation is one of the negative impacts of a college education. Overeducation may lead to job dissatisfaction, adverse work place behavior, deteriorating health, and decreased labor productivity.

8. T, This arises from the three-tiered structure of institutions of higher learning. It is likely that educational costs increase more than tuition as individuals move up the tier. Further it is likely that students from higher-income families are over-represented at these institutions. This results in tuition subsidies being directly related to income.

9. F, False, the returns to education tend to be higher for less developed countries and at lower levels of education in general. For less developed countries, the higher rates of return to education are due to the relative shortages of educated people at all levels in those societies.

Multiple Choice

1.	B	5.	D	9.	A
2.	C	6.	A	10.	D
3.	B	7.	D	11.	C
4.	A	8.	C	12.	B

13. B	18. A	23. A
14. B	19. B	24. C
15. D	20. A	25. A
16. C	21. D	26. D
17. A	22. C	

Fill-in Questions

1. future value; present value; discount factor
2. present value decision rule; rate of return; decision rule; rate of return
3. monetary benefits and costs; nonmonetary benefits and costs
4. social benefits; Social costs; external benefits; External costs; Student benefits; student rate of return; social rate of return
5. socially justified investment; student rate of return without government support

Educational Reform: The Role of Incentives and Choice

Objectives of the Chapter

After you have mastered this chapter you will understand:

1. That U. S. students do not compare favorably to international students in the fields of math and science.

2. That spending per pupil and student teacher ratios are not the causes of the problem of poor performance.

3. The two rationales for public support of primary and secondary schools.

4. That the student's decision to invest more effort into academic achievement is based on marginal benefits versus marginal costs. In order to increase achievement, marginal costs must be lowered or marginal benefits must be increased.

5. That high-stakes testing creates an incentive for students to increase achievement. There are benefits associated with increasing achievement in this way, but there are also costs. It is not known if benefits outweigh costs.

6. That requiring more courses as a condition for graduation is probably not an effective approach to the problem.

7. The three principles of economic organization and that the organization of the U. S. public school system is not consistent with these principles.

8. The major approaches and provisions of the No Child Left Behind Act.

9. The concepts of school choice and school vouchers.

Key Terms

commutative justice

distributive justice

high-stakes testing

general knowledge

specific knowledge

tacit knowledge

local knowledge

assembled knowledge

economic approach to organization

No Child Left Behind Act

school choice

vouchers

True False Questions

For these statements, indicate whether they are true or false. Defend your answer.

1. In terms of primary and secondary education, US public schools consistently rank among the best in the world.

    TRUE or FALSE

2. Thomas Jefferson was one of the early supporters of public primary education.

    TRUE or FALSE

3. If graduation rates are high, government will most likely need to subsidize K - 12 education in order to have the efficient level provided.

    TRUE or FALSE

4. It is possible that increased opportunities for part-time employment have decreased achievement levels.

    TRUE or FALSE

5. High-stakes testing may increase achievement levels.

    TRUE or FALSE

6. If the study of automobile mechanics becomes more difficult due to increasing technological complexity, the marginal benefits of achievement will decline.

    TRUE or FALSE

7. Typically, increases in per pupil spending are associated with increases in educational achievement.

    TRUE or FALSE

8. The economic organization of the typical American public school tends to mimic that of a market economy.

    TRUE or FALSE

9. Vouchers help to increase school choice.

    TRUE or FALSE

Multiple Choice

Check yourself. Choose the best answer. Answers are found at end of chapter.

1. Which of the following questions is correct?
   a. Evidence shows that U. S. public school performance is among the best in the world.
   b. In the U. S., students of advanced math and science perform relatively better than students of advanced math and science in other nations.
   c. Other countries tend to spend relatively more per pupil than does the U. S.
   d. Evidence indicates there is no relationship between spending per pupil and educational achievement.

2. The line labeled A represents:

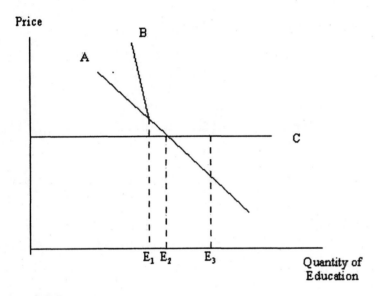

   a. supply.
   b. marginal social cost.
   c. demand.
   d. marginal social benefit.

3. The efficient level of education is represented by:

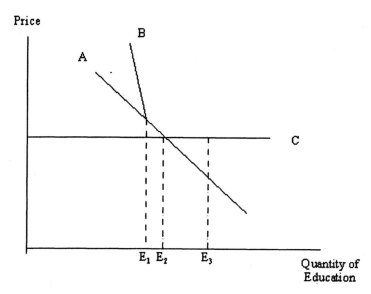

a. E_1.
b. E_2.
c. E_3.
d. somewhere between E_1 and E_2.

4. At education levels below E_1:

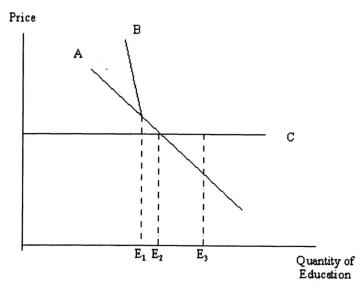

a. marginal social benefit exceeds marginal private benefit.
b. marginal private benefit exceeds marginal social cost.
c. marginal external benefits are zero.
d. marginal external benefits are negative.

5. Some people advocate government support of K - 12 education because such education can:
   a. generate negative external benefits.
   b. generate positive external benefits.
   c. generate negative external costs.
   d. generate positive external costs.

6. Your authors argue that educational attainment will increase as long as:
   a. the marginal benefit of achievement is equal to the marginal cost of achievement.
   b. the marginal cost of achievement is greater than the marginal benefit of achievement.
   c. the marginal benefit of achievement is greater than the marginal cost of achievement.
   d. the marginal benefit of achievement is greater than the marginal external benefit of education.

7.

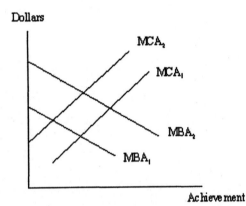

A shift from MBA_1 to MBA_2 is interpreted as:
   a. a decrease in the marginal benefit of achievement.
   b. a decrease in the marginal cost of achievement.
   c. an increase in the marginal benefit of achievement.
   d. an increase in the marginal cost of achievement.

8.

Dollars

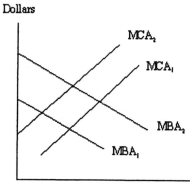

A shift from MCA$_1$ to MCA$_2$ could be caused by:
a. increased opportunities for part-time employment.
b. tying graduation to achievement test scores.
c. a decrease in the time spent watching television.
d. tying driving privileges to educational achievement.

9. Which of the following will lead to an increase in the marginal benefit of achievement?
a. an increase in the size of high school textbooks
b. a decrease in the real wage of high school graduates
c. an increase in the popularity of video games
d. tying driving privileges to educational achievement.

10. Achievement testing where demonstration of achievement is important for completion of high school and subsequent employment is:
a. low-takes testing.
b. superior-stakes testing.
c. mid-range testing.
d. high-stakes testing.

11. Which of the following is NOT a characteristic of high-stakes testing?
a. The tests are universal tests.
b. The tests use relative performance standards.
c. The tests are internationally referenced.
d. The test are analytically oriented.

12. Which of the following statements is correct?
a. U.S. officials have responded to poor test scores by requiring high-stakes testing.
b. Requiring students to take more courses will not necessarily increase educational achievement.
c. Requiring all students to take a common core of classes will increase educational achievement.
d. Underperforming students are typically required to repeat classes.

13. Knowledge that is easy to transfer to another person is:
    a. scientific knowledge.
    b. tacit knowledge.
    c. general knowledge.
    d. specific knowledge.

14. After making spending several months mountain biking, Joan has developed a new seat that is more comfortable for female riders. This is an example of:
    a. tacit knowledge.
    b. general knowledge.
    c. overall knowledge.
    d. public knowledge.

15. The three market organizing principles that lead to success when specific knowledge is important are:
    a. the assignment of property rights, the lack of reward for profitable decisions, and the ability to evaluate decision results.
    b. the assignment of property rights, a reward for profitable decisions, and the ability to evaluate decision results.
    c. the assignment of decision rights, the lack of reward for profitable decisions, and the ability to evaluate decision results.
    d. the assignment of decision rights, a reward for profitable decisions, and the ability to evaluate decision results.

16. Your text states that the inefficiency of the U. S. public school system is:
    a. largely a result of too much competition.
    b. largely a result of too much regulation.
    c. largely a result of the system's organization and a lack of competition.
    d. largely are result of teacher incompetence.

17. The justice that emerges from voluntary exchange is referred to as:
    a. distributive justice.
    b. equality justice.
    c. commutative justice.
    d. equality of outcome.

18. Applying the economic perspective to education would imply that:
    a. parents and students consider the social costs and benefits when making their choices.
    b. parents and students assess the benefits and costs of academic achievement by comparing the marginal private benefits with the marginal private costs.
    c. all parents and students have the same perception of the marginal costs and benefits associated with academic achievement.
    d. Individual costs are the same for all individuals

19. An increase in MCA reflects:
    a. a decline in the opportunity costs of achievement and an increase in the difficulty of learning.
    b. the impact of reducing expenditures and increasing the pupil-teacher ratio.
    c. an increase in the opportunity costs of achievement or an increase in the difficulty of learning.
    d. an increase in the opportunity cost of achievement or a decrease in the difficulty of learning.

20. High stakes testing encompasses all of the following characteristics except one. Which one?
    a. They use relative performance standards such as curves.
    b. They determine the degree to which the test taker has mastered a broad subject area.
    c. They are internationally referenced.
    d. They are analytically oriented.

21. In a state-owned enterprise, decisions are likely to be less than optimal because
    a. decision-making is decentralized.
    b. the incentives for evaluations are strong.
    c. decision-makers may lack specific knowledge.
    d. efficient decisions are always adequately rewarded.

22. The No Child Left Behind Act
    a. allows policy makers in Washington to set educational goals.
    b. requires standardized testing.
    c. increases competition by allowing parents to pull children from failing schools.
    d. all of the above.

23. Subsidies that would allow low income families to choose between public, charter, or private schools for their children are known as:
    a. vouchers.
    b. high stakes funds.
    c. commutative justice.
    d. curves.

Fill-in Questions

1. _____ is a norm for a market economy based on voluntary exchange. In addition to commutative justice, a market economy also needs _____ . This later type of justice deals with equality of opportunity.

2. The text indicates that _____ can increase educational achievement. Such testing would raise the marginal benefit of educational achievement by tying achievement to high school completion and subsequent employment. High-stakes testing would use achievement tests to determine the degree to which the test-taker has mastered a broad subject area.

3. Knowledge that is easy to transfer to another person is known as _____ . On the other hand, _____ is costly to transfer to another person. Typically, the head of a state department of education does not possess the specific knowledge needed to make good decisions for the organization's dispersed units.

4. The primary education initiative of the George W. Bush Administration, _____ allows the federal government to set goals for schools throughout the country, and requires _____ as a means of evaluation and increasing the marginal benefit of achievement.

5. Many states are adopting _____ as a policy to provide parents with more options for their children. One program, known as _____ , would provide subsidies to low income families to allow them to choose between public, charter, or private schools.

Problems Applying Economic Concepts

Use the following diagram to answer questions 1-4.

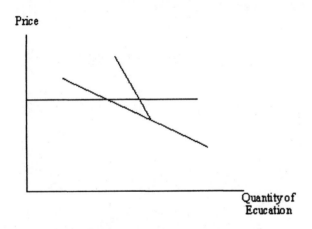

1. Correctly label all curves in the diagram.

2. Show the efficient level of education.

3. Show the level of education the private market will provide.

4. Because there are _____, the quantity of education provided by the market will be _____ the efficient quantity of education.

5. Using the economic analysis of achievement as presented in the text, show the effects of a) an increase in parental rewards provided for high grades and b) an increase in the popularity of providing service to the community through volunteer work. Explain.

Problems Applying Economic Concepts Solutions

1.

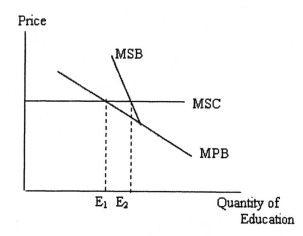

2. The efficient quantity of education occurs at E_2 where MSB and MSC are equal.

3. The market will provide E_1 of education where D=MPB=MSC.

4. Because there are ___*marginal external benefits*___, the quantity of education provided by the market will be ___*less than*___ the efficient quantity of education.

5.

   a. An increase in parental rewards for high grades will lead to an increase in the marginal benefit of achievement. Academic effort will increase. Graphically:

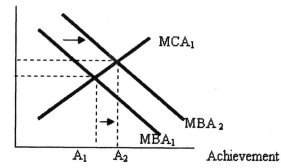

   b. An increase in the popularity of community service would increase the marginal cost of achievement. The level of academic achievement would decline:

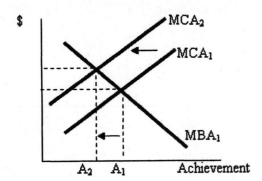

Internet Exercises

1. To examine the Bush administration viewpoint on the No Child Left Behind Act, visit the following web sites: http://www.ed.gov/nclb/landing.jhtml and http://www.whitehouse.gov/news/reports/no-child-left-behind.html. What are the major provisions of the No Child Left Behind Act? What was it supposed to accomplish?

2. To read some critics of the No Child Left Behind Act, visit the following web sites: http://www.nea.org/esea/index.html and http://nochildleft.com/. According to these groups, what's wrong with the No Child Left Behind Act?

Solutions

True False Questions

1. F, False, although the United States rank among the highest in terms of spending per pupil, we often rank among the lowest in terms of student achievement. For example, The Third International Mathematics and Science Study showed that American students were close to last in math and science scores.

2. T, True, in many of his writings, Jefferson was a strong supporter of public education, both as a means of individual development and to support the development of civil and democratic society.

3. F, Many agree that K - 12 education generates marginal external benefits. However, some argue that these marginal external benefits decline as graduation rates increase. In this case, if graduation rates are low then the MSB of K - 12 education will be greater than the MPB and the market provided output will be less than the efficient quantity. However, if graduation rates are high, the MSB may equal MPB. The quantity of education provided by the private market will be equal to the efficient quantity, and no government intervention will be required.

4. T, Increased opportunities for part-time employment increases the value of alternative uses of time required for studying. This leads to an increase in the opportunity cost of achievement. An increase in the opportunity cost of achievement will raise the marginal cost of achievement. Because it costs more for an additional unit of achievement, achievement levels will fall.

5. T, High-stakes testing focuses on achievement testing with demonstration of achievement important for completing high school and for subsequent employment opportunities and college admission. If high-stakes testing works, these connections will lead to higher achievement levels. It is possible that increased opportunities for part-time employment have decreased achievement levels.

6. F, False, an increase in the difficulty of learning will lead to an increase in the marginal cost of achievement. If everything else is held constant, an increase in the marginal cost of achievement will lead to a decrease in achievement.

7. F, In a random sample of the United States and 21 other countries, per pupil spending was highest in the United States. Comparisons of the United States with these other countries showed the United States ranking in the lower end in terms of math and science achievement levels. If graduation rates are low, government will most likely need to subsidize K - 12 education in order to have the efficient level provided.

8. F, False, a market economy tends to decentralize decision-making, so that decisions are made by those with specific knowledge of the situation. The market provides evaluation and rewards. The economic organization of a typical public school is closer to a state-owned enterprise, where decision-making is centralized to those without specific knowledge, and there is little incentive for evaluation and rewards.

9. T, True, vouchers provide a student with a sum of money that can be use for either private, charter, or regular public schools. Especially for low income families, vouchers can expand the range of options available for primary and secondary education, and increase competition among schools.

Multiple Choice

1. D
2. C
3. B
4. A

5. B
6. C
7. C
8. A

9. D
10. D
11. B
12. B

13. C	17. C	21. C
14. A	18. B	22. D
15. D	19. C	23. A
16. C	20. A	

Fill-in Questions

1. Commutative justice; distributive justice
2. high-stakes testing
3. general knowledge; specific knowledge
4. The No Child Left Behind Act; standardized testing
5. school choice; vouchers

Poverty: Old and New Approaches to a Persistent Problem

Objectives of the Chapter

After you have mastered this chapter you will understand:

1. The scope of the poverty problem and how poverty is defined and how the poverty rate is computed.

2. The relative effectiveness of the various government programs in reducing long-term poverty.

3. How the major poverty programs like food stamps, the earned income tax credit, and TANF work.

4. How food stamp benefits are determined.

5. How unemployment policies have affected the level of poverty.

6. The difference between the post and pre transfer poverty rates.

7. The importance of programs such as childcare assistance and medical protection in making work pay.

8. The impact of discrimination on wage differentials between races and genders.

9. The various proposals to make fathers pay.

Key Terms

poor person

official poverty threshold

money income

poverty rate

transfer

income-tested transfer

cash transfer

noncash transfer

pre-transfer poverty rate

Gross Income (GI)

deductible (D)

basic benefit (BB)

benefit (B)

benefit reduction rate (BRR)

break-even gross income (BEGI)

target efficiency

minimum wage

wage subsidy

True False Questions

For these statements, indicate whether they are true or false. Defend your answer.

1. Since Lyndon Johnson declared war on poverty in 1964, the official poverty rate at first declined, and then fluctuated, but has been generally lower than before 1964.

    TRUE or FALSE

2. The decline in poverty in the United States has reduced the relative income gap between the upper income group and the other income groups.

    TRUE or FALSE

3. The elderly have seen their relative share of poverty decline over the last four decades.

    TRUE or FALSE

4. An important demographic cause of poverty is the increasing transfer of employment opportunities from service industries to manufacturing industries.

    TRUE or FALSE

5. The underlying causes of poverty are entirely economic in nature.

    TRUE or FALSE

6. The break-even gross income occurs when a household is just able to pay all of its bills.

    TRUE or FALSE

7. By providing a credit against income tax liability, the Earned Income Tax Credit acts as a significant source of income for the working poor.

    TRUE or FALSE

8. Some analysts believe that more people are induced to become poor by the historical and current welfare programs.

    TRUE or FALSE

9. Well-designed programs to reduce poverty can be successful regardless of the state of the economy.
   TRUE or FALSE

10. White males have always earned more in salary and benefits than other socioeconomic groups in American society.
    TRUE or FALSE

11. Labor market discrimination is a significant source of poverty in the United States.
    TRUE or FALSE

Multiple Choice

Check yourself. Choose the best answer. Answers are found at the end of the chapter.

1. Which of the following would NOT be included in money income?
   a. earnings before taxes
   b. interest and dividend income
   c. food stamp benefits
   d. unemployment benefits

2. Examples of welfare programs would not include:
   a. TANF payments.
   b. food stamps.
   c. the earned income tax credit .
   d. the regressive nature of the sales tax.

3. The poverty rate is the:
   a. ratio of poverty income to the median income.
   b. number of people below the poverty line.
   c. percentage of persons below the poverty line.
   d. official definition of a subsistence level of income times 3.

4. Since the onset of the war on poverty in the mid 1960s, the poverty rate of the non-elderly:
   a. has steadily declined.
   b. b. has remained virtually the same.
   c. has increased.
   d. is lower during recessions and higher during periods of expansion.

5. The poverty threshold level defines poverty by calculating the cost of feeding a family and multiplying it by:
   a. two.
   b. three.
   c. four.
   d. five.

6. Which of the following statements regarding poverty is correct?
   a. There are more poor blacks than poor whites.
   b. The percentage of women heads of household in poverty is lower than for male heads of household.
   c. The percentage of blacks in poverty is higher than for whites.
   d. All of these are correct.

7. Programs whose benefits decline as income increases are called:
   a. social security programs.
   b. income-tested programs.
   c. social insurance programs.
   d. earned income tax credit programs.

8. The official poverty rate of elderly people:
   a. has declined substantially over the last 40 years.
   b. has increased as the number of elderly has increased as a percentage of the total population.
   c. will increase dramatically because the baby boom is nearing retirement.
   d. has remained virtually unchanged over the past 35 years.

9. Since 1959, the official poverty rate has fallen for
   a. the elderly.
   b. persons living in female-headed households.
   c. persons living in black and Hispanic households.
   d. all of the above.

10. The poverty threshold income level is:
    a. adjusted for increases in real per capita income.
    b. invariant to differences in size and composition of the family.
    c. adjusted for price changes.
    d. the highest income level that would keep a family in the low income group.

11. The number of poor people divided by the U.S. population yields the:
    a. break even level of poverty.
    b. break even gross income.
    c. discount premium.
    d. poverty rate.

12. Which demographic group has the highest poverty rates?
    a. Black heads of household.
    b. Unmarried white males.
    c. Female heads of household.
    d. Young married couples.

13. The pre-transfer poverty rate is:
    a. the number of people that would still be in poverty after all welfare benefits are counted.
    b. a good measure of the actual number of people in poverty after price adjustments are made.
    c. an estimate of what the poverty rate would be without cash transfer income.
    d. equal to the number of people in poverty times the labor force participation rate.

14. Which of the following would NOT account for the increased income inequality of recent years?
    a. The progressive income tax.
    b. The shift from goods production to service sector jobs.
    c. The declining union membership.
    d. Changes in family composition.

15. Welfare programs where the transfer falls as a recipient's income increases are referred to as:
    a. pre-transfer programs.
    b. break-even income programs.
    c. income-tested programs.
    d. entitlements.

16. The basic benefit refers to the:
    a. ratio of the decrease in benefits to the increase in income.
    b. break-even gross income level.
    c. target efficiency rate.
    d. the maximum benefit received when gross income is less than or equal to the deductible.

17. The break-even gross income level is defined as:
    a. the amount a person receives when the earned income tax credit is equal to zero.
    b. income that excludes entitlement payments.
    c. the level of gross income where food stamp benefits become zero..
    d. the basic benefit package.

18. In general, the lower the break-even gross income relative to the poverty rate, the:
    a. greater the target efficiency.
    b. lower the target efficiency.
    c. larger the ratio of means payments to income.
    d. smaller the ratio of means payments to income.

19. Suppose that a family of four has a monthly gross income of $400. For food stamps, the basic benefit is $500, the deductible is $200, and the benefit reduction rate is 0.25. For this family, the monthly food stamp benefit is
    a. $500
    b. $450
    c. $300
    d. $400

20. Suppose that a family of four has a monthly gross income of $400. For food stamps, the basic benefit is $500, the deductible is $200, and the benefit reduction rate is 0.25. For this family, the break-even gross income is
    a. $500
    b. $2000
    c. $2200
    d. $1200

21. The earned income tax credit (EITC) refers to:
    a. the taxes that must be paid against earned income.
    b. the tax credits that poor people receive for earning income.
    c. a refundable credit against the tax liability.
    d. the credit that a family in poverty receives per family member.

22. The temporary assistance for needy families, TANF, was designed to replace:
    a. the earned income tax credit.
    b. child care tax credits.
    c. social security payments for the elderly.
    d. AFDC.

23. According to the temporary assistance for needy families, (TANF), households are limited to how many years over their lifetimes?
    a. two.
    b. four.
    c. five.
    d. ten.

24. Which of the following is NOT a program that would reward workers for their efforts?
    a. An increase in the time frame for receiving TANF.
    b. Raising the minimum wage.
    c. Providing wage subsidies.
    d. Expanding the earned income tax credit.

25. Which of the following statements is true?
    a. Each family head that receives TANF must find work within two years or face the loss of benefits.
    b. Some estimates suggest that up to ¼ of the nation's welfare recipients may be unemployable.
    c. The Wisconsin experience suggests that it usually takes up to 18 months to prepare a person to leave welfare for good.
    d. All of the statements are true.

26. The federal program that provides the states with money to help low-income working families pay for childcare is the:
    a. Child and Dependent Care Tax Credit.
    b. Dependent Care Assistance Program.
    c. Earned Income Tax Credit.
    d. Child Care and Development Fund.

27. The Dependent Care Assistance Program is a federal program that:
    a. allows an employer to provide up to $5,000 in assistance to employees to help pay for child care expenses.
    b. provides a block grant to states to help low-income working families pay for childcare.
    c. provides a tax credit for child care expenses.
    d. provides an earned income tax credit for working families.

28. One of the problems with wage subsidies is that they:
    a. cannot be targeted towards low-income families.
    b. reduce the opportunity cost of leisure.
    c. require employers to pay more than an employer is worth.
    d. do not guarantee increased work effort.

29. The majority of studies seem to indicate that discrimination:
    a. is the single largest factor accounting for wage differences between men and women.
    b. affects only black workers.
    c. accounts for a relatively small portion of the existing wage differences between men and women.
    d. explains why Hispanics have a smaller wage gap than do blacks.

30. Which of the following would explain why discrimination does NOT have much to do with poverty?
    a. Females tend to be employed in lower-paying occupations.
    b. Earning differentials between white males and others is smaller among individuals with less education.
    c. The largest group of people in poverty is families headed by white males.
    d. Poverty rates persist even though earnings differentials have narrowed over time.

31. In child support assurance programs,
    a. a family is guaranteed a certain amount of child support regularly and on time each month.
    b. the government collects the funds owed by the noncustodial parent.
    c. if the government is unable to collect, or if the amount collected is less than the guarantee, than the government makes up the difference.
    d. all of the above.

Fill-in Questions

1. _____ includes earnings before taxes, interest, dividends, and private and government cash transfers. The _____ is an estimate of what the poverty rate would be without the income provided by cash transfers. _____ are the programs in which the transfer falls as a recipient's income increases. To be eligible for food stamps, gross household income cannot exceed _____ percent of the relevant poverty line for the particular household.

2. The _____ is the amount that people receive when their gross income is equal to or less than the _____ . The break-even gross income is an indicator of the _____ of a transfer program.

3. The three most common sources of public support for low-income families are _____ _____ , _____ , _____ _____ . Since each of these is an income-tested transfer, they may discourage _____ among recipient households. The replacement of the _____ program with TANF in 1996 was a clear signal that Congress desired to replace welfare with work.

4. The authors conclude that _____ plays a minimal role in causing poverty in the United States. More important explanations for poverty include the _____ occupation, and demographic factors such as education or head of household.

Problems Applying Economic Concepts

1. Suppose that the deduction for essential needs is $150, the benefit reduction rate is 0.20 and the basic benefit is $500. Based on this information what is the break-even level of gross income?

2. Suppose the monthly poverty threshold is $1,500 for a family of 4 and the break-even level of gross income is $2,650. What percent is the break-even level of gross income relative to the poverty threshold?

3. Suppose that the deduction for essential needs is $150, the benefit reduction rate is 0.20 and the basic benefit is $500. Based on this information what is the benefit received by a family with an income of $500 per month? $1000? $2000? $3000? What happens to the benefit as income increases?

4. If the cost of basic nutrition for a family of four is $450 per month, then what is the poverty threshold?

Problems Applying Economic Concepts Solutions

1. BEGI = (BB + D(BRR))/BRR; therefore, BEGI = ($500 +$150(.2))/0.2 = $2,650

2. $2,650 / $1,500 = 177 percent of the poverty threshold

3. The relevant equation to determine the benefit is

$$B = 500 - 0.2(GI - 150).$$

By plugging in the appropriate values for GI, you can derive the following table:

Gross Income	Benefit
500	430
1000	330
2000	130
3000	0

As shown in the table, there is an inverse relationship between gross income and the food stamp benefit received.

4. To determine the poverty threshold, the cost of basic nutrition is multiplied by 3. This is because when the poverty threshold was first developed in 1963 by Mollie Orshansky, the cost of food made up 1/3 of a typical family's budget. So in this example, the poverty threshold is

$$450 \times 3 = \$1350.$$

Internet Exercises

1. To learn about poverty statistics, visit the Census Bureau's poverty page at http://www.census.gov/hhes/www/poverty/poverty.html. From here, answer the following questions: a. Click on "History of the Poverty Measure". Briefly, how was the poverty threshold developed? b. Click on "Overview". What is the current poverty rate? What are trends for different socioeconomic groups? c. "Click on "Poverty Thresholds". What is the current poverty threshold?

2. To explore ways that you can help to reduce poverty personally, or for volunteer opportunities near you, check out some of these websites: http://www.charityguide.org/volunteer/poverty.htm, http://www.foodsecurity.org/, http://www.faireconomy.org/, http://www.secondharvest.org/, http://www.bread.org/, http://www.hungeractionnys.org, http://www.nerahn.org/, http://hungeraction.net/, and http://www.actionagainsthunger.org/.

Solutions

True False Questions

1. T, True, the War on Poverty at first was very successful in reducing the official poverty rate, from 17.3% in 1964 to 11.1% in 1973. The official poverty rate has fluctuated since then, reaching 12.7% in 2004, still well below the rate of 17.3% in 1964.

2. F, Despite the large number of welfare and income transfer programs, the upper income groups have seen their relative percentage of total income increase. Further, all of the other income groups have had their relative shares of total income decline.

3. T, True, before 1982, the poverty rate among the elderly was higher than the general population, but since then, the elderly have fared relatively better than the average population in terms of poverty rates.

4. F, False, the change has been in the opposite direction. Job opportunities have switched from manufacturing to service industries. Since manufacturing jobs tend to pay much higher wages than service industry jobs, the movement to the service sector has reduced wages among lower-income workers.

5. F, There are a myriad of factors that contribute to poverty. Demographic factors such as female head of households, lack of job skills and training, lack of education, and large families all contribute to the problems of poverty.

6. F, False, in the Food Stamp program, the break-even gross income occurs when a household is no longer eligible for food stamp benefits. This occurs currently at an income of $1371 per month.

7. T, True, the Earned Income Tax Credit (EITC) provides a credit towards a household's income tax liability for households with income less than $33,692 (for 2003). This tax refund check may be the biggest check that the family will see all year.

8. T, There is at least some evidence to suggest that the innumerable welfare programs reduce the incentive for some individuals and families to leave the welfare rolls. Additionally, in at least some states, families receive higher incomes on welfare when non-cash benefits are included than they could earn in relatively low-paying jobs.

9. F, False, since the pre-transfer poverty rate seems to be highly influenced by the rate of unemployment, economic conditions that promote low rates of unemployment will provide the conditions for a reduction in poverty. If real GDP is falling drastically, even the best designed programs will be unable to reduce poverty.

10. T, True, differences in earnings reflect a variety of factors that distinguish one group from another, including discrimination, that tend to favor white males. For example, white males earn 27% more than black males and 22% more than white females.

11. F, False, even though an earnings penalty does exist that can be attributed to racial and gender discrimination, most studies have shown that this earnings penalty would be too small in and of itself to cause poverty. Many other factors, such as education, occupation, and head of household, provide better explanations for the causes of poverty.

Multiple Choice

1. C
2. D
3. C
4. B
5. B

6. C
7. B
8. A
9. D
10. C

11. D
12. C
13. C
14. A
15. C

16. D	22. D	28. D
17. C	23. C	29. C
18. A	24. A	30. C
19. B	25. D	31. D
20. C	26. D	
21. C	27. A	

Fill-in Questions

1. Gross money income; pre-transfer poverty rate; Income-tested transfers; 130
2. basic benefit; deduction for essential needs; target efficiency
3. Food; Stamps; the Earned Income Tax Credit; and; TANF; work effort; AFDC
4. labor market discrimination; unemployment rate

Tracking and Explaining the Macroeconomy

Objectives of the Chapter

After you have mastered this chapter you will understand:

1. How the nation's output is measured using the concept of GDP.

2. The importance of distinguishing between nominal and real magnitudes.

3. How price indexes are constructed and interpreted.

4. Why it is difficult to compare the nation's output in one year with its output in another year or to compare the output of one country with that of another country.

5. That the nation's level of economic activity doesn't increase steadily, so that the economy suffers from business cycles.

6. How aggregate demand and supply curves are defined and derived and how to apply them with regard to the determination of the GDP deflator, real GDP, and employment.

Key Terms

gross domestic product (GDP)

final goods

intermediate goods

personal consumption expenditures

gross private domestic investment

capital stock

government purchases of goods and services

net exports of goods and services

exports

imports

price index

nominal GDP

real GDP

GDP deflator

business cycle

expansion phase

peak

contraction phase

trough

aggregate demand curve

real balance effect

interest rate effect

foreign trade effect

fiscal policy

money supply

monetary policy

aggregate supply curve

True False Questions

For these statements, indicate whether they are true or false. Defend your answer.

1. Intermediate goods, such as the tires on a brand new automobile, are included in GDP since they represent productive activity in the economy that year.

   TRUE or FALSE

2. During 2006, A. New Automobile Company produced 1,500,000 automobiles. 500,000 automobiles are unsold at the end of the year. These unsold automobiles should be counted as a part of GDP.

   TRUE or FALSE

3. The underground economy includes such industries as coal and silver mining operations and oil and natural gas extraction.

   TRUE or FALSE

4. When calculating GDP, exports should be excluded because they are consumed by citizens of other countries.

   TRUE or FALSE

5. Gross Private Domestic Investment includes the purchase of new physical capital by firms, newly produced structures, and business inventory changes.

   TRUE or FALSE

6. Economists generally assume that the consumption of goods and services provides individuals with utility or welfare. Although GDP is a measure of the nation's output, many other factors also affect utility. Hence GDP is not an accurate measure of that economy's welfare.

   TRUE or FALSE

7. In the base year, a price index will always be equal to 100.

   TRUE or FALSE

8. The longest economic expansion in United States history occurred in your lifetime.

   TRUE or FALSE

9. In the long run, over the course of several years, the effects of natural disasters such as Hurricane Katrina and terrorist attacks such as 9/11 will lead to reductions in GDP.

   TRUE or FALSE

10. The aggregate demand curve has a negative slope because as the price level falls, goods and services become relatively cheaper. As a result, more goods and services are purchased.

    TRUE or FALSE

11. Fiscal policy includes the federal government's attempts to control the money supply and interest rates.

    TRUE or FALSE

12. An increase in resource prices will lead to a decrease (leftward shift) in the aggregate supply curve.

    TRUE or FALSE

13. Along the upward-sloping range of the aggregate supply curve, an increase in aggregate demand will lead to an increase in the price level and real GDP.

    TRUE or FALSE

Multiple Choice

Check yourself. Choose the best answer. Answers are found at the end of the chapter.

1. Which of the following would be included in US GDP?
   a. the value of the spark plugs Tim buys in order to do a tune-up on his car in New York.
   b. the purchase of a new summer home in the Canadian Rockies.
   c. the purchase of a used car in Los Angeles.
   d. the purchase of a used home in Boston.

2. The value of all final goods and services produced in an economy during a year is referred to as:
   a. net domestic product.
   b. gross domestic product.
   c. value of domestic product.
   d. net domestic income.

3. Which of the following is included in US GDP?
   a. the purchase by an American consumer of sweaters that were produced in Norway by a Norwegian company
   b. the production of tires by Goodyear in Ohio that are purchased by General Motors
   c. a cashmere sweater that your Aunt knits for you
   d. the production of tires by Goodyear in Ohio that are purchased by you

4. One reason why GDP may not be an accurate measure of the quality of life is because
   a. those countries with higher per capita GDPs tend to have higher literacy rates.
   b. GDP increases if the sale of bicycles declines.
   c. GDP decreases if the sale of SUVs increases.
   d. If people decide to consume more leisure, GDP will decline.

5. Which of the following would be considered an intermediate good?
   a. a home produced last year, but not sold.
   b. a new heavy-duty mixer bought by Delectable Delights Bakery to mix donut dough.
   c. the buttons used on a pair of Levi Button-Down blue jeans.
   d. a new car.

6. Which of the following would NOT be considered a part of government purchases?
   a. government payments to elderly individuals through the Medicare program.
   b. government purchases $300 worth of hammers.
   c. government purchases new computers.
   d. local government purchases of paper for a copier.

7. Personal consumption expenditures would include all of the following except:
   a. a household's purchase of a new refrigerator.
   b. a household's expenditures for medical services.
   c. a household's expenditures for clothing.
   d. a household's purchase of a new home.

8. Which of the following would be included as gross private domestic investment?
   a. purchase of IBM stock.
   b. a new factory built by a firm.
   c. a refrigerator purchased by a household.
   d. a purchase of a used car.

9. Suppose that during 2006 a nation's net private domestic investment was $3.5 billion. This would imply that:
   a. a total of $3.5 billion was spent on capital stock during the year.
   b. the nation's capital stock decreased by over $3.5 billion during the year.
   c. after accounting for depreciation, the nation's capital stock grew by $3.5 billion during the year.
   d. the nation's structures and equipment depreciated by $3.5 billion during the year.

10. Suppose that a firm's business inventories were $2 million at the beginning of 2006 and $2.5 million at the end of 2006. As a result:
    a. $2.5 million will be added to gross private domestic investment.
    b. $2 million will be added to gross private domestic investment.
    c. $0.5 million will be added to gross private domestic investment.
    d. there will be no change in gross private domestic investment. A firm's inventory is only counted as a part of net investment.

11. The consumption of fixed capital refers to:
    a. the deduction made from GDP in order to allow for the purchase of new issues of stocks and bonds.
    b. the allowance made for depreciation of and accidental damage to the nation's capital stock.
    c. the allowance made for the purchase of used equipment.
    d. the allowance made for the trade of equipment between the United States and other countries.

12. Suppose gross domestic investment is $625 billion. The consumption of fixed capital is $600 billion. Net investment is:
    a. -$25 billion.
    b. $25 billion
    c. $600 billion
    d. $1,225 billion.

13. Suppose federal government purchases of goods and services is $350 billion, state government purchases of goods and services is $375 billion, and local government purchases of goods and services is $200 billion. What figure would GDP use for government purchases?
    a. $925 billion.
    b. $725 billion.
    c. $550 billion.
    d. $350 billion.

14. Suppose the United States exports $800 billion of goods and services and imports $820 billion of goods and services. For the purposes of GDP, net exports are:
    a. $1,620 billion.
    b. $800 billion.
    c. $20 billion.
    d. -$20 billion.

15. The least stable component of GDP is:
    a. government purchases.
    b. net exports.
    c. gross private domestic investment.
    d. consumption.

16. Suppose that during 2000, real GDP increased by $25 billion. Which of the following is necessarily correct?
    a. price increased.
    b. quantity increased.
    c. price decreased, but quantity increased
    d. both price and/or quantity increased.

17. Suppose that nominal GDP increased from $11,700 billion in 2004 to $12,500 billion in 2006. Suppose that over this same period real GDP did not change. In this instance:
    a. price decreased and quantity was constant.
    b. quantity decreased and price was constant.
    c. price increased and quantity was constant.
    d. quantity increased and price was constant.

18. Suppose nominal GDP in 2004 is $8,000 billion. If the GDP deflator is 125, real GDP is:
    a. $10,000.
    b. $100.
    c. $6,400.
    d. $6405.

19. Real GDP may not accurately reflect economic activity because it does not include:
    a. the value of services.
    b. the value of illegal activities.
    c. the value of nondurables.
    d. the value of used goods that are exchanged.

20. Which of the following would NOT be included in GDP?
    a. a drug store sells Valium to a customer.
    b. the money you pay to the person delivering your newspaper.
    c. the money you pay a gardener to maintain the grounds of your home.
    d. the money paid for the illegal sale of marijuana.

21. In the diagram, the letters A, B, C, and D, represent which phases of the business cycle?

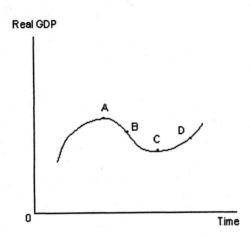

    a. expansion, peak, contraction, and trough, respectively.
    b. peak, contraction, trough, and expansion, respectively.
    c. expansion, contraction, trough, and peak, respectively.
    d. contraction, trough, expansion, and peak, respectively.

22. In the diagram, unemployment is likely to be the lowest at point:

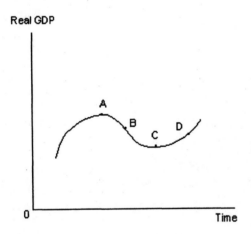

    a. A.
    b. B.
    c. C.
    d. D.

23. The effect of excluding non-market activity would probably cause the relatively largest underestimate of GDP in:
    a. India.
    b. Great Britain.
    c. Japan.
    d. the United States.

24. Business cycles are:
    a. caused by the government deficit.
    b. easily predicted by using the composite index of leading indicators.
    c. recurring fluctuations in the level of economic activity.
    d. fluctuations in the level of economic activity that occur every six months.

25. During the past three quarters real GDP has risen by 1.7 percent and the unemployment rate has decreased from 5.5 to 5.1 percent. Economists predict that in the next quarter GDP will show an increase of 2.5 percent and unemployment may decrease to 4.9 percent. The economy is most likely:
    a. at the peak of the business cycle.
    b. in a contraction phase.
    c. in an expansion phase.
    d. at the trough of the business cycle.

26. Which of the following accounts for the negative slope of the aggregate demand curve?
    a. the real balance effect.
    b. the interest rate effect.
    c. the international trade effect.
    d. all of these.

27. If the interest rate increases:
    a. households will borrow less and aggregate demand will fall.
    b. households will borrow less and aggregate demand will rise.
    c. households will borrow more and aggregate demand will fall.
    d. households will borrow more and aggregate demand will rise.

28. If firms or households become more optimistic about the future:
    a. there will be an upward movement along a given aggregate demand curve.
    b. the aggregate demand curve will shift to the left.
    c. there will be a downward movement along a given aggregate demand curve.
    d. the aggregate demand curve will shift to the right.

29. The function showing the total output of final goods and services that will be produced at each price level is the:
    a. aggregate supply curve.
    b. aggregate demand curve.
    c. GDP curve.
    d. business phase curve.

30. The positively sloped portion of the aggregate supply curve occurs because:
    a. input prices are flexible.
    b. profits fall as the price level rises due to the flexibility of input prices.
    c. profits increase as the price level rises due to sticky input prices.
    d. profits remain unchanged as the price level changes due to sticky input prices.

31. If aggregate demand is AD_3, the equilibrium price level and real GDP will be:

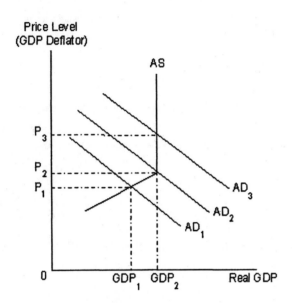

    a. P_1 and GDP_1, respectively.
    b. P_2 and GDP_2, respectively.
    c. P_3 and GDP_1, respectively.
    d. P_3 and GDP_2, respectively.

32. Suppose aggregate demand is AD_1. The economy is:

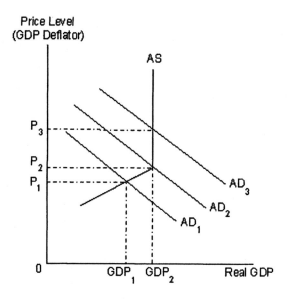

a. experiencing full employment.
b. experiencing a recession.
c. experiencing inflation.
d. cannot be determined without further information.

33. Suppose aggregate demand is currently AD$_2$. If the Federal Reserve undertakes expansionary monetary policy:

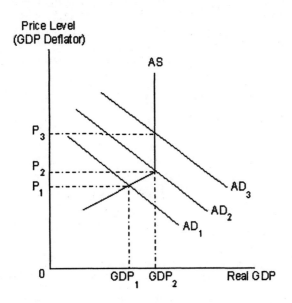

a. the price level will increase, but real GDP will remain unchanged.
b. real GDP will increase, but the price level will remain unchanged.
c. both the price level and real GDP will increase.
d. both the price level and real GDP will fall.

34. Suppose the economy is currently producing below the full employment level of GDP. The government undertakes expansionary fiscal policy. As a result:
a. the equilibrium price level is constant, but real GDP increases.
b. the equilibrium price level increases, but real GDP is constant.
c. both the equilibrium price level and real GDP increase.
d. both the equilibrium price level and real GDP decrease.

35. Increases in aggregate demand when the economy is producing at the full employment level of GDP will cause:
a. increases in the price level.
b. increases in output and the price level.
c. increases in the price level but decreases in the level of output.
d. decreases in the price level and increases in the level of output.

36. An increase in the price level will tend to:
a. a rightward shift in the aggregate demand curve.
b. a leftward shift in the aggregate demand curve.
c. a movement upward along a stationary demand curve.
d. a movement downward along a stationary demand curve.

37. Based on the real balances effect, a decrease in the price level will:
    a. shift the aggregate demand curve to the right.
    b. lead to an downward movement along a stationary aggregate demand curve.
    c. shift the aggregate demand curve to the left.
    d. lead to a rightward shift in the aggregate supply curve.

38. All of the following will result from a decline in the price level except an increase in:
    a. the real value of wealth.
    b. household real wealth.
    c. the real value of money balances.
    d. aggregate demand.

39. The interest rate effect refers to:
    a. the inverse relationship between the interest rate and the level of investment.
    b. the impact of price changes on household wealth.
    c. the impact of government borrowing on the interest rate.
    d. the impact of price changes on the interest rate and investment spending.

40. Which of the following events will cause an increase in aggregate demand?
    a. the end of the Iraqi War.
    b. an increase in interest rates.
    c. a decline in the value of the dollar.
    d. an increase in income taxes.

41. Expansionary fiscal policy may be accomplished through
    a. a decrease in income taxes.
    b. a decrease in G.
    c. an increase in income taxes.
    d. an increase in the money supply.

42. Aggregate supply depicts the relationship between:
    a. aggregate output and aggregate income.
    b. unemployment and the price level.
    c. the price level and aggregate output.
    d. the price level and the interest rate.

43. The vertical portion of the aggregate supply curve follows from the existence of:
    a. an increase in the price level.
    b. full employment.
    c. crowding out.
    d. insufficient aggregate demand.

Fill-in Questions

1. _____ , the market value of all final goods and services produced in an economy over the relevant time span, does not include goods purchased for resale or _____ . In order to avoid the problem of double counting the nation's output, only _____ , goods purchased for (or available for) final use are included in GDP.

2. GDP consists of four components. The largest of these components is households' purchases of durable and nondurable goods and services or _____ . _____ , firms' purchases of equipment, changes in business inventories, and the purchases of all newly produced structures, is a second component of GDP. A third component of GDP is the purchase of goods and services by federal, state, and local governments. This component is known as _____ . _____ , payments made to individuals or institutions that involve no production and exchange of goods and services, are not included as a part of government purchases. The final component of GDP, _____ , is the amount by which foreign spending on domestically produced goods and services is greater (less) than domestic spending on goods and services produced abroad. Net exports is found by subtracting _____ from _____ .

3. If one is interested in additions to a nation's _____ or additions to a nation's accumulation of structures, producers' durable equipment, and business inventories, the variable that must be examined is _____ . Net private domestic investment is derived by subtracting _____ from gross private domestic investment.

4. Economists often adjust variables so as to hold prices constant. In order to do this, a _____ must be used. The particular price index used to adjust GDP for price changes is called the _____ . GDP that has been adjusted for price changes is referred to as _____ . _____ has not been adjusted for price changes.

5. Real GDP has grown over time, however, it has not been a steady growth. Instead, real GDP has fluctuated from year to year. These fluctuations in the general level of economic activity are referred to as _____ . Business cycles consist of four phases. The low and high points of the business cycle are known respectively as the _____ and _____ . During the _____ of the business cycle, GDP is increasing and unemployment is falling while during the _____ of the business cycle, GDP is falling and unemployment is rising.

6. The _____ shows the total amount of final goods and services that will be purchased at each price level. This function is negatively sloped. The _____ , the interest rate effect, and the effect of changes in the price level on the relative prices of exports and imports all help to explain the negative slope of the aggregate demand curve.

7. Changes in the price level will cause movements along a given aggregate demand curve. Changes in other factors will cause the aggregate demand curve to shift. Changes in _____ , households' spendable income, _____ (changes in government spending and taxes), and _____ (changes in nation's money supply in an attempt to achieve economic goals) will all shift the aggregate demand curve.

8. _____ will cause an increase in aggregate demand. If the Federal Reserve increases the _____ they are said to be undertaking _____ _____ . Like expansionary fiscal policy, expansionary monetary policy will also increase aggregate demand. If the government pursues _____ or if the Federal Reserve undertakes _____ , the aggregate demand curve will shift to the left. In this case, aggregate demand is said to be decreasing.

9. The _____ shows the total output that firms are willing to produce at various price levels. The positively sloped portion of the aggregate supply curve is drawn on the assumption that input prices are sticky. The vertical portion of the aggregate supply curve is drawn on the assumption that input prices are flexible.

Problems Applying Economic Concepts

1. Use the information in the following table to calculate GDP.

Item	Amount
Wheat	$3,900,000
Automobiles	6,500,00
Tires used in production of automobiles	800,000
Social Security	1,500,000
Highway system	3,250,000
Residential housing	8,250,000
Leisure	3,500,000
Volunteer services	1,750,000
Government purchases	2,225,000

Item	Amount
Consumption	$3,000
Gross investment	1,000
Consumption of fixed capital	425
Government purchases	800
Government transfers	1,750
Exports	700
Imports	320

2. What is net investment?

Item	Amount
Consumption	$3,000
Gross investment	1,000
Consumption of fixed capital	425
Government purchases	800
Government transfers	1,750
Exports	700
Imports	320

3. What are net exports?

Item	Amount
Consumption	$3,000
Gross investment	1,000
Consumption of fixed capital	425
Government purchases	800
Government transfers	1,750
Exports	700
Imports	320

4. What is GDP?

Year	Units of Good Produced	Price per Unit
1999	4 million bagels	$1.00
1999	2 million pounds of cream cheese	$0.50
2000	5 million	$1.20
2000	4 million pounds of cream cheese	$0.85

5. What is nominal GDP for 1999 and 2000?

Year	Units of Good Produced	Price per Unit
1999	4 million bagels	$1.00
1999	2 million pounds of cream cheese	$0.50
2000	5 million	$1.20
2000	4 million pounds of cream cheese	$0.85

6. What is the real GDP deflator? (Assume 1999 is the base year.)

Year	Units of Good Produced	Price per Unit
1999	4 million bagels	$1.00
1999	2 million pounds of cream cheese	$0.50
2000	5 million	$1.20
2000	4 million pounds of cream cheese	$0.85

7. What is real GDP for 2000?

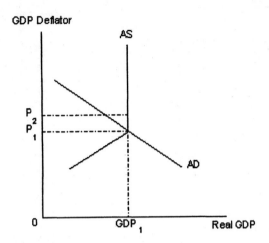

8. If the GDP deflator is currently P_2, explain why there will be a tendency for the deflator to decrease to P_1.

9. Fill in the blanks in the following table.

Year	Nominal GDP In Billions of Current Dollars	Real GDP In Billions of 1992 Dollars	GDP Deflator
1998	4,800.0	4,000.0	___
1999	5,500.0	___	130
2000	___	4,850.0	135

10. Assume that an economy produces four goods, dates, plates, crates and gates. Dates are their food source. Plates and crates are used for carrying the food; they are good substitutes for each other. The quantities and prices for each of the goods in years one and two are given by the following table:

	YEAR 1				YEAR 2	
good	quantity	price	good	quantity	price
dates	600	$3	dates	800	$4
plates	400	$1	plates	600	$1
crates	300	$2	crates	200	$4
gates	200	$6	gates	300	$8

a. What is nominal GDP in year 1?

b. What is real GDP in year 1?

c. What is nominal GDP in year 2?

d. What is real GDP in year 2? (Use year 1 as the base year.)

e. What is the percentage increase in nominal GDP? Real GDP?

  f. What is the GDP price deflator?

11. Using aggregate demand and aggregate supply analysis, show the effects of the following events:

  a. deflation

  b. an increase in investment spending

  c. an increase in the average wage rate

  d. an income tax cut

Problems Applying Economic Concepts Solutions

1. GDP is equal to the market value of all final goods and services produced in an economy over the relevant time span. Thus, the goods that should be included are wheat, automobiles, the highway system, residential housing, and government purchases of computers. This leads to a value of GDP = $3,900,000 + $6,500,000 + $3,250,000 + $8,250,000 + $2,225,000, or $24,125,000.

2. Net investment is equal to gross investment less the consumption of fixed capital. Thus, net investment = $1,000 - $425 or $575.

3. Net exports are equal to exports less imports. Thus, net exports = $700 - $320, or $380.

4. The four components of GDP are consumption, gross private domestic investment, government purchases, and net exports. Thus, GDP = $3,000 + $1,000 + $800 + ($700 - $320), or $5,180.

5. Nominal GDP for 1999

$$= (4,000,000 \times \$1.00) + (2,000,000 \times \$0.50)$$
$$= \$4,000,000 + \$1,000,000$$
$$= \$5,000,000$$

Nominal GDP for 2000
$$= (5,000,000 \times \$1.20) + (4,500,000 \times \$0.85)$$
$$= \$6,000,000 + \$3,4000,000$$
$$= \$9,400,000$$

6. The GDP deflator

$$= \frac{[(4,000,000)(\$1.20) + (2,000,000)(\$0.85)]}{[(4,000,000)(\$1.00) + (2,000,000)(\$0.50)]}$$
$$= \frac{\$4,800,000 + \$1,700,000}{\$4,000,000 + \$1,000,000}$$
$$= \frac{\$6,500,000}{\$5,000,000}$$
$$= 1.30$$

7. Real GDP for 2000

> = nominal GDP x 100
>   real GDP
> = nominal GDP
>   GDP deflator
> = 9,400,000
>   1.30
> = 7,230,769

8. If the GDP deflator is currently P_2, there will be a tendency for the deflator to decrease to P_1. At P_2, the aggregate quantity supplied exceeds the aggregate quantity demanded. Buyers are not willing to purchase all of the goods and services that firms are willing to produce. This puts a downward pressure on prices. The price level will fall until the equilibrium price of P_1 is reached. At this price aggregate quantity demanded and aggregate quantity supplied are equal.

9.

> GDP deflator for 1998
> = nominal GDP x 100
>   real GDP
> = 4,800 x 100
>   4,000
> = 1.2 x 100
> = 120
>
> Real GDP for 1999
> = nominal GDP
>   GDP deflator
> = 5,500
>   1.25
> = \$4,400 billion
>
> Nominal GDP for 2000
> = real GDP x GDP deflator
> = 4,850 x 1.30
> = \$6,305 billion

10.

a. Nominal GDP in year 1 = (600 x 3) + (400 x 1) + (300 x 2) + (200 x 6) = 4000

b. Real GDP in year 1 = nominal GDP in year 1 = 4000 (Year 1 is the base year.)

c. Nominal GDP in year 2 = (800 x 4) + (600 x 1) + (200 x 4) + (300 x 8) = 7000

d. Real GDP in year 2 = (800 x 3) + (600 x 1) + (200 x 2) + (300 x 6) = 5200

e. Percentage increase in nominal GDP = [(7000 – 4000)/4000] x 100 = 75%
   Percentage increase in real GDP = [(5200 – 4000)/4000)] x 100 = 30%

f. GDP price deflator = nominal GDP/real GDP = 7000/5200 = 1.346

11.

a.

A decrease in the price level will not shift either AD nor AS, it will just lead to movements along the curves. Overconsumption would result.

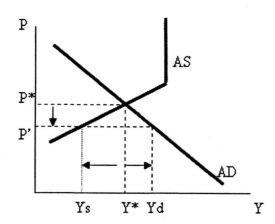

b.

An increase in investment spending will shift AD to the right, so both prices and real GDP increase:

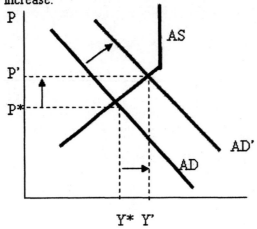

c.

An increase in the average wage rate will lead to a decrease in AS, since the price of a resource has increased. Real GDP declines and the price level rises.

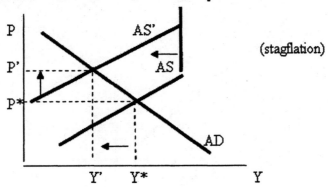

(stagflation)

d.

An income tax cut will increase consumption spending, which will lead to an increase in AD, so that both P and Y increase. The graph is similar to b).

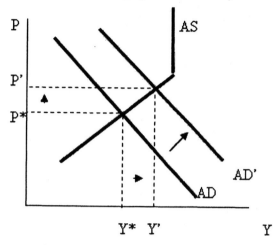

In a supply-side model, an income tax cut would also increase after-tax wages, so that labor supply and aggregate supply would both increase. The graph is similar to b).

Internet Exercises

1. Go to the Bureau of Economic Analysis web page at: http://www.bea.gov. Click on "Gross Domestic Product" to get to the GDP data page. There are many ways to access the data from here, but the easiest way without printing the data is to click on "text" under "Selected NIPA Tables". From here, scroll down to answer the following questions:

   a. Table 1.1.1 shows the percent change in real GDP What was the percent change in real GDP in the most recent year? How has real GDP been changing in the past two years? What are the major categories in which GDP is measured?

   b. From Table 1.1.5, find nominal GDP in the two most recent years.

   c. From Table 1.1.6, find real GDP in the two most recent years.

   d. Look at Table 1.7.5. What does it show? How does the table go from GDP to personal income?

   e. Look at Table 2.1. What are the major components of personal income?

   f. Use Table 1.1.9 to find the implicit price deflators for the two most recent years. What do these numbers mean?

2. Go to the following website to read about the alternative measure of economic welfare developed by the Friends of the Earth: http://www.foe.co.uk/campaigns/sustainable_development/progress/. From there, read the "Introduction", "Replacing GDP", and "ISEW explained".

   a. According to the website, is GDP a good measure of economic welfare? Why or why not?

b. Briefly, what is the Index of Sustainable Economic Welfare? How is it calculated? Is it a better measure of the standard of living? Why or why not?

Solutions

True False Questions

1. F, False, although such items as tires are considered intermediate goods because they are an output of one firm that are used as an input for another firm, they are not included in GDP. If intermediate goods were included in GDP, then double-counting would occur.

2. T, GDP attempts to measure the value of production in an economy, not sales. Since these automobiles were produced in 2000, they should be included in this year's GDP. They would be counted as a part of inventory. Inventory is one component of GDP.

3. F, False, even though these commodities are produced underground, that is not what is meant by the underground economy. The underground economy includes illegal markets, such as illicit drugs, bookmaking, and prostitution, and those who work without declaring their income. The underground economy is not included in the calculation of GDP.

4. F, Exports should be included in the measure of GDP. GDP measures the value of the output produced by an economy. Exports use the productive resources of the nation. Hence, they should be included in GDP.

5. T, True, Gross Private Domestic Investment measures total spending by firms in the economy on physical capital goods and structures. Changes in inventory are included as investment since GDP measures production, not sales. Goods produced but not sold are treated as if the firm invested in its own inventory.

6. T, GDP is not an accurate measure of social welfare. It excludes many goods and services that are produced and consumed in the economy. For example, any goods produced in the underground economy or as nonmarket transactions are excluded from GDP. Further, GDP does not reflect the intangibles that people value such as leisure time. Because of this, GDP is not an accurate measure of social welfare.

7. T, True, a price index is defined as (price in current year/price in base year) x 100. Since in the base year, the same set of prices are used to measure both the current year and the base year, then in the base year, the price index is equal to 100. This makes it easy to compare percent changes to the base year.

8. T, True, the longest economic expansion in US history occurred between March 1991 and March 2001, lasting ten years between quarters of declining real GDP.

9. F, False, while such disasters tend to reduce GDP in the year or two after they happen, in the long run, GDP is increased. In the gulf region, the costs of the rebuilding efforts are likely to greatly exceed the original output lost due to the hurricanes. As another example, in April 2006 the rebuilding of the World Trade Center, now dubbed "Freedom Tower", began, at a cost of unforeseeable billions of dollars.

10. F, When the price level falls in the aggregate demand model, the price of goods and services (on average) is falling. Thus we cannot say that more goods and services will be purchased because they are relatively less expensive. Instead, the aggregate demand curve is negatively sloped because of the real balance effect, the interest rate effect, and the effect of changes in the price level on exports and imports.

Suppose the price level falls. According to the real balance effect, the real value of assets that have fixed dollar values will increase. As a result, consumers will purchase more goods and services. According to the interest rate effect, as the price level falls the real money supply increases. This will cause the interest rate to fall. When the interest rate falls, firms will invest in more plant and equipment. Consumers will purchase more durables and housing. Finally, a decrease in the price level will cause the relative price of exports to fall and the relative price of imports to increase. As a result, net exports will increase. These three effects account for the negative slope of the aggregate demand function.

11. F, False, fiscal policy includes changes in government spending or taxes that are meant to influence the macroeconomy. Monetary policy is changes in the money supply and interest rates.

12. T, True, if resource prices increase, then firms will require a higher price level to be willing to produce any given level of real GDP. So the relevant portion of the aggregate supply would decrease, or shift to the left. The price level would rise and real GDP would fall.

13. T, True, if the aggregate supply curve is upward sloping, then an increase in aggregate demand will lead to a movement upward along the aggregate supply curve so that both the price level and real GDP increase. Draw a graph and see for yourself!

Multiple Choice

1. A	16. B	30. C
2. B	17. C	31. D
3. D	18. C	32. B
4. D	19. B	33. A
5. C	20. D	34. C
6. A	21. B	35. A
7. D	22. A	36. C
8. B	23. A	37. B
9. C	24. C	38. D
10. C	25. C	39. D
11. B	26. D	40. C
12. B	27. A	41. A
13. A	28. D	42. C
14. D	29. A	43. B
15. C		

Fill-in Questions

1. Gross domestic product (GDP); intermediate goods; final goods

2. personal consumption expenditures; Gross private domestic investment; government purchases of goods and services; Government transfer payments; net exports of goods and services; imports; exports

3. capital stock; net private domestic investment; consumption of fixed capital

4. price index; GDP deflator; real GDP; Nominal GDP

5. business cycles; trough; peak; expansion phase; contraction phase

6. aggregate demand curve; real balance effect

7. disposable income; fiscal policy; monetary policy

8. Expansionary fiscal policy; money supply; expansionary; monetary policy; contractionary fiscal policy; contractionary monetary policy

9. aggregate supply curve

CHAPTER **13**

Unemployment: The Legacy of Recession, Technological Change, and Free Choice

Objectives of the Chapter

After you have mastered this chapter you will understand:

1. That unemployment has both economic and noneconomic costs and that these costs are different for society and the individual.

2. How the unemployment rate is calculated and how unemployment rates vary among demographic groups.

3. That three types of unemployment--frictional, structural, and cyclical--exist, and these differ both in terms of costs and policy implications.

4. How the full employment, or natural, unemployment rate is defined.

5. How fiscal and monetary policies can be applied to achieve and/or maintain full employment.

6. The differences between active and passive macroeconomic policies.

7. That a significant increase in the minimum wage has an adverse effect on unemployment, particularly among teenagers.

8. That for various reasons, the unemployment rate in most European countries is much higher than the unemployment rate in the United States.

9. The concepts of the marginal product of labor and the value of marginal product of labor.

10. That in a competitive labor market, firms will maximize profits by hiring labor until the wage rate is equal to the value of the marginal product of labor. This means that the demand for labor curve is equivalent to the value of marginal product for labor curve.

Key Terms

unemployment rate
civilian labor force
frictional unemployment
structural unemployment

cyclical unemployment

full employment

natural rate of unemployment

recession

demand shock

maximum potential real GDP

stagflation

active macroeconomic policy

passive macroeconomic policy

expansionary fiscal policy

expansionary monetary policy

automatic stabilizers

Euro area

True False Questions

For these statements, indicate whether they are true or false. Defend your answer.

1. The economy is said to be experiencing full employment when there is no unemployment.

   TRUE or FALSE

2. The unemployment rate is measured as the percentage of the population that is actively seeking but not finding work.

   TRUE or FALSE

3. The unemployment rate can vary significantly among various demographic groups.

   TRUE or FALSE

4. Expansionary fiscal and monetary policies are not the best methods to deal with structural unemployment.

   TRUE or FALSE

5. Frictional unemployment results from the lack of employment opportunities during a cyclical downturn of the economy.

   TRUE or FALSE

6. In order to help the working poor, the minimum wage should be increased.

   TRUE or FALSE

7. Expansionary fiscal or monetary policies will lead to rightward shifts of the aggregate demand curve.
   TRUE or FALSE

8. In Europe, the rates of unemployment tend to be higher than those in the United States because there is less flexibility in labor markets.
   TRUE or FALSE

9. In a competitive labor market, the supply curve is the same as the marginal product of labor curve.
   TRUE or FALSE

Multiple Choice

Check yourself. Choose the best answer. Answers are found at the end of the chapter.

1. A non-economic cost of unemployment is best exemplified by:
   a. the output that Buddy would have produced if he had been working.
   b. the income that Sally would have earned if she had been working.
   c. the money government must pay to Rob in the form of unemployment benefits.
   d. the depression Laura suffers as a result of Rob being unemployed.

2. Each of the following would be considered a member of the civilian labor force except:
   a. Jim who worked 18 hours as an unpaid employee in a family business.
   b. Teresa, a sixteen year old who works part-time at Fast Food Burger Emporium.
   c. John who is not employed, would like to be, but is no longer seeking employment.
   d. Mark who was previously employed full-time, but is now on strike.

3. Suppose the unemployment rate increases by 0.5 percent. The group most adversely affected by this will be:
   a. teens.
   b. females.
   c. African-Americans.
   d. Hispanics.

4. Suppose the population is 250,000, the labor force is 180,000, and the number of unemployed is 9,000. The unemployment rate is:
   a. 2.0 percent.
   b. 2.5 percent.
   c. 4.3 percent.
   d. 3.44 percent.

5.

Discouraged workers	30,000
Homemakers	45,000
Individuals working part-time	25,000
Individuals working full-time	155,000
Individuals seeking employment	15,500
Full-time college students	37,000

The number of people in the civilian labor force is:
a. 445,000.
b. 400,000.
c. 352,500.
d. 323,500.

6. Scott has worked at MI Industries for the past five years. A downturn in the economy has forced the company to layoff some of its work force. Scott is among those who loses his job during the cutbacks. Scott is currently experiencing:
a. structural unemployment.
b. underemployment.
c. frictional unemployment.
d. cyclical unemployment.

7. Earl has worked on the assembly line at Rust Belt Industries for the past twenty years. He recently lost his job because Rust Belt has employed a new technology that requires less labor. Although there are numerous jobs listed in the paper, Earl still remains unemployed. Earl is most likely experiencing:
a. structural unemployment.
b. cyclical unemployment.
c. frictional unemployment.
d. temporary unemployment.

8. Gina recently moved to Metropolis. She had a job offer, but did not accept it because she wants a higher paying position with better benefits. Gina is most likely experiencing:
a. structural unemployment.
b. frictional unemployment.
c. cyclical unemployment.
d. overemployment opportunities.

9. Which of the following statements is correct?
    a. The full employment rate of unemployment occurs when the only type of unemployment occurring is cyclical unemployment.
    b. The natural rate of unemployment tends to be constant over time.
    c. The full employment rate of unemployment occurs when the level of cyclical unemployment is zero.
    d. The full employment rate of unemployment will change as the composition of the labor force changes, but the natural rate of unemployment is constant.

10. The economy is experiencing full employment when:
    a. the frictional rate of unemployment is zero.
    b. the structural rate of unemployment is zero.
    c. when the cyclical rate of unemployment is zero.
    d. when the overall unemployment rate is 2 percent.

11. Which of the following most likely caused the natural rate of unemployment to increase during the 1970s?
    a. An increase in the proportion of the labor force that is over 19 years of age.
    b. A decrease in the proportion of the labor force that is Hispanic.
    c. An increase in the proportion of the labor force that is Caucasian.
    d. An increase in the number of females entering the labor force.

12. Suppose the economy is currently experiencing problems with cyclical unemployment. If wages and other input prices are sticky, government might:
    a. increases taxes to deal with the problem.
    b. increase government spending to deal with the problem.
    c. decrease the growth rate of the money supply to deal with the problem.
    d. increase taxes to deal with the problem.

13. Which of the following is most likely to result in a decrease of structural unemployment?
    a. job training programs.
    b. increases in government spending.
    c. decreases in taxes.
    d. increases in the growth rate of the money supply.

14. Suppose aggregate supply is currently given by AS_1. If wages and other input price are flexible, we would expect:

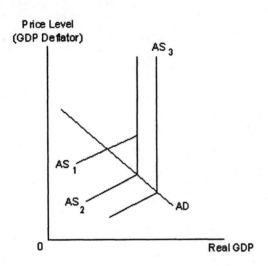

a. the aggregate demand curve to shift to the right and unemployment to be eliminated.
b. the aggregate demand curve to shift to the left and unemployment to be eliminated.
c. the aggregate supply curve to shift to AS_2 and unemployment to be eliminated.
d. the aggregate supply curve to shift to AS_3 and unemployment to be eliminated.

15. Suppose aggregate supply is currently given by AS_2. If government wants to move the economy to full employment, it could:
a. increase taxes.
b. decrease taxes.
c. leave taxes unchanged.
d. decrease the money supply.

16. Which of the following will cause an increase (rightward shift) in the aggregate demand curve?
a. a decline in government spending.
b. a decline in the money supply.
c. a decline in income taxes.
d. an increase in income taxes.

17. Suppose minimum wage legislation causes the wage for low-skill workers to increase from W_1 to W_2. As a result:

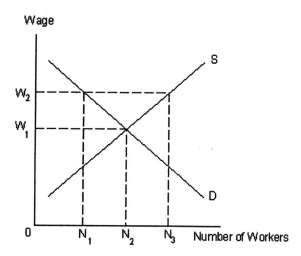

a. the level of employment will increase from N_1 to N_2.
b. the level of employment will increase from N_3 to N_1.
c. the level of employment will fall from N_1 to N_3.
d. the level of employment will fall from N_2 to N_1.

18. If a minimum wage of W_2 is imposed, there will be unemployment of:
a. $N_3 - N_1$.
b. $N_2 - N_3$.
c. $N_1 - N_2$.
d. $0 - N_1$.

19. Minimum wage legislation most adversely affects:
a. high-skilled labor.
b. teenagers and the structurally unemployed.
c. the structurally and frictionally unemployed.
d. teenagers and the cyclically unemployed.

20. Expansionary fiscal and monetary policies are best used to address
a. a, structural unemployment.
b. permanent unemployment.
c. frictional unemployment
d. cyclical unemployment.

21. A computerized national job bank has been suggested to deal with:
a. structural unemployment.
b. frictional unemployment.
c. cyclical unemployment.
d. discouraged workers.

22. Which of the following statements is correct?
    a. Unemployment rates are lower in Europe than in the United States.
    b. Long-term unemployment is less of a problem in Europe than in the United States.
    c. Unemployment rates are higher in Europe than in the United States.
    d. Most economists believe expansionary fiscal and monetary policies should be used to deal with unemployment in Europe.

23. Unemployment rates in most European countries are relatively high because:
    a. minimum wages are higher in Europe than in the United States.
    b. European labor unions tend to be more powerful than labor unions in the United States.
    c. unemployment benefits in Europe tend to be higher than unemployment benefits in the United States.
    d. all of these.

24. The unemployment rate is computed as:
    a. (total population / total employment) x 100.
    b. (civilian labor force / total employment) x 100.
    c. (number of persons unemployed / civilian labor force) x 100.
    d. number of persons unemployed x civilian labor force.

25. The type of unemployment that occurs because of the normal job search process is referred to as:
    a. the natural rate of unemployment.
    b. frictional unemployment.
    c. structural unemployment.
    d. cyclical unemployment.

26. The full employment rate of unemployment is:
    a. zero.
    b. equal to the frictional rate of unemployment plus the structural rate of unemployment.
    c. equal to the frictional rate of unemployment minus the aggregate unemployment rate.
    d. higher than the natural rate of unemployment.

27. When the level of economic activity declines, _____ occurs.
    a. cyclical unemployment.
    b. frictional unemployment.
    c. structural unemployment.
    d. natural unemployment.

28. Which of the following is an example of a supply shock?
    a. an increase in consumer spending due to stock market exuberance.
    b. an increase in government spending due to war.
    c. a large, rapid increase in petroleum prices.
    d. all of the above.

29. Automatic stabilizers
    a. are a type of passive macroeconomic policy.
    b. are features of government taxation and expenditures that automatically increase aggregate demand during a recession.
    c. include progressive income taxes and unemployment insurance.
    d. all of the above.

30. In a competitive labor market, increases in the value of the marginal product of labor
    a. ill lead to a leftward shift of the labor demand curve.
    b. will cause the firm to hire less labor.
    c. will cause the firm to hire more labor.
    d. will have no effect on the amount of labor hired.

Fill-in Questions

1. The _____ is used to measure the magnitude of the unemployment problem in the economy. It is the percentage of the _____ that is unemployed. The civilian labor force includes both the number of persons employed as well as the number of persons who are unemployed.

2. There are several different types of unemployment. One type of unemployment, _____ , is caused by structural changes in the economy. Temporary unemployment experienced by individuals entering the labor force or changing jobs is another type of unemployment. This is referred to as _____ . Finally, unemployment may be characterized by a lack of jobs. This type of unemployment is referred to as _____ , and is caused by the drop in economic activity that occurs during the contraction phase of the business cycle. _____ are designed to reduce cyclical unemployment.

3. Full employment is defined in terms of these types of unemployment. For example, _____ or the _____ is said to exist when the economy is experiencing no cyclical unemployment. The natural rate of unemployment is considered to be the sum of _____ and _____ unemployment, or the rate of unemployment that exists in the absence of _____ .

4. In a competitive labor market, the demand curve for labor is similar to the _____ .

Problems Applying Economic Concepts

1. Using the information given in the table, calculate the number of persons in the civilian labor force.

Persons between 16 and 65 years of age	500,000
Persons 16 years and older working part-time	80,000
Persons 16 years and older working full-time	225,500
Persons between 16 and 65 not working, but actively seeking employment	15,000
Persons over 65 not working, but actively seeking employment	4,500
Homemakers	35,000
Persons between 16 and 65 years who are institutionalized	25,000

2. Using the information given in the table, calculate the number of persons who are unemployed.

Persons between 16 and 65 years of age	500,000
Persons 16 years and older working part-time	80,000
Persons 16 years and older working full-time	225,500
Persons between 16 and 65 not working, but actively seeking employment	15,000
Persons over 65 not working, but actively seeking employment	4,500
Homemakers	35,000
Persons between 16 and 65 years who are institutionalized	25,000

3. Using the information given in the table, calculate the unemployment rate.

Persons between 16 and 65 years of age	500,000
Persons 16 years and older working part-time	80,000
Persons 16 years and older working full-time	225,500
Persons between 16 and 65 not working, but actively seeking employment	15,000
Persons over 65 not working, but actively seeking employment	4,500
Homemakers	35,000
Persons between 16 and 65 years who are institutionalized	25,000

4. Using the information given in the table, find the number of persons in the civilian labor force.

Persons over 65 not actively seeking employment	20,000
Persons 16 years and older not working because of labor disputes	15,000
Persons 16 years and older not working because of bad weather	7,000
Persons 16 years and older not actively seeking employment	55,000
Persons 16 years and older actively seeking employment	25,125
Persons 16 years and older who are working part-time or full-time	287,875
Persons 16 years and older who are discouraged workers	4,500
Military personnel	35,000

5. Using the information given in the table, calculate the unemployment rate.

Persons over 65	
not actively seeking employment	20,000
Persons 16 years and older	
not working because of labor disputes	15,000
Persons 16 years and older	
not working because of bad weather	7,000
Persons 16 years and older	
not actively seeking employment	55,000
Persons 16 years and older	
actively seeking employment	25,125
Persons 16 years and older	
who are working part-time or full-time	287,875
Persons 16 years and older	
who are discouraged workers	4,500
Military personnel	35,000

6. Suppose the level of frictional unemployment is 1.5 percent, the level of structural unemployment is 3.0 percent and the level of cyclical unemployment is 2.1 percent. What is the full employment or the natural rate of unemployment?

7. Suppose that the economy of Workerville consists of the following people:

> Alice reports to her union hall everyday seeking carpentry work, but has been unable to find employment this month. .
> Bert works full-time as a high school teacher.
> Charlotte is employed part time as an engineering consultant.
> David is a drug addict who stays at home all day selling crack.
> Ethel is a professional golfer.
> Fred is serving three years in the state penitentiary for embezzlement.
> Grace volunteers five hours per week at the local nursing home, but she is not actively seeking paid employment.
> Hank works for 4 hours per week delivering pizzas.
> Irene was just laid off from her job as a dot.com executive and she is actively seeking another form of employment.
> Jim works as a self-employed architect.
> Karen works full-time as a police officer, and she moonlights as a security guard.
> Larry has a part-time job working nights and weekends as a party clown.
> Michelle is a retired CEO.
> Nick is a firefighter who is actively seeking employment but is currently without a job.

What is the size of the labor force in Workerville? What is the rate of unemployment? Explain.

8. Assume that the market for unskilled fast food workers is given by the following equations:

demand: $P = 8.00 - .002Q$
supply: $P = 2.00 + .001Q$

where P is the price of labor (wage rate per hour) and Q is the quantity of labor hours per day.

a. Find the equilibrium price and quantity. Show graphically.

b. Suppose that the government imposes a minimum wage of $6.00 per hour. What is the result in the market? Is there a shortage or surplus? Of how much?

Problems Applying Economic Concepts Solutions

1. The number of persons in the civilian labor force is 325,000 (80,000 + 225,000 + 15,000 + 4,500).

2. The number of persons who are unemployed is 19,500 (15,000 + 4,500).

3. The unemployment rate is 6 percent [(19,500/325,000) x 100].

4. The number of persons in the civilian labor force is 335,000 (15,000 + 7,000 + 25,125 + 287,875).

5. The unemployment rate is 7.5 percent [(25,125/335,000) x 100].

6. The full employment or the natural rate of unemployment is the frictional rate of unemployment plus the structural rate of unemployment. In this instance the natural rate of unemployment is 4.5 percent (1.5 + 3.0).

7. The following people would be included in the labor force:

   Alice, Bert, Charlotte, Ethel, Hank, Irene, Jim, Karen, Larry and Nick, so the size of the labor force is 10. Of those ten people, three are actively seeking work but not working (Alice, Irene, and Nick), so the unemployment rate is 3/10 = 30%.

8.

   a.

$$8.00 - .002Q = 2.00 + .001Q$$
$$-.003Q = -6.00$$
$$Q^* = 2000$$

$$P^* = 8.00 - .002(2000) = 4.00$$
$$P^* = 2.00 + .001(2000) = 4.00$$
(check)

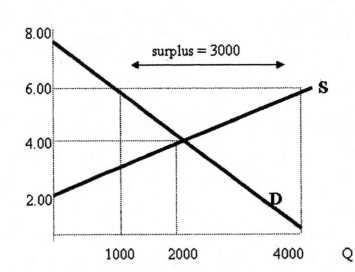

b. A minimum wage would impose a surplus in the market. In the labor market, a surplus is known as unemployment. To find the quantities supplied and demanded, plug the price of 6.00 into the demand and supply equations, and solve for Q:

$$6.00 = 8.00 - .002Q$$
$$-2.00 = -.002Q$$
$$Q_d = 1000$$

$$6.00 = 2.00 + .001Q$$
$$4.00 = .001Q$$
$$Q_s = 4000$$

Since the quantity demanded is only 1000 while the quantity supplied is 4000, then there is a surplus of 3000 labor hours. In this simple model, unemployment results

Internet Exercises

1. Visit the Bureau of Labor Statistics Home Page (http://www.bls.gov) to find out about recent trends in unemployment. From the BLS home page, first click on "US economy at a glance", under "at a glance tables".

    a. What is the current rate of unemployment? Do you notice any trends in the unemployment rate over the past two years?

    b. By clicking on the appropriate links from the BLS home page, verify that, for the most recent month available,

    Unemployment Rate = (Unemployed/Labor Force) x 100.

2. To learn about how the BLS calculates the rate of unemployment and other related statistics, go to the following web page: http://www.bls.gov/bls/employment.htm. Briefly, how does the BLS measure the unemployment rate? What are some relevant issues mentioned on the site?

Solutions

True False Questions

1. F, There are three types of unemployment: frictional, structural, and cyclical. Frictional unemployment is caused by people entering the labor force or changing jobs. Structural unemployment is a mismatch between the skills of the unemployed and the skills needed to fill available jobs. Structural unemployment is caused by technical or structural changes in the economy. Cyclical unemployment is caused by the drop in economic activity that occurs during the contraction phase of the business cycle. Economists argue that stabilization policy can be used to eliminate this cyclical unemployment. However, no policy will stop people from entering the labor force or changing jobs. Likewise, one would not wish to eliminate technical changes. Thus, full employment is said to occur when only frictional and structural unemployment exist.

2. F, False, the unemployment rate is measured as the percentage of the labor force (not population) that is actively seeking but not finding a job.

3. T, The unemployment rate for teenagers tends to be much higher than the overall unemployment rate. For example, the unemployment rate for teenagers in 1994 was three times the overall unemployment rate. The unemployment rate for females (in recent periods) has been lower than the unemployment rate for males. The unemployment rate for minority groups (with the exception of Asian-Americans) is higher than the unemployment rate of the non-minority group. For example, the unemployment rate for blacks is more than twice that of whites.

4. T, Structural unemployment is caused by a mismatch between the skills of the unemployed and available jobs. Fiscal and monetary policy can stimulate aggregate demand, thereby increasing the number of workers firms are willing to hire; however, if individuals do not have the requisite skills, they will not be hired. Instead of creating more jobs, the better method of dealing with structural unemployment is to provide people with training so they can fill jobs that are currently available.

5. F, False, frictional unemployment results when potential workers first enter the labor force by looking for a job or when workers are between jobs to search for better employment opportunities. Cyclical unemployment is the type of unemployment that increases during a recession.

6. F, If the minimum wage rises above the equilibrium wage, the quantity of labor demanded will fall. As a result, workers will be laid off their jobs. Also, in response to the higher wage rate, the quantity of labor supplied will increase. These two effects work to increase the level of unemployment among unskilled workers. Thus, increases in the minimum wage create unemployment for the very group it is trying to help.

7. T, True, Expansionary fiscal or monetary policies increase one of the components of aggregate demand, either consumption, investment, government spending, or net export spending. The increase in spending causes an increase, or rightward shift, in the aggregate demand curve.

8. T, True, as pointed out in the text, Europe tends to have more impediments to hiring and impediments to accepting employment that introduce more rigidities into the labor market. Obstacles to hiring in Europe include minimum wages, the strength of labor unions, high taxes, and large required severance payments. Disincentives for accepting employment include the comparative generosity of unemployment benefits and relatively high income taxes.

9. F, False, in a competitive labor market, the demand curve is equivalent to the value of marginal product of labor curve, since firms will maximize profits by hiring a quantity of labor where the wage rate is equal to the value of marginal product of labor. The supply of labor depends on households' decisions between income and leisure.

Multiple Choice

1. D	11. D	21. B
2. C	12. B	22. C
3. A	13. A	23. D
4. B	14. C	24. C
5. A	15. C	25. B
6. D	16. C	26. B
7. A	17. D	27. A
8. B	18. A	28. D
9. C	19. B	29. D
10. C	20. D	30. C

Fill-in Questions

1. unemployment rate; civilian labor force
2. structural unemployment; frictional unemployment; cyclical unemployment; Stabilization policies
3. full employment; natural rate of unemployment; frictional; structural; cyclical unemployment
4. value of marginal product curve for labor

Inflation: A Monetary Phenomenon

Objectives of the Chapter

After you have mastered this chapter you will understand:

1. How inflation is defined and measured.

2. The differences between the Consumer Price Index and the GDP Price Deflator.

3. That the Consumer Price Index has a number of limitations as a measure of the cost of living.

4. That it is important to distinguish between unanticipated and anticipated inflation.

5. That inflation affects the economy in many different ways.

6. How the money supply is defined and that the Federal Reserve controls the nation's money supply.

7. How to explain inflation in terms of the quantity theory and aggregate supply-aggregate demand frameworks.

8. That with the income velocity of money and output growth rates constant, the inflation rate is determined by the growth rate of the money supply.

9. That to reduce the inflation rate the growth rate of the money supply must be reduced.

10. That supply-side policies, even if they are successful in raising the nation's output growth rate, are unlikely to significantly reduce the inflation rate.

11. That incomes policy has many shortcomings as a means to control inflation and that the experience of the United States with wage-price guidelines and controls has been very discouraging.

12. The structure of the US banking system, and the different types of depository institutions.

13. The money creation process and the tools of monetary policy that the Federal Reserve can use to control the money supply.

Key Terms

inflation

deflation

consumer price index (CPI)

cost-of-living adjustment (COLA) clause

unanticipated inflation

anticipated inflation

indexing

creditor

debtor

hyperinflation

medium of exchange

money

currency (cash)

demand deposits

money supply

central bank

quantity theory of money

equation of exchange

income velocity of money

supply-side policies

incomes policy

depository institutions

national banks

state banks

member banks

vault cash

required reserves

excess reserves

money creation

open market operations

reserve requirements

discount rate

True False Questions

For these statements, indicate whether they are true or false. Defend your answer.

1. Deflation occurs when there is a decline in the long term inflation rate.

   TRUE or FALSE

2. The Consumer Price Index measures the prices of a fixed basket of goods and services purchased by a typical urban household.

   TRUE or FALSE

3. Unanticipated inflation occurs when economic decision makers guess incorrectly about price changes, believing that the inflation rate will be lower than it actually turns out to be.

   TRUE or FALSE

4. Inflation causes income to be redistributed from debtors to creditors. Because government is a huge debtor, it has implemented strict policies to deal with inflation.

   TRUE or FALSE

5. Inflation benefits those who earn income from export-producing sectors, such as agriculture or aviation.

   TRUE or FALSE

6. An increase in the CPI of 4 percent does not imply that each individual's cost of living has increased by 4 percent.

   TRUE or FALSE

7. An important function of money is the discouragement and prevention of theft.

   TRUE or FALSE

8. Households and firms tend to reduce their holdings of money during periods of high inflation.

   TRUE or FALSE

9. Legalized domestic markets provide the most important sources of demand for US currency.

   TRUE or FALSE

10. According to the quantity theory of money, an increase in the money supply will cause a decline in the income velocity of money.

    TRUE or FALSE

11. If an economy is highly monopolized, it will tend to have a higher inflation rate than an economy with a more competitive market structure.

    TRUE or FALSE

12. The distinction between a rise in the price level and inflation is an important one.

    TRUE or FALSE

13. Fiscal policy can be an effective means to fight inflation over the long run.

    TRUE or FALSE

14. The target for the discount rate is set by the FOMC.

    TRUE or FALSE

15. The Federal Reserve Bank of New York is where open market operations are actually carried out.

    TRUE or FALSE

16. The tools of monetary policy include open market operations, changing the discount rate, and changing reserve requirements.

    TRUE or FALSE

Multiple Choice

Check yourself. Choose the best answer. Answers are found at end of chapter.

1. Inflation refers to:
    a. a continuing increase in the price level.
    b. a once-and-for-all increase in the price level.
    c. an increase in average prices.
    d. an increase in the price of all goods and services.

2. A once-and-for-all decrease in the price level is referred to as:
    a. disinflation.
    b. under inflation.
    c. deflation.
    d. a decrease in the price level.

3. The broadest based price index is:
    a. the CPI.
    b. the GDP deflator.
    c. the crude materials PPI.
    d. the COLA index.

4. The CPI tends to overstate increases in the cost of living because:
    a. it is based on a fixed basket of goods and services.
    b. it accounts for quality changes.
    c. it only includes final goods bought by families.
    d. only the prices of some of the goods and services measured by the CPI change.

5. Suppose the GDP deflator in 2000 was 120. The GDP deflator in 2001 is 124.68. The rate of inflation over this period was:
   a. 9.62 percent.
   b. 4.68 percent.
   c. 3.9 percent.
   d. 2.68 percent

6. Inflation will have the greatest effect on the distribution of income and wealth if:
   a. prices and incomes rise by the same percentage.
   b. all workers are covered by COLA's.
   c. it is anticipated.
   d. it is unanticipated.

7. Anne will most likely be harmed by inflation if:
   a. she works in real estate and is paid on a commission basis.
   b. she is a creditor.
   c. she receives Social Security benefits that are indexed for inflation.
   d. she holds most of her wealth in the form of real estate.

8. Suppose that both creditors and debtors correctly anticipate that the inflation rate will rise to 4.5 percent. In this case:
   a. there will be a tendency for the interest rate to fall.
   b. there will be a tendency for the interest rate to increase.
   c. debtors will gain at the expense of creditors.
   d. creditors will gain at the expense of debtors.

9. John borrows $1,000 from Amy for one year at an interest rate of 6 percent. During the year the rate of inflation decreases from 6 percent to 5 percent. The price decrease was unexpected. As a result of the fall in prices:
   a. income is redistributed from John to Amy.
   b. income is redistributed from Amy to John.
   c. both Amy and John will benefit as a result of the increase in the rate of inflation.
   d. Amy will be harmed by the inflation because she is paid back dollars that are worth less (have less purchasing power.)

10. Some individuals argue that the federal government has little incentive to pursue anti-inflationary policies because:
   a. government is a huge creditor.
   b. indexation of the federal tax system causes tax revenues to increase with inflation.
   c. government is a huge debtor.
   d. the federal personal income tax system has recently been indexed for inflation.

11. A high and variable rate of inflation would most likely cause:
    a. a nation's money supply to become more stable.
    b. government's tax revenues to fall.
    c. an increase in the capital stock, as the higher interest rates will encourage investment.
    d. a decrease in the goods and services produced in the nation.

12. Suppose the United States is experiencing a relatively high inflation rate. In this instance:
    a. the relative price of U.S. exports will increase.
    b. the relative price of U.S. exports will decline.
    c. the relative price of imports into the U.S. will increase.
    d. foreign firms competing with U.S. companies will be harmed.

13. If a country experiences hyperinflation:
    a. its monetary unit will become more valuable.
    b. its monetary system may fail.
    c. it should pursue expansionary monetary policy to deal with the inflation.
    d. it should pursue expansionary fiscal policy to deal with the inflation.

14. Paul saves some money each month so at the end of the year he can travel to Europe. In this instance money is functioning as:
    a. a unit of account.
    b. a store of value.
    c. a medium of exchange.
    d. a medium of value.

15. Which of the following is the best example of money functioning as a medium of exchange?
    a. Meena compares the price of a pound of hamburger and a pound of chicken.
    b. Bob saves money for a summer vacation.
    c. Brooke purchases a winter coat.
    d. Selwyn tries to determine if a 2006 Ford Focus or a 2006 Toyota Prius is the better buy.

16. Currency is valuable to us because:
    a. it is accepted as payment for goods and services.
    b. it is backed by gold.
    c. it has an intrinsic value.
    d. all of these.

17. M1 is defined as:
    a. currency held by the nonbank public.
    b. currency held by the nonbank public and demand deposits.
    c. currency held by the nonbank public, demand deposits, and other checkable deposits.
    d. currency held by the nonbank public, demand deposits, other checkable deposits, and travelers' checks.

18. The largest component of M1 is:
    a. currency.
    b. demand deposits.
    c. travelers' checks.
    d. other checkable deposits.

19. According to the quantity theory of money, inflation is caused by:
    a. a too rapid increase in aggregate supply.
    b. supply shocks.
    c. a too rapid increase in the money supply.
    d. decreases in the income velocity of money.

20. In deriving the quantity theory of money, it is assumed that:
    a. M is constant.
    b. V is constant.
    c. P is constant.
    d. nominal GDP is constant.

21. According to the quantity theory of money, an increase in the money supply will cause:
    a. a proportional increase in the income velocity of money.
    b. a proportional decrease in the income velocity of money.
    c. a proportional increase in nominal GDP.
    d. a proportional increase in real GDP.

22. Suppose the rate of growth in the money supply is 7 percent and the rate of growth in real GDP is 4.5 percent. Then the rate of inflation is:
    a. 2.5 percent.
    b. 4.5 percent.
    c. 7 percent.
    d. 11.5 percent.

23. The equation of exchange states that:
    a. M = P x GDP.
    b. M x P = V x GDP.
    c. M x GDP = V x P.
    d. M x V = P x GDP.

24. There is a direct link between the growth rate in the money supply and inflation only if:
    a. the income velocity of money is constant.
    b. the income velocity of money is variable.
    c. the growth rate in output is constant.
    d. both the growth rates of the income velocity of money and output are constant.

25. Suppose aggregate demand grows more rapidly than aggregate supply. We know that:
    a. inflation will occur.
    b. deflation will occur.
    c. hyperdeflation will occur.
    d. the price level will remain constant.

26. Suppose the economy is initially in equilibrium at point A. The monetary authorities allow the money supply to grow at 6 percent per year while output grows at 3 percent per year. The economy will most likely move to a new equilibrium at point:

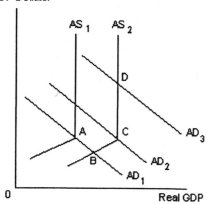

GDP Deflator

AS₁ AS₂

D

A C AD₃

B AD₂

AD₁

0 Real GDP

    a. A.
    b. B.
    c. C.
    d. D.

27. Suppose that over several years both the money supply and real output grow at a constant rate of 3 percent. During this same period, the income velocity of money falls. The most likely result will be:
    a. inflation.
    b. deflation.
    c. disinflation.
    d. under-employment.

28. Supply-side policies are an ineffective way to deal with inflation because:
    a. it is difficult to increase the growth rate in aggregate supply.
    b. supply-side policies do not deal with the root cause of inflation, union activity, that results in increased wages.
    c. supply-side policies work so rapidly that they can cause a demand shock.
    d. increases in aggregate supply are accompanied by decreases in employment.

29. Economists generally oppose wage and price controls because:
    a. such controls do not deal with the root cause of inflation, a too rapid growth in the money supply.
    b. such controls can be costly to administer.
    c. such controls can result in a misallocation of resources.
    d. all of these.

30. Most economists do not think unions are a large contributor to inflation because:
    a. union activity causes the aggregate supply curve to shift to the left.
    b. unions have significant bargaining power.
    c. union activity will not alter wages in general.
    d. union activity causes a large increase in aggregate demand.

31. All of the following are shortcomings of the CPI except which of the following?
    a. It is an index for the typical urban household.
    b. It is a broad based measure hence is subject to the aggregation problem.
    c. It overstates the increase in the cost of living because it is based on a fixed market basket of goods and services.
    d. It does not fully account for changes in quality.

32. Demand deposits are considered money because:
    a. they are backed by gold.
    b. because they are backed by the full faith and credit of the U.S. government.
    c. they are acceptable in exchange as payment for goods and services.
    d. the bank will always have enough on hand to cover the full value of all customer deposits.

33. The interest rate that is charged when one bank borrows the deposits of another bank is called the:
    a. federal funds rate.
    b. prime rate.
    c. discount rate.
    d. basis point rate.

34. Suppose that nominal GDP is equal to $9 trillion and the money supply is equal to $3 trillion. Then, according to the equation of exchange,
    a. inflation will result.
    b. velocity is equal to 3.
    c. velocity is equal to 27.
    d. real GDP is equal to $6 trillion.

35. The functions of money include
    a. providing intrinsic value to the owner of the currency.
    b. allowing international exchange to take place.
    c. acting as a store of value.
    d. all of the above.

36. Coins and currency are included in
    a. M1 only.
    b. M2 only.
    c. M3 only.
    d. M1, M2 and M3.

37. When money functions as a medium of exchange,
    a. it reduces the transactions costs of buying and selling.
    b. it helps to avoid the necessity of bartering, which requires a double coincidence of wants.
    c. it allows for the creation of wealth in the economy through exchange.
    d. all of the above. *

38. Which of the following statements is false?
    a. The tools of monetary policy available to the Fed include open market operations, changing the discount rate, and changing reserve requirements.
    b. Money is measured by the concepts of M1, M2 and M3.
    c. Wampum and furs were early forms of money in North America.
    d. Fiat money has intrinsic value in that it has important uses besides its use as money.

39. The only state with two Federal Reserve Banks is
    a. Alaska.
    b. Missouri
    c. Kansas.
    d. New York.

40. Which of the following is not a part of the Federal Reserve System?
    a. the Board of Governors
    b. the Federal Open Market Committee
    c. the twelve regional Federal Reserve Banks
    d. the Federal Deposit Insurance Corporation

41. Reserve requirements are set by
    a. the Board of Governors.
    b. the Federal Advisory Council.
    c. the Federal Open Market Committee.
    d. the twelve regional Federal Reserve Banks.

42. Which of the following is not a function of Federal Reserve Banks?
    a. issuing currency
    b. clearing checks
    c. examining state member banks
    d. setting the target for the Federal Funds rate.

43. In a simple banking model with no excess reserves, time deposits, nor cash drain, assume that $1000 open market purchase leads to an increase in deposits of $5000. What is the reserve ratio?
   a. 0.1
   b. 0.2
   c. 5
   d. 10

44. Which of the following will lead to an increase in the money supply?
   a. an increase in the required reserve ratio.
   b. an increase in required reserves.
   c. a decline in desired excess reserves.
   d. a Christmas sale at Wal-Mart.

45. The FOMC consists of
   a. the 7 members of the Board of Governors plus 7 regional bank presidents.
   b. the 7 members of the Board of Governors, the Federal Reserve Bank of New York president, plus four other rotating district bank presidents.
   c. the 12 district bank presidents plus the Federal Advisory Council.
   d. the chair of the Federal Reserve Board, the Speaker of the House of Representatives, and the majority leader of the Senate.

46. Suppose that in a simple deposit multiplier model, that the reserve ratio is equal to 0.1 (10%). Which of the following statements is true?
   a. An increase in reserves of $100 will lead to an increase in deposits of $10.
   b. An increase in reserves of $100 will lead to an increase in deposits of $100.
   c. An increase in reserves of $100 will lead to an increase in deposits of $1000.
   d. an increase in reserves will have no effect on deposits.

Fill-in Questions

1. A continuing increase in the price level is referred to as _____ , while a continuing decrease in the price level is called _____ . Price indexes have been developed to measure changes in prices. The GDP deflator is the broadest based price index. The _____ is often used as a measure of the cost of living. It is the basis for wage adjustments that occur when workers are covered by contracts that have a _____ .

2. Inflation has several different effects on the economy. These effects are generally greater if the economy experiences _____ . If there is _____ , the effects on the economy are much smaller.

3. One effect on inflation is a redistribution of income. For example, during periods of inflation the value of the dollar falls. This means that a _____ , a person who owes money, will pay back a

_____ , a person to whom money is owed, with dollars that are worth less. Thus, income is redistributed from the creditor to the debtor.

4. A redistribution of income can also occur if a person is living on a fixed income. In order to mitigate this problem, social security benefits are _____ so that they change as the price level changes.

5. If _____ occurs, an economy's monetary system can be destroyed. Hyperinflation is generally caused by government printing huge amounts of money.

6. Money has three basic functions. It can serve as a unit of account, a store of value or a _____ . This latter function is extremely important. A modern economy would be unable to function without a medium of exchange.

7. Anything that is generally accepted as final payment for goods, services, and debt is _____ . The _____ , M1, is defined as currency, demand deposits, other checkable deposits, and travelers' checks.

8. _____ refers to paper money or coins, while _____ refer to noninterest bearing checking accounts at commercial banks. The rate of growth in the money supply is controlled by the _____ .

9. The _____ argues that the money supply is the principal determinant of nominal GDP. It is based on the _____ . According to this equation $M \times V = P \times GDP$. In this equation, M is the money supply, V is the _____ , P is the price level and GDP is real GDP. V indicates the number of times the money supply is used to purchase final goods and services during a year.

10. Supply-side policies and incomes policy are not thought to be very effective in dealing with inflation. _____ do not cause the aggregate supply curve to increase fast enough to have a significant impact on inflation. _____ deal with the outcome of inflation by restraining wages and prices; however, they do not deal with the root cause of inflation, a too rapid increase in the money supply.

11. Through the process of _____ , an increase in reserves through an open market purchase can be multiplied into a much larger increase in the money supply as banks are able to lend out _____ . The tools of monetary available to the Fed include _____ , changes in the _____ and changes in _____ .

Problems Applying Economic Concepts

1. The CPI in 1999 was 120.75. In 2002, it was 115.0. What was the rate of inflation over the period? (Calculate to the nearest hundredth.)

2. Suppose the GDP deflator was 175 in 1999 and 189 in 2002. What was the rate of inflation over the period?

3. Given the information in the following table, find M1.

Currency	$750
Travelers' checks	25
Demand deposits	2,625
Other checkable deposits	820
Time deposits less than $100,000	300
Time deposits $100,000 or more	646
Repurchase agreements	225
Eurodollars	195

4. Suppose velocity is 10 and nominal GDP is $2,400 billion. What is the money supply?

5. Suppose the rate of growth of the money supply is 6.25 percent. If velocity is constant, what is the growth rate of nominal GDP?

6. Suppose the growth rate of real GDP is 3.5 percent and the growth rate of the money supply is 5 percent. If velocity is constant, what is the rate of change in the GDP deflator?

7. Use a graph of demand and supply to explain why wage and price controls may result in a misallocation of resources.

8. Suppose that you and your friends decide to construct a price index for college students. After careful research, you find the following information on prices for selected goods in 1990 and 2000:

GOOD	1990 PRICES	2000 PRICES
pens	$.25	$1.00
notebooks	1.00	3.00
textbooks (average price)	25.00	60.00
pizza	4.00	10.00
compact disks	7.50	20.00
16 ounce bottle of soda	.40	1.00

According to your research, the average student consumes 20 pens, 6 notebooks, 8 textbooks, 25 pizzas, 10 compact disks, and 10 bottles of soda per semester.

Construct a student price index for 1990 and 2000. Assume that 1990 is the base year. How much (by what percentage) did student prices change in the ten-year period?

9. Suppose that in a simple money multiplier model with no cash drain or excess reserves, that the reserve ratio is 0.2. What is the effect on the money supply of an open market sale of $50,000?

Problems Applying Economic Concepts Solutions

1. The rate of inflation is calculated as:

   Inflation rate = $\frac{CPI_1 - CPI_0}{CPI_0}$ x 100

   CPI_1 is the latest period's price level and CPI0 is the earlier period's price level. Using this equation we find the rate of inflation:

   Inflation rate = $\frac{120.75 - 115.00}{115.5}$ x 100

   Inflation rate = percent.

2.

   Inflation rate = $\frac{189 - 175}{175}$ x 100

   Inflation rate = 8 percent.

3. M1 is defined as currency, travelers' checks, demand deposits, and other checkable deposits. According to this definition, M1 is $4,220 (750 + 25 + 2,625 + 820).

4. The money supply is equal to nominal GDP divided by velocity. The money supply is 240 (2,400/10).

5. If velocity is constant, the growth rate in nominal GDP is equal to the growth rate in the money supply, or 6.25 percent.

6. The rate of change in the GDP deflator is equal to the difference between the growth rate in the money supply and the growth rate in real GDP, or 1.5 percent (5.0 - 3.5).

7.

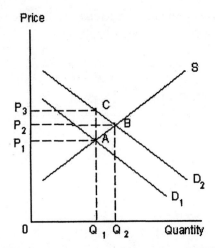

Suppose this market is initially in equilibrium at point A. If demand increases to D_2, the quantity of the product exchanged would increase to Q_2 and the price would increase to P_2. Suppose that price controls fix price at P_1. Firms now have no incentive to increase production. As a result, too few resources will be allocated to the production of this good (as indicated by the fact that consumers would be willing to pay a price of P_3 for quantity Q_1.) It follows that if too few resources are allocated to the production of this good, too many resources will be allocated to the production of other goods and services.

8. First, we must calculate the cost of each market basket in each year:

GOOD	1990 PRICES	Q	P x Q	2000 PRICES	Q	P x Q
pens	$.25	20	5.00	$1.00	20	20.00
notebooks	1.00	6	6.00	3.00	6	18.00
textbooks (average price)	25.00	8	200.00	60.00	8	480.00
pizza	4.00	25	100.00	10.00	25	250.00
compact disks	7.50	10	75.00	20.00	10	200.00
16 ounce bottle of soda	.40	10	4.00	1.00	10	10.00
			390.00			978.00

Cost of market basket in 1990 = $390
Cost of market basket in 2000 = $978

$$\text{Student Price Index} = \frac{\text{Cost of market basket in current year}}{\text{Cost of market basket in base year}} \times 100$$

For 1990 = (390/390) x 100 = 100
For 2000 = (978/390) x 100 = 250.77

So student prices have increased by 150.7% from 1990 to 2000:

$$\% \text{ change in student price index} = \frac{\text{SPI (2000)} - \text{SPI (1990)}}{\text{SPI (1990)}} \times 100$$

$$= \frac{250.77 - 100}{100} \times 100 = 150.7$$

Note that for a price index, quantity is held constant while the price varies.

9. In the simple money creation model, the money multiplier is equal to

$$1/r = 1/0.2 = 5.$$

An open market sale would create a decline in bank reserves, as banks pay for the purchase of securities by drawing down reserves. The total change in the money supply is

$$\Delta M = 1/r \times \Delta R$$

so $\quad\quad \Delta M = 5 \times -5,000 = -\$25,000$

In this simple model, an open market sale of $5,000 will reduce the money supply by $25,000.

Internet Exercises

1. Visit the Bureau of Labor Statistics Home Page (http://www.bls.gov) to find out about recent trends in inflation as measured by the CPI and PPI. From the BLS home page, first click on "US economy at a glance", under "at a glance tables".

    a. What are the current rates of inflation? Do you notice any trends in the inflation rates?

b. Go back to the home page and click on "Consumer price index". Then click on "Tables created by BLS", and then click on "Table containing history of CPI-U U.S.". What was the CPI in 1913? July 1983? 2000? The most recent month this year? What does the most recent figure mean?

2. Go to the Fed's website about the history of banking, www.federalreserveeducation.org/fed101/history. Installing FlashPlayer will allow you to see the pictures. After reading through the site, please answer the following questions:

   a. Who were Carter Glass and H. Parker Willis?

   b. What does the Humphrey-Hawkins bill require?

   c. When did Alan Greenspan become Chairman of the Board of Governors? How old were you? When did he retire? Who replaced him?

   d. What change occurred in January 2003?

3. This question asks you to read the minutes from the latest FOMC meeting. Go to the following website: www.federalreserve.gov/fomc/minutes/20050503.htm. To navigate, start at the BOG home page, www.federalreserve.gov and click on "monetary policy". Then click on "Federal Open Market Committee." Then click on, "Meeting calendar, statements, and minutes." Then click on the latest date. While you're at the site, you can also read about the tools of monetary policy. After reading the minutes, answer the following questions:

   a. How does the FOMC view the current state of the economy?

   b. What does the FOMC forecast for the future of the economy?

   c. What is the target for the federal funds rate? What is the discount rate?

Solutions

True False Questions

1. F, False, deflation is a sustained decrease in the average level of prices over time. It occurs when the overall price level is declining, not when the inflation rate is declining. A decline in the inflation rate is known as disinflation.

2. T, True, the CPI includes the prices of about 80,000 goods and services purchased by a typical urban household. Since it looks at a fixed basket of goods and services, it may overstate price increases when consumers are able to substitute to relatively lower-priced goods in the face of price increases. The inability to reflect changes in consumption patterns is known as a substitution bias.

3. T, True, when workers, savers, lenders, or landlords underestimate the future rate of inflation, economic decisions will be made incorrectly. Those who receive payments from fixed-price contracts will see the purchasing power of those payments declining with unanticipated inflation.

4. F, Inflation causes a redistribution of income from creditors to debtors. Because debtors repay their debts with dollars that are worth less, they benefit from inflation. Government is a huge debtor. Some argue that because inflation benefits debtors, government has been lax in dealing with inflation.

5. F, False, if American prices are increasing compared to foreign prices, then foreigners will purchase less American products, and those in export-industries will be harmed.

6. T, If an individual does not purchase the "typical" basket of goods and services, an increase in the CPI can either over- or understate increases in the cost of living. Also, because the CPI is based on a fixed basket of goods and services, it will tend to overstate the cost of living. This occurs because individuals tend to change consumption patterns in response to a change in prices. Specifically, individuals tend to purchase less of the relatively more expensive goods and services and more of the relatively less expensive goods and services. Finally, the CPI will overstate increases in the cost of living because it makes no adjustment for changes in the quality of products.

7. F, False, the functions of money include a medium of exchange, store of value, and unit of account. Most forms of money, such as coins and currency, actually encourage theft, since the instrument is payable to the bearer on demand. Checks and most forms of electronic money provide means to discourage theft.

8. T, True, during periods of high inflation, the purchasing power of money will be declining, so households will attempt to reduce their holdings of money and attempt to hold more real assets whose value may be more closely keeping pace with inflation.

9. F, False, legalized domestic markets are able to utilize other payment systems such as checks and electronic funds transfers. More than 70% of US currency is held by foreigners outside the United States, and the underground economy provides an important source of demand for $100 bills.

10. F, False, in quantity theory, the income velocity of money is assumed to be constant, as is real GDP. So any increase in the money supply will lead to an increase in the price level. This is seen from the equation of exchange, $M \times V = P \times GDP$. IF V and GDP are constant, then any change in the money supply will lead to a proportionate change in the price level.

11. F, It is true that an economy that is highly monopolized will tend to have higher prices than a more competitive economy. However, there is no reason to believe that prices in the less competitive economy will continue to increase at a faster rate than prices in the competitive economy. Because inflation deals with continuing increases in the price level and not high prices, this statement is false.

247

12. T, The distinction between an increase in the price level and inflation is important. A once-and-for-all increase in the price level does not require policy action. Inflation, a continuous increase in the price level, will continue until action is taken to stop it. Thus, inflation does require action on the part of policy-makers.

13. F, False, contractionary fiscal policy may be able to temporarily offset the effects of an expansionary monetary policy, but there are limits to how much government spending can be reduced or taxes raised. In the long run, fiscal policy cannot be used as an anecdote to expansionary monetary policy.

14. F, False, the Federal Open market Committee sets the target for the federal funds rate. The discount rate is set by the 12 regional; Federal reserve bank presidents, in consultation with the Board of Governors.

15. T, True, since the bond markets are located in the financial district of New York City, physically close to the Federal Reserve Bank of New York, this is where the actual day-to-day trading of bonds occurs.

16. T, True, the quantity of bank reserves can be changed through buying or selling Treasury securities, changing=g the discount rate, or changing reserve requirements. The change in bank reserves then leads to multiplied changes in the money supply.

Multiple Choice

1. A	17. D	32. C
2. C	18. B	33. A
3. B	19. C	34. B
4. A	20. B	35. C
5. C	21. C	36. D
6. D	22. A	37. D
7. B	23. D	38. D
8. B	24. A	39. B
9. A	25. A	40. D
10. C	26. D	41. A
11. D	27. B	42. D
12. A	28. A	43. B
13. B	29. D	44. C
14. B	30. C	45. B
15. C	31. B	46. C
16. A		

Fill-in Questions

1. inflation; deflation; consumer price index (CPI); cost-of-living adjustment (COLA) clause

2. unanticipated inflation; anticipated inflation

3. debtor; creditor

4. indexed

5. hyperinflation

6. medium of exchange

7. money; money supply

8. Currency (cash); demand deposits; central bank or Federal Reserve
9. quantity theory of money ; equation of exchange; income velocity of money
10. Supply-side policies; Incomes policies
11. money creation; excess reserves; Open market operations; discount rate; reserve requirements

Sustained Budget Deficits: Is This Any Way to Run a Government?

Objectives of the Chapter

After you have mastered this chapter you will understand

1. The differences between the unified budget, off-budget, and on-budget balances.

2. The differences between the budget deficit, the national debt, and the public debt.

3. The difference between mandatory and discretionary outlays.

4. The effects of recent trends in the federal government's deficit and debt.

5. The reasons why the deficit is unsustainable in the long run.

6. How to calculate the fiscal imbalance.

7. That depending on the circumstances deficits can (1) cause inflation, (2) reduce the nation's growth rate because they raise interest rates and therefore lower investment, and (3) increase the balance-of-payments deficit by altering the value of the dollar.

8. That the national debt has harmful effects both to present and future generations.

9. That running deficits during recessions has some beneficial effects in the short run, but the justification disappears when the economy is at full employment.

10. How you will be affected in the future by the consequences of the fiscal decisions made in the past and present, and what policies might help to mitigate such effects.

Key Terms

budget

unified budget

budget balance

discretionary outlay

mandatory outlay (entitlement)

budget deficit

budget surplus

off-budget balance

on-budget balance

national debt

public debt

intra-governmental debt

baseline forecast

alternative minimum tax

Medicare

Medicaid

Social Security

fiscal imbalance

national savings

foreign investment in the United States

United States' foreign investment

sources of investment funds

uses of investment funds

True False Questions

For these statements, indicate whether they are true or false. Defend your answer.

1. A mandatory outlay consists of spending that depends on specific criteria over which the government has little control.

   TRUE or FALSE

2. The portion of the Federal budget that contains Social Security expenditures is known as the on-budget balance.

   TRUE or FALSE

3. Suppose Zambena has a national debt of $100 billion and GDP of $2,000 billion. Massorno, on the other hand has a national debt of $100 million and GDP of $1,000 million. Economists would be more concerned with Zambena's national debt because it is larger than Massorno's.

   TRUE or FALSE

4. Most official forecasts of the US federal government finances predict a quick end to deficit spending, and then surpluses which should continue well into the twenty-first century.

   TRUE or FALSE

5. Due to the National Income Accounting identities, saving is the sum of gross private domestic investment and net exports.

TRUE or FALSE

Multiple Choice

Check yourself. Choose the best answer. Answers are found at end of chapter.

1. Which of the following is a receipt in the federal unified budget?
   a. national defense
   b. corporate income taxes
   c. Social Security outlays
   d. net interest

2. The national debt refers to:
   a. the amount by which government expenditures exceed government revenues over the business cycle.
   b. the amount by which government expenditures exceed government revenues during the fiscal year.
   c. the aggregate of federal deficits and surpluses that have occurred over time.
   d. the aggregate of federal deficits that have occurred over time.

3. A difference between the national debt and public debt is that
   a. the national debt includes only debt held by foreign nations.
   b. the public debt includes the debt that the government owes to itself.
   c. the national debt includes the debt that the government owes to itself.
   d. the public debt includes only internally-held debt.

4. The baseline forecast
   a. is published annually by the CBO.
   b. assumes no change in fiscal legislation.
   c. provides the CBO's best predictions about future federal fiscal performance.
   d. all of the above.

5. The primary sources of the federal government's long-run fiscal problems include:
   a. Medicaid, Medicare, and Social Security.
   b. progressive income taxes that are indexed to inflation.
   c. large projected increases in aerospace spending.
   d. the financing of presidential elections.

6. Suppose the economy is in equilibrium at point A. To increase AD and bring the economy closer to full employment, the government should:

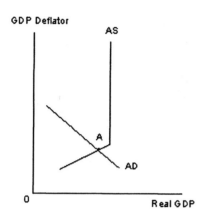

   a. allow revenues to exceed expenditures.
   b. allow expenditures to exceed revenues.
   c. balance the budget.
   d. decrease expenditures.

7. Suppose the economy is in equilibrium at point A. A decrease in government expenditures would:

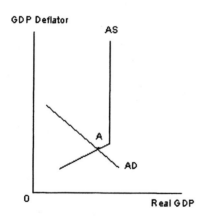

   a. help to mitigate the effects of recession.
   b. make the recession worse.
   c. help to mitigate the effects of inflation.
   d. make the inflation worse.

8. The unemployment rate is 3.8 percent. The government incurs a deficit and finances it by selling Treasury securities to the private sector. Which of the following is most likely to result?
   a. The interest rate will increase, and private investment will fall.
   b. The interest rate will increase, but private investment will not be affected.
   c. The interest rate will decrease, and private investment will fall.
   d. The interest rate will decrease, but private investment will not be affected

9. If the federal government finances a deficit by selling U.S. Treasury securities to the private sector:
    a. the demand for loanable funds will increase and the interest rate will fall.
    b. the demand for loanable funds will decrease and the interest rate will rise.
    c. both the demand for loanable funds and the interest rate will increase.
    d. both the demand for loanable funds and the interest rate will fall.

10. An increase in the interest rate caused by a budget deficit will:
    a. cause the relative price of imports and exports to rise.
    b. cause the relative price of exports to increase and the relative price of imports to decrease.
    c. cause the relative price of imports to increase and the relative price of exports to decrease.
    d. cause the relative price of imports and exports to decrease.

11. One of the main problems with a large national debt is that:
    a. it may cause the government to go bankrupt.
    b. large sums of money must be raised to ultimately repay the debt.
    c. the repayment of interest causes a burden in that there will be fewer goods and services available.
    d. the debt may slow the rate of capital formation and lower future standards of living.

12. When citizens of another country hold the national debt:
    a. there is no burden associated with the debt.
    b. there is no redistribution of income.
    c. there is a redistribution of income from U.S. citizens to foreigners.
    d. there is a redistribution of income from bondholders to taxpayers.

13. In international payments accounting, the flow of dollars into the United States, exports plus foreign investment in the United States, must be equal to
    a. imports.
    b. imports plus U.S. foreign investment.
    c. investment plus saving.
    d. the flow of dollars out of China.

14. As a result of the national debt, marginal tax rates will be higher than otherwise. These higher marginal tax rates are likely to result in:
    a. decreased work incentives.
    b. increased saving.
    c. increased investment.
    d. all of these.

15. The argument that the national debt is a burden may be valid for the portion of national debt that is:
    a. viewed as financial capital.
    b. internally held.
    c. externally held.
    d. held by banks instead of private citizens.

16. When the government incurs a deficit and finances it by selling securities:
    a. the resulting higher interest rates may reduce private investment.
    b. taxes must be raised to cover the debt.
    c. the macroeconomy automatically falls into a recession.
    d. inflation must necessarily occur.

17. A discretionary program is one for which the government:
    a. must define eligibility and set the entitlement.
    b. sets a spending limit annually.
    c. must be continued from year to year.
    d. has no control over in setting its annual budget.

18. The long-run effects of sustained deficit spending include:
    a. higher trade deficits.
    b. lower growth of real GDP.
    c. higher rates of inflation.
    d. all of the above.

Fill-in Questions

1. A _____ is the amount by which government expenditures exceed government revenues while a _____ is the amount by which government revenues exceed government expenditures in a given period of time. The _____ refers to the aggregate of the federal deficits and surpluses that have accumulated over time. Economists are more concerned with the size of the debt relative to GDP than the absolute size of the debt.

2. The _____ includes what the government owes to itself, while the _____ is what the government owes to others, both domestically and foreign.

3. The demand for _____ can increase if the government finances the deficit by issuing Treasury securities to the private sector. This increase can cause the interest rate to rise and result in a decline in private investment spending.

4. In the short run, budget deficits can help to stimulate the economy by increasing _____ . In the long run, however, budget deficits can be problematic since they may cause higher _____ , lower rates of _____ , and higher rates of _____ .

Problems Applying Economic Concepts

1. Given the following information find the size of the deficit and the national debt for each year. Assume that prior to 1992 the country's budget was balanced annually. All numbers are in billions of dollars.

Year	Government Revenues	Government Expenditures	Deficit	Debt
1992	$303.9	$305.7	$ _____	$ _____
1993	306.0	306.0	_____	_____
1994	308.9	307.0	_____	_____
1995	309.2	309.0	_____	_____
1996	311.0	313.6	_____	_____
1997	314.9	317.3	_____	_____
1998	314.6	318.9	_____	_____
1999	313.5	320.1	_____	_____
2000	314.9	319.5	_____	_____

2. Suppose that after many years of balancing the budget a country then runs a deficit of $1.3 billion in one year and a deficit of $2.9 billion the next year. What is the country's national debt?

3. Given your knowledge of deficits, surpluses, and debt, fill in the blanks in the following table. All figures are in billions of dollars. Assume that prior to 1997, the national debt was zero.

Year	Government Revenues	Government Expenditures	Deficit	Debt
1997	$415.6	$ _____	$2.8	$ _____
1998	_____	417.5	_____	1.7
1999	_____	418.9	-0.1	_____
2000	422.3	_____	_____	1.9

4. Using a graph of the loanable funds market, explain how government deficits financed by borrowing from the public will affect this market.

5. Suppose that the government of Smallville currently has $1000 in financial assets. It expects to collect $2000 in tax revenue at the end of each year for each of the next two years, and to make $3000 in expenditures at the end of each year for each of the next two years. Calculate the fiscal imbalance for the next two years, assuming that interest rates are 10%.

Problems Applying Economic Concepts Solutions

1.

Year	Government Revenues	Government Expenditures	Deficit	Debt
1992	$303.9	$305.7	$1.8	$1.8
1993	306.0	306.0	0.0	1.8
1994	308.9	307.0	-1.9	-0.1
1995	309.2	309.0	-0.2	-0.3
1996	311.0	313.6	2.6	2.3
1997	314.9	317.3	2.4	4.7
1998	314.6	318.9	4.3	9.0
1999	313.5	320.1	6.6	15.6
2000	314.9	319.5	4.6	20.2

The deficit is found by subtracting government revenues from government expenditures. A negative number indicates a surplus. The national debt is the accumulated total of federal deficits and surpluses over time. To find the national debt for any year, simply sum the deficits and surpluses.

2. The national debt will be $4.2 billion ($1.3 + $2.9).

3.

Year	Government Revenues	Government Expenditures	Deficit	Debt
1997	$415.6	$418.4	$2.8	$2.8
1998	418.6	417.5	-1.1	1.7
1999	419.0	418.9	-0.1	1.6
2000	422.3	422.6	0.3	1.9

4.

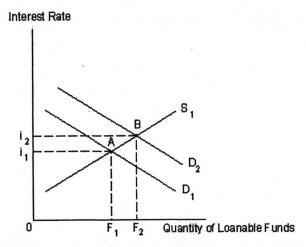

Interest Rate

S₁

B

A

D₂

D₁

0   F₁ F₂   Quantity of Loanable Funds

The demand and supply of loanable funds is initially given by D_1 and S_1, respectively. Equilibrium in this market occurs at point A with the equilibrium rate of interest equal to i_1 and the quantity of funds exchanged equal to F_1. If government finances a deficit by borrowing from the public, the demand for loanable funds will increase to D_2. A new equilibrium emerges at point B. Associated with this new equilibrium is a higher interest rate i_2. The quantity of funds exchanged increases to F_2.

5.

The fiscal imbalance is given by the following equation:
$$FI = PVFO - PVFR - CVFA \quad \text{where}$$
FI = fiscal imbalance
PVFO = present value of future outlays
PVFR = present value of future receipts
CVFA = current value of financial assets.
So
$PVFO = 3000/(1.1) + 3000/((1.1)^2) = 5206.61$
$PVFO = 2000/(1.1) + 2000/((1.1)^2) = 3471.07$
$FI = 5206.61 - 3471.07 - 1000 = 735.54$.
So Smallville has a fiscal imbalance of $735.54 over the next two years.

Internet Exercises

1. Go to the White House web site to read the latest budget message from the president.
    Go to www.whitehouse.gov and type "budget message" in the search box and click on
    "search" to find the most recent budget message from the president. (For 2006, the link is
    http://www.whitehouse.gov/omb/budget/fy2007/pdf/budget/message.pdf). What issues and initiatives
    are discussed in the president's budget message? How concerned does the president seem about
    debts and deficits?

2. Go to the Bureau of Economic Analysis web page at http://www.bea.gov. Click on "Overview of the U.S. economy". Then click on "Summary XLS table". Scroll down to "Federal Government Finances" and "Balance of Payments". Examine the table to answer the following questions:

   a. What was the federal government budget deficit for the two most recent quarters? (Net Federal Government saving).

   b. What was the balance of payments trade deficit? (Use the current account data.)

   c. How have these two variables been moving in the past two years?

3. Go to the Congressional Budget office website at www.cbo.gov. Click on "Monthly Budget Review". How is the federal government doing so far this fiscal year?

Solutions

True False Questions

1. T, True. Mandatory outlays are controlled by legislation or regulations that determine the eligibility requirements for a government entitlement, usually based on age, income, or disability. Congress has more control over discretionary spending, since it depends on appropriations limits that are set annually by Congress.

2. F, False, The on-budget balance includes the portions of the Federal Budget except for Social Security and the US Postal Service. The off-budget balance includes the Social Security and US Postal Service accounts. The unified budget balance is the sum of the on-budget balance and the off-budget balance. Since the off-budget balance has been in surplus and the on-budget balance has been in deficit, the unified budget deficit is smaller than the on-budget deficit.

3. F, Economists are more concerned with the size of the debt relative to the economy. Zambena's national debt is 5 percent of its GDP while Massorno's debt is 10 percent of its GDP. Because Massorno's debt is larger relative to the economy, economists would be more concerned with it than with Zambena's.

4. F, False, the CBO baseline forecast predicts rising deficits at least until 2075, based on no change in current fiscal legislation. The deficit is forecast to rise from 0.9% of GDP in 2015 to 18.3% of GDP in 2075.

5. T, True, starting from the GDP identity: GDP = C + Id + G + NX or GDP − C − G = Id + NX or S = Id + NX. The left hand side of the equation, GDP − C − G, is national saving, or what is left of income after subtracting consumption and government spending. This must be equal to the sum of domestic investment and net exports, Id + NX.

Multiple Choice

1. B
2. C
3. C
4. D
5. A
6. B
7. B
8. A
9. C
10. B
11. D
12. C
13. B
14. D
15. C
16. A
17. B
18. D

Fill-in Questions

1. budget deficit; budget surplus; national debt
2. national debt; public debt
3. loanable funds
4. aggregate demand; trade deficits; growth of real GDP; inflation

Social Security: Leading Issues and Approaches to Reform

Objectives of the Chapter

After you have mastered this chapter you will understand:

1. The principal features of the Social Security system.

2. How to calculate and interpret the primary insurance amount.

3. The effect of Social Security on the income and wealth of the elderly.

4. The effects of Social Security on early retirement decisions.

5. The factors affecting the ability of Social Security to influence private savings.

6. The meaning of the real rate of return on Social Security, and how to determine if the rate of return is adequate.

7. How employers may be able to shift the burden of Social Security taxes to employees.

8. The problems created by the baby boom generation and legacy debt.

9. How the Social Security Trust Funds are likely to behave over the next 75 years, and why.

10. Alternative approaches to limiting the size of the long-run deficit of the trust fund.

Key Terms

wage indexing factor

average indexed monthly earnings (AIME)

principal insurance amount (PIA)

inflation indexing

early retirement penalty

delayed retirement credit

substitution effect of a wage decrease

income effect of a wage decrease

wealth substitution effect

Social Security wealth

induced retirement effect

cost rate

income rate

baby boom generation

legacy debt

True False Questions

For these statements, indicate whether they are true or false. Defend your answer.

1. The Social Security payroll tax is the largest source of revenue for the U.S. federal government.

   TRUE or FALSE

2. Since Social Security is designed to make the retirement decision an actuarially fair choice, most economists believe that Social Security in itself has little effect on the age of retirement.

   TRUE or FALSE

3. The more elastic (flatter) the supply of labor, the greater the effect of the payroll tax on hours worked.

   TRUE or FALSE

4. The real rate of return on Social Security is below what could be earned on private investments.

   TRUE or FALSE

5. The rate of poverty among the elderly has not been affected much by Social Security.

   TRUE or FALSE

6. The wealth substitution effect occurs when higher interest rates cause consumers to substitute saving for consumption spending.

   TRUE or FALSE

7. The income effect of a wage decrease occurs when a decline in wages causes workers to increase their labor hours supplied to make up for the reduction in the hourly wage.

   TRUE or FALSE

8. If labor supply is infinitely inelastic (vertical), then employers will be unable to shift any of the payroll tax burden on to employees.

   TRUE or FALSE

9. Legacy debt has been declining since the 1930s as the original recipients of Social Security have eventually been dying off and no longer receiving benefits.

   TRUE or FALSE

10. In his 2005 State of the Union Address, President Bush introduced a plan to reform Social Security by allowing for the establishment of individual savings accounts and the price indexing of benefits rather than wage indexing.

    TRUE or FALSE

Multiple Choice

Check yourself. Choose the best answer. Answers are found at the end of the chapter.

1. Social Security expenditures are financed primarily by:
   a. the federal individual income tax.
   b. payroll taxes.
   c. interest earned on assets in the social security trust fund.
   d. corporate income taxes.

2. In general, Social Security benefits are:
   a. relatively more generous for males.
   b. relatively more generous for single individuals.
   c. relatively more generous for high-income individuals.
   d. relatively more generous for low-income individuals.

3. The amount a person receives at the normal or full retirement age is called the:
   a. average indexed monthly earnings.
   b. primary insurance amount.
   c. indexed factor.
   d. payroll tax.

4. If workers believe that Social Security will provide them with enough retirement income they may spend a larger share of their pre-retirement earnings. This behavior is referred to as the:
   a. wealth substitution effect.
   b. induced retirement effect.
   c. primary insurance effect.
   d. payroll tax effect.

5. If workers decide to retire earlier because of Social Security, they are exhibiting the:
   a. wealth substitution effect.
   b. primary insurance effect.
   c. induced retirement effect.
   d. payroll tax effect.

6. Ralph's monthly benefit from Social Security was reduced because he retired at age 63. This is an example of Social Security's:
   a. declining gross replacement rate.
   b. delayed retirement penalty.
   c. income retirement penalty.
   d. delayed retirement penalty.

7. Suppose the labor supply curve is positively sloped. In this instance a payroll tax will:
   a. increase the number of hours worked.
   b. increase the after-tax wage.
   c. decrease the after-tax wage.
   d. increase savings.

8. An increase in the Social Security tax causes Jennifer's take-home wage to fall. As a result, Jennifer decreases the number of hours she works. This is an example of:
   a. the substitution effect of a wage decrease.
   b. the income effect of a wage decrease.
   c. the opportunity cost of a wage decrease.
   d. the salaried effect of a wage decrease.

9.

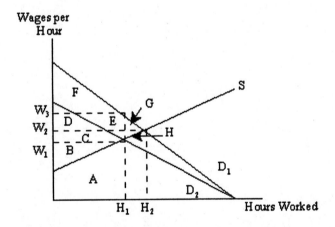

Suppose a payroll tax shifts the demand for labor from D_1 to D_2. The employees' equilibrium wage and hours worked after the shift would be:
   a. W_1 and H_1, respectively.
   b. W_2 and H_2, respectively.
   c. W_1 and H_1, respectively.
   d. W_3 and H_1, respectively.

10.

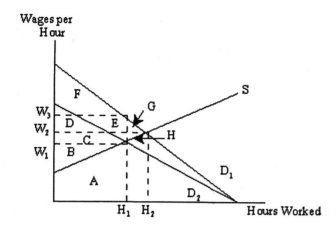

If a payroll tax shifts the demand for labor from D_1 to D_2, government raises:
a. D + C + E in tax revenue. (correct answer)
b. D + C + E + G + H in tax revenue. (This was marked as correct but is not)
c. D + C + E + G + H + F in tax revenue.
d. A + B + D + C in tax revenue.

11.

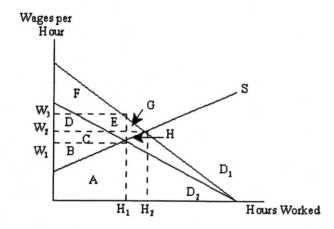

If a payroll tax shifts the demand for labor from D_1 to D_2, the before-tax wage paid by employers:
a. will increase from W_1 to W_3.
b. will increase from W_2 to W_3.
c. will decrease from W_3 to W_1.
d. will decrease from W_3 to W_2.

12.

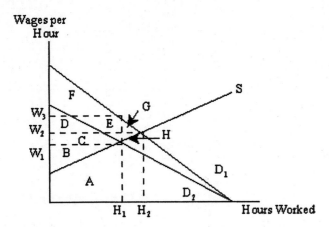

If a payroll tax shifts the demand for labor from D_1 to D_2, the portion of the payroll tax borne by employers will be represented by area:

a. F.

b. D + C + E.

c. C + H.

d. D + E.

13. Dan expects to receive Social Security benefits upon retirement. As a result he saves less money now. This is an example of:

a. the wealth substitution effect.

b. the induced consumption effect.

c. the saving offset effect.

d. the reduced saving effect.

14. Which of the following would be most likely to cause savings to increase in response to the payment of Social Security benefits?

a. the wealth substitution effect.

b. the induced retirement effect.

c. pension alternative effect.

d. the income substitution effect.

15. The substitution effect of a wage decrease occurs when

a. a decrease in the hourly wage rate causes an individual to work more hours to make up for the decline in wages.

b. a decrease in the hourly wage rate causes an individual to work less hours since the return to labor hours has declined.

c. a decrease in the hourly wage rate causes an increase in the saving rate.

d. a decrease in the hourly wage rate causes an increase in the quantity demanded of labor.

16. Which of the following statements is correct?
    a. The present value of Social Security benefits is greater than the present value of Social Security taxes.
    b. The rate of return an individual can earn on Social Security is approximately equal to the rate of return that can be earned when investing in the stock market.
    c. The rate of return an individual can earn on Social Security is less than the rate of return that can be earned on U. S. Treasury securities.
    d. Considering non-monetary benefits will cause the individual's rate of return on Social Security to fall.

17. An increase in fertility rates will:
    a. increase the Social Security deficit.
    b. decrease the Social Security deficit.
    c. have no impact on the Social Security deficit.
    d. first increase and then decrease the Social Security deficit.

18. Projections of Social Security indicate that:
    a. the surplus will continue to grow until about 2013.
    b. the surplus will continue to shrink until about 2013.
    c. the surplus will continue to grow until about 2025.
    d. the surplus will continue to shrink until about 2025.

19. The Social Security Trust Fund surplus is expected to be depleted by:
    a. 2006.
    b. 2013.
    c. 2041.
    d. 2075.

20. In order to prevent exhaustion of the Social Security trust fund:
    a. the retirement age for Social Security should be decreased.
    b. the tax for Social Security should be increased.
    c. the penalty for early retirement should be decreased.
    d. the age at which benefits become available should be decreased for females, but increased for males.

21. Using the Social Security surplus to increase investment will most likely:
    a. put pressure on future legislators to increase the Social Security payroll tax.
    b. put pressure on Congress to allow trustees to invest directly in private securities.
    c. increase future GDP.
    d. decrease future GDP.

22. Which of the following best explains why the social security system may experience financial difficulties in the future?
    a. Social security revenues have been invested in risky stock market investments rather than in safer investment devices.
    b. The social security system does not receive any interest on the money that it lends to the Treasury.
    c. The funds in the social security have generally been kept in a lock box which is unavailable for other purposes.
    d. The number of workers paying into the system is expected to decline relative to the number of retirees collecting benefits.

23. The social security program is principally
    a. a government financed insurance program which is similar to all other insurance plans.
    b. a forced savings program whereby current workers will receive only the amount they have placed in the accounts plus interest.
    c. an income transfer system designed to tax current workers in order to provide benefits for current retirees.
    d. a voluntary savings and investment program run by the government.

24. The costs of the payroll tax fall on:
    a. employers.
    b. low income unemployed workers.
    c. minimum wage recipients.
    d. employed workers.

25. The cost of an employee to an employer equals the wage paid to the employee:
    a. plus the employer's contribution to Social Security.
    b. less the employer's contribution to Social Security.
    c. only.
    d. plus the total Social Security Bill.

26. The principal impact of social security is that it:
    a. decreases the supply of labor.
    b. increases the demand for labor.
    c. decreases the demand for labor.
    d. increases the level of employment.

27. On balance those currently receiving Social Security retirement benefits receive:
    a. more than they and the employer have contributed.
    b. less than they and the employer have contributed.
    c. an amount equal to what they have contributed plus an amount equal to that paid by the employer.
    d. a predetermined portion of what they have contributed.

28. Which of the following would NOT reduce the benefit costs of the Social Security program?
    a. The use of a more accurate measure of inflation to index benefits.
    b. An increase in the normal retirement age.
    c. A decrease in the normal retirement age.
    d. A change in the method used to index pre-retirement earnings.

29. President Bush's proposed reforms for Social Security, as outlined in his State of the Union Address of 2005, included the introduction of
    a. more government control over the Social Security Trust fund.
    b. individual saving accounts.
    c. an increase in the retirement age to 70 years.
    d. an increase in the employer share of payroll taxes.

30. The proposed reforms by Diamond and Orszag, as outlined in the text,
    a. adjust Social Security for what they consider to be the principal sources of fiscal imbalance, including increased life expectancy and increasing earnings inequality.
    b. include a series of tax increases and benefit reductions.
    c. would provide, if adopted, fiscal solvency to the Social Security system over a 100-year time horizon.
    d. all of the above.

Fill-in Questions

1. The Social Security payroll tax is currently levied on earnings up to $94,300 at a rate of _____ which is split evenly between _____ and _____ .

2. Social Security benefits can vary depending on the age of retirement. If an individual retires between the ages of 62 and 65, benefits are subject to a(n) _____ . On the other hand, benefits will increase if an individual delays retirement. In this case, they receive a(n) _____ .

3. There is some concern about the effects of Social Security taxes on the number of hours worked. Social Security taxes decrease net take-home pay. This can lead to a _____ . As the wage falls, the number of hours worked decreases because leisure time becomes relatively less expensive. The decrease in net take-home pay can also lead to a(n) _____ . In this instance, the decrease in take-home pay causes income to fall. The individual works more hours in order to maintain income. Your authors argue that Social Security tax may have no impact on the number of hours worked. In this case, the two effects cancel each other out.

4. Social Security may also affect household savings. The _____ causes household savings to fall as _____ is substituted for other types of wealth. The _____ causes household savings to increase as households save more in order to finance increased years of retirement. Analysts argue that several factors can impact the projected Social Security deficit. Increases in GDP will cause the projected deficit to fall. Likewise, increases in _____ , the average number of children born to women in their lifetime, can also cause projected deficits to fall.

5. Potential remedies for the long run fiscal problems include fixing the current system or allowing private accounts. Diamond and Orszag suggest that the current system can become fiscally sound by increasing _____ and implementing three types of _____ . Recent proposals for reform from President Bush include investing Social Security trust funds in private securities, either investing the funds in _____ (stocks) or establishing _____ .

Problems Applying Economic Concepts

1. Doris had an annual income of $40,000 at age 50. Suppose that the Average National Wage was $40,000 when Doris was 50, and the Average National Wage was $50,000 when Doris was 60. Find the Indexed Earnings for Doris at age 50.

2. Ethel turns 62 in the year 2006. Find her Primary Insurance Amount for the following levels of Average Indexed Monthly Earnings:

    a. AIME = $500.

    b. AIME = $1,000

    c. AIME = $10,000

3. The pretax equilibrium wage is _____ while the imposition of a payroll tax causes a new equilibrium wage of _____ to emerge.

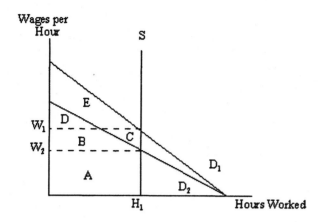

4. The value of output produced by labor (with or without a payroll tax imposed) is given by area _____.

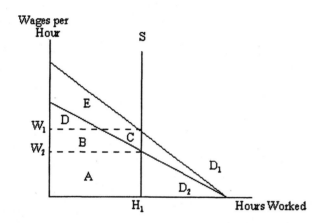

5. Before the imposition of a payroll tax, the income earned by labor is represented by area _____.

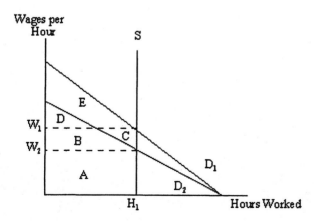

6. After the imposition of a payroll tax, the income earned by labor is represented by area _____.

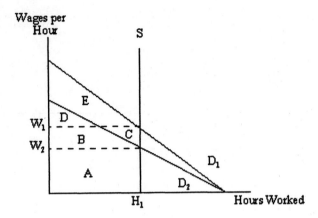

7. In this instance, the entire tax is borne by _____.

8.

Suppose that Joe is willing to work for 50 hours per week regardless of the wage rate, so his labor supply curve is vertical at 50 hours. Suppose that the demand for Joe's labor is given by the following equation:

$$\text{demand: } W = 125 - H$$

where W is the hourly wage rate and H is the number of hours worked per week.

a. What is the equilibrium wage rate? Hours worked?

b.

Suppose that a payroll tax of 25% is imposed on employers, so that the demand curve shifts to

$$\text{demand(t): } W = 100 - 0.8H.$$

What wage will Joe receive with the tax?

c. Show a) and b) graphically. Who pays the tax?

Problems Applying Economic Concepts Solutions

1. Since Indexed Earnings are given by the following equation,

Since Indexed Earnings are given by the following equation,

$$IE_a = E_a \left(ANW_{60} / ANW_a \right)$$

where IE_a = Indexed Earnings at age a
            E_a = Earnings at age a
            ANW_{60} = Average National Wage at age 60
            ANW_a = Average National Wage at age a.

then IE_{50} = \$40,000 (50,000/40,000) = \$40,000 x 1.25 = \$50,000.

2. For someone turning 62 in the year 2006, the Primary Insurance Rate formula is provided in the text: PIA = 0.9(first $656 AIME) + 0.32($656<AIME<3955) + 0.15(AIME over 3955). So

    a.

    $$\text{AIME} = \$500: \qquad \text{PIA} = 0.9(500) = 450$$
    $$\text{PIA/AIME} = 0.9$$

    b.

    $$\text{AIME} = \$1,000: \qquad \text{PIA} = 0.9(656) + 0.32(344) = 590 + 110 = 700$$
    $$\text{PIA/AIME} = 0.7$$

    c.

    $$\text{AIME} = \$10,000: \qquad \text{PIA} = 0.9(656) + 0.32(3299) + 0.15(6045)$$
    $$= 590 + 1056 + 907 = 2553$$
    $$\text{PIA/AIME} = 0.2553$$

    Note that as average monthly income increases, the principal insurance amount also increases. Benefits are relatively more generous to low-income individuals, since PIA/AIME increases as AIME declines.

3. W_1, W_2

4. A + B + C + D + E

5. A + B + C

6. A

7. labor

    a.

    If H = 50, then the equilibrium wage rate is
    $$W = 125 - (50) = \$75$$

    b.

    If a payroll tax of 25% is imposed, the wage received by Joe will equal:
    $$W = 100 - 0.8(50) = \$60.$$
    The amount of the payroll tax equals 0.25 x $60 = $15.

    c. Since Joe's wage has declined by the entire amount of the $15 tax (from $75 to $60), then Joe pays the entire tax. Whenever labor supply is infinitely inelastic, then a payroll tax will be borne entirely by employees. Graphically,

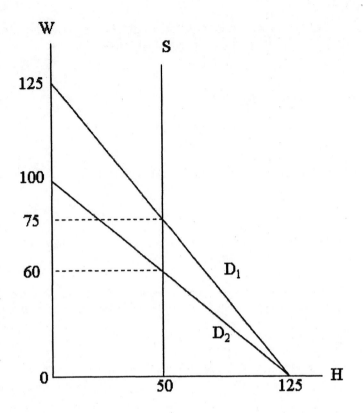

Internet Exercises

Go to the Social Security Administration's website at www.ssa.gov/qa.htm and read the FAQs about Social Security. Also, browse through the most recent Trustee's Report Summary that is available. How does the Social Security Administration view the future of the trust fund? Are current recipients in danger of losing their benefits? What about future recipients? What about you?

Solutions

True False Questions

1. F, False, the Social Security payroll tax is the second largest source of revenue for the federal government, behind the personal income tax.

2. T, True, because of the early retirement penalty that permanently reduces benefits if an employee retires early, there is less inducement for early retirement. In addition, the delayed retirement credit encourages people to work beyond the retirement age. Due to the penalty for early retirement and the credit for late retirement, the decision to retire is actuarially fair in terms of Social Security benefits. For this reason, the existence of Social Security itself should have little effect on the choice of when to retire.

3. T, If the labor supply curve is vertical, the payroll tax will have no effect on the number of hours worked. The more elastic (flatter or less vertical) the labor supply curve, the greater will be the effect of the payroll tax on hours worked.

4. T, The present value of Social Security taxes exceeds the present value of Social Security benefits. This means that the rate of return on Social Security is less than what could be earned if the money were invested in long-term U. S. Treasury securities. Like Social Security, these securities are essentially risk free. It should be noted, however, that Social Security does offer some additional non-monetary benefits not found in the private sector. For example, Social Security offers protection against poverty and inflation. If these factors are taken into account the rate of return on Social Security increases. It is possible that the real rate of return on Social Security is comparable to that which could be earned on truly comparable private investments, if they existed.

5. F, Social Security benefits are an important source of family income for retired workers, especially for low-income retirees. It is relatively more generous to low-wage workers than to high-wage workers. This is because the program was deliberately designed to provide a safety net for the elderly poor. Estimates show that more than 45% of the elderly would live in poverty in the absence of Social Security. In addition, statistics show that the poverty rate of the elderly is below the poverty rate for the population as a whole.

6. F, False, the wealth substitution effect occurs when workers substitute Social Security wealth for private sources of wealth, such as personal savings or private pensions. Social Security wealth is the present value of the stream of Social Security benefits received in the future.

7. T, True, the effects of a wage decrease include the substitution and income effects. Workers face a choice between income and leisure. The wage rate is the opportunity cost of consuming an hour of leisure. When the hourly wage rate declines, leisure becomes less expensive, and workers will substitute more leisure for other goods that are now relatively more expensive. This is the substitution effect. The income effect occurs when the decline in income from a wage decrease results in workers being able to afford less leisure, so they consume less leisure and work more.

8. F, False, if the labor supply curve is vertical, employers will be able to shift the entire burden of the tax on to employees. Since the quantity of labor supplied doesn't respond to changes in the wage rate, employers can reduce hourly wages by the full amount of the tax without losing any hours of labor supplied.

9. F, False, the legacy debt has been increasing, which is one explanation for the rising costs of Social Security over time. The legacy debt is the debt left by a cohort when their discounted benefits over time are greater than their total discounted contributions plus interest over time. As each generation has to pay the legacy debt of the past generations, the legacy debt accumulates.

10. T, True, President Bush proposed significant reforms to Social Security in his State of the Union Address of February, 2005. The proposal was based on "Plan B" of the President's Commission on Strengthening Social Security, which contained the ideas of individual savings accounts and price indexing of benefits.

Multiple Choice

1. B
2. C
3. B
4. A
5. C
6. D
7. C
8. A
9. C
10. B
11. B
12. D
13. A
14. B
15. B
16. C
17. B
18. C
19. C
20. B
21. C
22. D
23. A
24. D
25. A
26. C
27. A
28. C
29. B
30. D

Fill-in Questions

1. 12.4%; employers; employees
2. early retirement penalty; delayed retirement credit
3. substitution effect of a wage decrease; income effect of a wage decrease
4. wealth substitution effect; social security wealth; induced retirement effect; fertility rates
5. payroll taxes; benefit reductions; equity; Individual Accounts

International Trade: Beneficial, but Controversial

Objectives of the Chapter

After you have mastered this chapter you will understand:

1. That U.S. participation in the world economy is increasing.

2. That trade among nations is based on comparative, not absolute, advantage.

3. That international trade is advantageous in that it allows countries to specialize in the production of goods in which they have a comparative advantage and exchange those goods for goods in which they have a comparative disadvantage.

4. That although economists view free trade as beneficial, many groups criticize free trade for destroying domestic jobs, exploiting foreign labor, sacrificing national defense, harming infant industries, or increasing trade deficits.

5. That tariffs, quotas, and voluntary export restraints serve as impediments to international trade, and create net welfare losses for society as a whole.

6. That society as a whole benefits from free trade, but some individuals are worse off.

7. The importance of the WTO, NAFTA, and GATT as frameworks for promoting free trade.

8. That the harm of free trade to specific individuals may be mitigated by various Trade Adjustment Assistance programs such as extended unemployment benefits or job retraining.

Key Terms

comparative advantage

comparative disadvantage

absolute advantage

absolute disadvantage

consumers' surplus

producers' surplus

net welfare gain

elasticity of substitution between varieties of a good

productivity

trade deficit

tariff

import quota

voluntary export restraints

General Agreement on Tariffs and Trade

World Trade Organization

embargo

North American Free Trade Agreement

European Union

trade adjustment assistance

True False Questions

For these statements, indicate whether they are true or false. Defend your answer.

1. In the past 25 years, U.S. exports have been relatively constant at 10% of GDP, while imports have increased from 10% to 15% of GDP.

   TRUE or FALSE

2. Suppose the average cost of producing shirts is higher in the United States than it is in Canada. The United States should import shirts from Canada.

   TRUE or FALSE

3. Import restrictions are harmful to all of society.

   TRUE or FALSE

4. Because the concept of comparative advantage is so well accepted, free international trade is the rule.

   TRUE or FALSE

5. Consumers' surplus in a market increases as the price of the good rises.

   TRUE or FALSE

6. NAFTA is an agreement that has lowered trade barriers between the United States, Canada, and Mexico.

   TRUE or FALSE

7. The primary function of the WTO is to support and maintain trade barriers between different countries around the world.

   TRUE or FALSE

8. Free trade inevitably leads to a loss of domestic jobs.

   TRUE or FALSE

Multiple Choice

Check yourself. Choose the best answer. Answers are found at the end of the chapter.

1. Which of the following best exemplifies absolute advantage?
   a. A unit of labor in the United States can produce more wheat than a unit of labor in Canada.
   b. A unit of labor in Canada can produce more apples than a unit of labor in the United States.
   c. The United States must give up fewer apples to produce a unit of wheat than Canada must give up.
   d. Workers in Japan are more productive than workers in the United States.

2. Which of the following statements is correct?

	Wheat	Sugar
United States	4	2
Philippines	1	4

   a. The United States has an absolute advantage in the production of wheat.
   b. The United States has an absolute advantage in the production of sugar.
   c. The United States has an absolute advantage in the production of both goods.
   d. The Philippines has an absolute advantage in the production of wheat.

3. In the United States, the opportunity cost of producing a unit of wheat is:

	Wheat	Sugar
United States	4	2
Philippines	1	4

   a. 4 units of sugar.
   b. 2 units of sugar.
   c. 1 unit of sugar.
   d. ½ unit of sugar.

4. Based on the above information:

	Wheat	Sugar
United States	4	2
Philippines	1	4

   a. the Philippines should produce wheat and trade for sugar.
   b. the Philippines should produce sugar and trade for wheat.
   c. the United States should produce sugar and trade for wheat.
   d. the United States should not trade with the Philippines.

5. Trade based on comparative advantage will:
   a. increase the well-being of the stronger trading partner.
   b. increase the well-being of the trading partner that has the absolute advantage.
   c. increase the well-being of the trading partner that has the absolute disadvantage.
   d. increase the well-being of both trading partners.

6. Who has an absolute advantage in making pizza?
   a. Anthony can make 12 pizzas or 6 calzones in an hour.
   b. Bernardo can make 10 pizzas or 5 calzones in an hour.
   c. Constantine can make 4 pizzas or 4 calzones in an hour.
   d. Dominic can make 4 pizzas or 8 calzones in an hour.
   e. Emil can make 3 pizzas or 1 calzone in an hour.

7. Who has a comparative advantage in making pizza?
   a. Anthony can make 12 pizzas or 6 calzones in an hour.
   b. Bernardo can make 10 pizzas or 5 calzones in an hour.
   c. Constantine can make 4 pizzas or 4 calzones in an hour.
   d. Dominic can make 4 pizzas or 8 calzones in an hour.
   e. Emil can make 3 pizzas or 1 calzone in an hour.

8. Which of the following statements is correct?
   a. Imports and exports are relatively more important in the United States than they were in the 1960s.
   b. The reason imports are not very important in the United States is because the United States imports less than other countries.
   c. The United States' main trading partner is Japan.
   d. During the 1980s, the level of exports generally exceeded the level of imports in the United States.

9. A tariff:
    a. places an upper limit on the amount of a good that may be imported into a country.
    b. is a tax levied on a good when it crosses a nation's border.
    c. encourages the growth of a country's more efficient industries.
    d. will cause the relative price of imports to decrease.

10. A tariff on cattle imported from Brazil is eliminated. The most likely effect of the elimination of the tariff will be to:
    a. decrease the price domestic producers receive for cattle.
    b. increase the quantity of cattle bought by domestic buyers.
    c. increase the quantity of cattle imported into the country.
    d. all of these.

11. Suppose a tariff is imposed on textiles imported into the United States. This will result in:
    a. a decrease in the price paid by domestic buyers.
    b. an increase in the amount of textiles sold by domestic producers.
    c. a decrease in the price received by domestic producers.
    d. an increase in the amount of textiles (both foreign and domestic) bought by domestic buyers.

12. Japan decides to limit the number of cars it sells to the United States. This is an example of:
    a. a tariff.
    b. a quota.
    c. a voluntary export restraint.
    d. a voluntary import restraint.

13. Trade restrictions cause:
    a. a decrease in the price of domestic goods.
    b. resources to remain in industries that have a comparative disadvantage.
    c. resources to flow to industries that have a comparative advantage.
    d. significant revenues to be generated for the federal government.

14. Which of the following statements is correct?
    a. A tariff generates revenue for the government. A quota does not.
    b. A quota generates revenue for the government. A tariff does not.
    c. Voluntary export restraints can actually cause the price of a good to fall.
    d. Trade barriers increase the welfare of society.

15. One difference between a tariff and a quota is that
    a. a quota is a tax on imports, while a tariff is a quantity restriction.
    b. a tariff is a tax on imports, while a quota is a quantity restriction.
    c. only tariffs lead to higher prices for products domestically.
    d. only quotas increase the quantity produced domestically.

16. Which of the following best exemplifies the decreasing cost argument for free trade?
    a. Tiny Land has only one bicycle manufacturer. Free trade increases the number of firms the manufacturer must compete with.
    b. As a result of free trade, the New and Improved Automobile Company is able to increase its production, thereby lowering its production costs.
    c. Free trade results in inefficient industries shutting down, thereby allowing resources to flow to more efficient industries.
    d. Before free trade, citizens of Limited Land consumed only bagels and lox. After free trade, citizens of Limited land also have cream cheese and sparkling water available to them.

17. "Trade restrictions must be imposed on Taiwan. It has begun exporting a large number of computer chips to the United States. We must have a reliable domestic supply of these chips available if war breaks out." This is an example of:
    a. the comparative advantage argument.
    b. the national defense argument.
    c. the productivity argument.
    d. the cheap labor argument.

18. Suppose strict trade restrictions are imposed in the automobile industry. The most likely result of this action will be to:
    a. increase employment in the automobile industry, but decrease employment in other industries.
    b. decrease employment in the automobile industry, but increase employment in other industries.
    c. increase the overall rate of unemployment.
    d. cause the rate of employment to increase in industries where the country has a comparative advantage.

19. The best way to protect American jobs is:
    a. through a system of import quotas.
    b. through a system of tariffs.
    c. to use monetary and fiscal policies that promote full employment.
    d. use a wide variety of trade restrictions including tariffs, quotas, and voluntary export restraints.

20. Which of the following might be used as an argument in support of free trade?
    a. Industry XYZ cannot compete with foreign firms because the foreign firms can hire labor more cheaply.
    b. Increasing trade restrictions can increase competition.
    c. Free trade can increase the diversity of products available to consumers.
    d. Feel Good industries produces a product that is vital to the nation's security.

21. Which of the following statements is correct?
    a. Since World War II, barriers to international trade have risen significantly.
    b. The GATT has been the major regional approach to reducing trade barriers.
    c. The European Union is the largest trading bloc in the world.
    d. NAFTA created a free-trade area that has a GDP greater than that of the European Union.

22. One explanation for the increasing U.S. trade deficits of the late 1990s is
    a. increasing productivity growth which raised U.S. rates of return.
    b. declining real interest rates in the United States.
    c. high rates of inflationary expectations.
    d. increases in tariffs and quotas.

23. The difference between what consumers would pay and the price they must pay refers to:
    a. the producer surplus.
    b. producer profits.
    c. the net gains from absolute advantage.
    d. the consumer surplus.

24. The difference between the price that producers receive and what is required to cover costs refers to:
    a. the producer surplus.
    b. the consumer surplus.
    c. the net gains from absolute advantage.
    d. the net gains from the combination of tariffs and quotas.

25. An important function of the WTO is to
    a. enforce tariff laws around the world.
    b. maintain and support trade barriers around the world.
    c. promote and maintain free trade around the world.
    d. provide a karaoke forum for world leaders.

Fill-in Questions

1. Recent trends in U.S. international trade include growing trade _____ as the amount of _____ as a percentage of GDP has remained relatively constant, while the share of _____ has increased from ten to fifteen percent of GDP.

2. Trade should be based on _____ . A country has a comparative advantage in a good or service if it can produce that good or service at a lower opportunity cost than its trading partner. A country has a(n) _____ in a good or service if it produces that good at a higher opportunity cost than its trading partner.

3. Comparative advantage is different than absolute advantage. A country is said to have a(n) _____ if it can produce a good or service at a lower cost than its trading partner. A country is said to have a(n) _____ if it produces a good or service at a higher cost than its trading partner.

4. Although free trade benefits society as a whole, nations often limit free trade by imposing trade restrictions. For example, a nation may place a tax or _____ on a good that crosses its borders. Nations may also place upper limits on the amount of goods that may be imported during any time period. Such a limit is known as a(n) _____ . Finally, nations may reach an agreement whereby the exporting nation voluntarily restricts the amount of goods they ship to the importing nation. This type of agreement is a(n) _____ . These trade restrictions work to increase the price of imports. As a result, resources are shifted from industries that have a comparative advantage to industries that have a comparative disadvantage.

5. The _____ is an international framework for promoting free trade and solving trade disputes. It was formed in 1995 as a successor to the _____ .

6. Some of the costs of free trade may be mitigated by _____ , which compensates the losers of free trade by providing re-employment services such as job training programs, and income support benefits, for workers who lose their jobs.

Problems Applying Economic Concepts

1. Which country has the absolute advantage in the production of bicycles? in the production of wine?

Country	Bicycles per day	Wine per day
France	2	6
Italy	7	7

2. Which country has the comparative advantage in the production of bicycles? in the production of wine?

Country	Bicycles per day	Wine per day
France	2	6
Italy	7	7

3. If France and Italy specialize according to the principle of comparative advantage, then France will produce (a) _____ and trade for (b) _____ while Italy will produce (c) _____ and trade for (d) _____.

Country	Bicycles per day	Wine per day
France	2	6
Italy	7	7

4. What is the opportunity cost of producing 1 unit of wheat in the United States? in England?

Country	Wheat per day	Cloth per day
United States	30	30
England	30	60

5. What is the opportunity cost of producing 1 unit of cloth in the United States? in England?

Country	Wheat per day	Cloth per day
United States	30	30
England	30	60

6. The United States will be willing to trade wheat for cloth if it can get more than (a) unit(s) of cloth for 1 unit of wheat. England will be willing to trade cloth for wheat if it can get more than (b) unit(s) of wheat for 1 unit of cloth.

Country	Wheat per day	Cloth per day
United States	30	30
England	30	60

7. You and your roommate Chris must clean your apartment before your parents visit for Parents' Weekend. By yourself, you can clean the entire apartment in two days, and Chris can clean the entire apartment in two days. Together, you could both clean the apartment in one day. Additionally, you can earn $100 per day working as a computer consultant, while Chris can earn $50 per day working as a disk jockey at the local radio station.

   a. Who has a lower opportunity in cleaning the apartment? Why?

   b. According to the principle of comparative advantage, who should clean the apartment? Explain.

8. Suppose that the United States and Saudi Arabia can each produce guns and oil. The quantities of each good that can be produced by each country in a year, assuming that all resources are devoted to the production of that good, are given by the table below. Guns are measured in units, and oil is measured in barrels.

	GUNS/YEAR	OIL/YEAR
UNITED STATES	600,000	600,000
SAUDI ARABIA	200,000	600,000

   a. For each country, what is the opportunity cost of producing one gun? One barrel of oil?

   b. Should each country specialize and trade? Why or why not? If so, then which country should specialize in what product?

   c. If your answer to b) is yes, then use PPC graphs to show that each country is better off through specialization and trade. Assume that each country completely specializes in that product in which it has a comparative advantage. Then show that through trade, each country can achieve a point that lies above its own PPC.

9. During the first term of the Bush Administration, tariffs were placed on imported steel in an attempt to protect domestic steel producers from foreign competition. Let's examine a hypothetical model to show the effects of the tariff on the U.S. market for steel.

   Suppose that the demand and supply conditions in the U.S. steel market can be described by the following equations:

   domestic demand: $P = 64 - 2Q$
   domestic supply: $P = 4 + Q$

   where P is the price in dollars and Q is measured as tons of steel.

   a. Assume that the U.S. does not trade with the rest of the world. (This situation is often referred to as autarky.) What is the equilibrium price and quantity in the U.S. steel market? What is the amount of consumer surplus? Producer surplus? Show graphically.

   b. Suppose that the U.S. now opens its steel market to the rest of the world. Assume that the world price of steel is $12, so that the world supply curve is a horizontal line at a price of $12. This assumes that the U.S. market is small enough relative to the rest of the world that the U.S. has no control over the world price. What is the amount of domestic consumption? Domestic production? How much is imported from the rest of the world? What is the amount of consumer surplus for U.S. consumers? What is the amount of producer surplus for U.S. producers? How much revenue is earned by importers?

c. Suppose now that the U.S. government imposes a tariff of $8.00 for each ton of steel imported from the rest of the world. What is the equilibrium price? What is the amount of domestic consumption? Domestic production? How much is imported from the rest of the world? What is the amount of consumer surplus? Producer surplus? Find the change in producer surplus (from b), tariff revenue, and the net welfare loss of the tariff. Show the net welfare loss on your graph from a).

Problems Applying Economic Concepts Solutions

1. Since the output of both goods is higher in Italy, Italy has the absolute advantage in the production of both goods.

2. In order to produce 1 bicycle, France must give up 3 (6/2) units of wine. In Italy, the opportunity cost of 1 bicycle is 1 (7/7) unit of wine. Thus, Italy has the comparative advantage in the production of bicycles. In order to produce 1 unit of wine, France must give up 1/3 (2/6) bicycles while Italy must give up 1 (7/7) bicycle. Thus, France has the comparative advantage in the production of wine.

3.

   a. Wine

   b. bicycles

   c. bicycles

   d. wine

4. In the United States, the opportunity cost of producing 1 unit of wheat is 1 (30/30) unit of cloth. In England, the opportunity cost of producing 1 unit of wheat is 2 (60/30) units of cloth.

5. In the United States, the opportunity cost of producing 1 unit of cloth is 1 (30/30) units of wheat. In England, the opportunity cost of producing 1 unit of cloth is ½ (30/60) units of wheat.

6.

   a. 2

   b. ½

7.

   a. Chris has a lower opportunity cost in cleaning the apartment, since he would be giving up less income to stay home for the day. Since it takes each of you two days to clean the apartment, your opportunity cost to clean the apartment would be $200, while Chris would only have to give up $100.

b. Chris should clean the apartment since he (or she) has a lower opportunity cost. Without specialization, you would each spend one day working and one day cleaning. In two days, you would both have a clean apartment, you would earn $100 for working one day, and Chris would earn $50. With specialization, Chris would clean the apartment in two days and you would work for two days. You would earn $200 by working for two days. If you paid Chris $60 to clean the apartment, you would both be better off. You would have a clean apartment and $140, rather than the $100 you could earn in one day without specialization. Chris would have a clean apartment and $60, rather than the $50 that he could earn in one day.

8.

   a.

United States: 600,000G = 600,000O   Saudi Arabia: 2000,000G = 600,000O
$$1G = 1O \qquad\qquad\qquad\qquad 1G = 3O$$
$$1O = 1G \qquad\qquad\qquad\qquad 1O = 1/3\ G$$

   b. Since the United States has a lower opportunity cost in producing guns (1O v 3O), then the United States should specialize in gun production. Since Saudi Arabia has a lower opportunity cost in producing oil (1/3 G v 1G), then Saudi Arabia should specialize in oil production.

   c. Both countries would be willing to trade 1 gun for 2 barrels of oil. (1O < 2O < 3O).

The maximum quantity of oil that Saudi Arabia can produce is 600,000 barrels per year, so assume that the United States trades 300,000 guns for 600,000 barrels of oil:

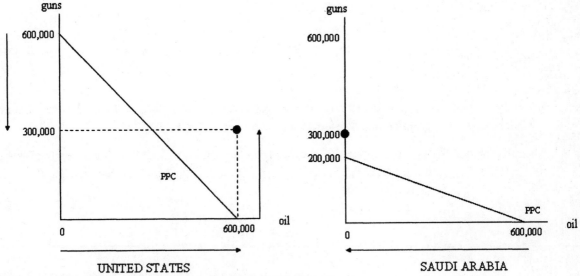

The trade makes both the United States and Saudi Arabia better off.

9.

   a. The equilibrium under isolation (autarky) is the intersection of the supply and demand curves:

$$64 - 2Q = 4 + Q$$
$$-3Q = -60$$
$$Q^* = 20$$
$$P^* = 4 + (20) = 24$$
$$P^* = 64 - 2(20) = 24 \text{ (check)}$$

Graphically,

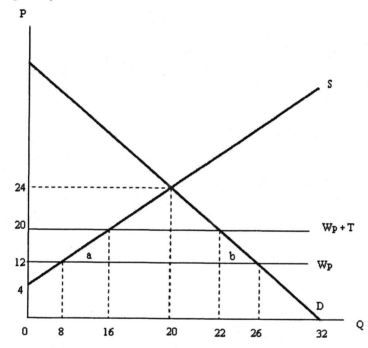

Consumers' surplus is given by the area of the triangle below the demand curve and above the price line of 24:

$$CS = \tfrac{1}{2} \times b \times h = \tfrac{1}{2}(20 - 0)(64 - 24) = 400.$$

Producers' surplus is given by the area of the triangle above the supply curve and below the price line of 24:

$$CS = \tfrac{1}{2} \times b \times h = \tfrac{1}{2}(20 - 0)(24 - 4) = 200.$$

b.

If trade with the rest of the world is allowed, the price in the United States will be the world price Wp = $12. At a price of $12, the quantity supplied by domestic producers is

$$12 = 4 + Q, \text{ so } Qs = 8.$$

At a price of $12, the quantity demanded is

$$12 = 64 - 2Q \text{ so } Qd = 26.$$

So American consumers will purchase 26 tons of steel, 8 tons from domestic producers, and 18 tons imported from foreign producers.

Consumers' surplus is now ½ (26 − 0) (64 − 12) = 676
Producers' surplus is now ½ (8 − 0) (12 − 4) = 32

Compared to isolation, consumers are better off under free trade, since consumers' surplus increases from 400 to 676. Domestic producers, however, are worse off under free trade, since producers' surplus has declined from 200 to 32. Foreign producers are able to sell 18 tons at $12 each, so foreign producers earn a total revenue of 18 x 12 = $216.

c.

If the U.S. government imposes a tariff of $8 on each ton of steel imported, then the price in the United States becomes the world price plus the tariff,

$$P = Wp + T = 12 + 8 = 20.$$

At a price of $20, the quantity supplied by domestic producers is given by

$$20 = 4 + Q \text{ so } Qs = 16.$$

At a price of $20, the quantity demanded is given by

$$20 = 64 - 2Q \text{ so } Qd = 22.$$

So U.S. consumers will purchase 22 tons of steel, 16 tons produced by domestic producers and 6 tons imported from foreign producers.

Consumers' surplus is equal to ½ (22 − 0) (64 − 20) = 484.
Producers' surplus is equal to ½ (16 − 0) (20 − 4) = 128.
Tariff revenue = $8 x 6 = $48. Foreign producers earn $12 x 6 = $72.
Producers are better off due to the tariff compared to free trade. Producers' surplus has increased by 1: − 32 = 96.
Consumers are worse off from the tariff compared to free trade. Consumers' surplus has declined by 6 − 484 = 192.
Of the $192 decline in consumers' surplus, $96 was captured by producers as an increase in producers' surplus. $48 was captured by government in the form of tax revenue. The remainder, 192 − 96 − 48 = is the net welfare loss of the tariff. Verify that $48 is the combined areas of triangles a and b, or the ne welfare loss (deadweight loss) of the tariff.
So tariffs make domestic producers better off at the expense of consumers and society as a whole.

Internet Exercises

Go to the WTO website at www.wto.org. After reading the homepage, click on "THE WTO" and "What is the WTO?" Then read "The WTO in Brief". There is a PDF version if you like. Next, visit the Global Exchange website at www.globalexchange.org/campaigns/wto and click on "Background" and then "Top Reasons to Oppose the WTO". After reading the articles, answer the following questions:

1. What is the WTO? Briefly describe its functions and structure.

2. What is GATT? How is the WTO related to GATT?

3. What are the advantages and disadvantages of the WTO? Overall, does the WTO help or harm the world?

4. Who are the likely beneficiaries of free trade? Who will pay the costs of free trade?

Solutions

True False Questions

1. T, True, while U.S. exports have been relatively constant as a share of GDP, imports from the rest of the world have increased. Because of this, the United States has seen growing trade deficits.

2. F, The fact that the United States produces shirts at a higher cost simply means that is has an absolute disadvantage. Trade should be based on the principle of comparative advantage. Thus, what is important for trade is the relative opportunity cost of producing shirts in the United States and Canada. Only if the United States has a comparative disadvantage should it import shirts from Canada.

3. F, Trade restrictions benefit certain groups in society. Specifically, trade restrictions benefit the producers of the good on which the trade restriction is placed. The restriction will drive up the price of imports and allow domestic producers to sell more of their product at a higher price.

4. F, Most countries, including the United States, restrict trade by imposing tariffs, quotas, and voluntary export restraints. The most common arguments against free trade stress that (1) new industries should be protected until they can become competitive, (2) industries essential for national defense should be protected, (3) protection is necessary to save jobs, and (4) American workers must be protected from cheap foreign labor. One of the main reasons such restrictions are successful is that the benefits of restrictions are concentrated on a fairly small group while the costs are spread over the entire population. This means benefits per person are high while costs per person are low. Individuals have little incentive to protest restrictions.

5. F, False, consumers' surplus is the benefit that consumers receive from participating in a market since the market price they must pay is less than the maximum price they would be willing to pay for different quantities of the good. With a linear demand curve, consumers' surplus is the area of the triangle below the demand curve and above the horizontal price line. As the price of the good increases, the area of that triangles declines, so consumers' surplus decreases.

6. T, NAFTA is the North American Free Trade Agreement. Following a 1988 agreement between Canada and the United States, talks began with Mexico regarding the formation of a free-trade area. In August 1992 an announcement was made that an agreement between the three nations had been reached. The agreement was approved by Congress and took effect January 1, 1994. The agreement eliminates tariffs over a 15-year time period. It also eliminates quotas and other trade restrictions. It should be noted that barriers only within the free-trade area will be lifted. Each country is free to maintain trade barriers against non-member countries.

7. F, False, the primary function of the WTO is to promote free trade and to provide a forum for trade disputes around the world. The WTO does not support, but tries to eliminate, trade barriers that restrict trade between countries.

8. F, False, while some jobs may be lost due to free trade, especially in those industries subject to intense import competition, other jobs will be created, especially in those industries that rely heavily on export revenue. There is nothing inevitable about free trade creating job losses; it depends on the relative sizes of the losses and gains.

Multiple Choice

1. A
2. A
3. D
4. B
5. D
6. A
7. E
8. A
9. B

10. D   16. B   22. A
11. B   17. B   23. D
12. C   18. A   24. A
13. B   19. C   25. C
14. A   20. C
15. B   21. D

Fill-in Questions

1. deficits; exports; imports
2. comparative advantage; comparative disadvantage
3. absolute advantage; absolute disadvantage
4. tariff; quota; voluntary export restraint (VER)
5. World Trade Organization; General Agreement on Tariffs and Trade
6. trade adjustment assistance

Financing Trade and the Trade Deficit

Objectives of the Chapter

After you have mastered this chapter you will understand:

1. That the large and persistent current account deficit is undesirable.

2. That exchange rates are determined by the demand for and supply of foreign exchange in currency markets.

3. The differences between fixed and flexible exchange rates.

4. That GDP and interest rates are important in determining exchange rates.

5. That fixed exchange rates require the intervention of central banks.

6. That some economists argue that flexible rates lead to greater economic stability and leave central banks free to pursue monetary policy.

7. That some economists believe that fixed exchange rates are more stabilizing on an economy and force central banks to practice monetary discipline.

8. The components of the Balance of Payments Accounts.

9. The issues involved in the introduction of the Euro.

10. The events surrounding the Mexican Peso Crisis of 1994 and Asian Financial Crisis of 1997, and that these crises started in financial markets, but soon spread to all areas of the affected economies.

11. That controls may be applied to capital outflows or inflows in order to prevent currency depreciation or appreciation.

Key Terms

exchange rate

flexible (floating) exchange rates

depreciation

appreciation

fixed exchange rates

balance of payments

balance of payments deficit

balance of payments surplus

devaluation

revaluation

True False Questions

For these statements, indicate whether they are true or false. Defend your answer.

1. Suppose that a dollar trades for 100 yen, and that a dollar trades for 0.5 euros. Then a euro should trade for 50 yen.

   TRUE or FALSE

2. As the value of the dollar falls compared to the yen, the amount of U.S. exports purchased by Japanese consumers will increase.

   TRUE or CHOICE F: FALSE

3. Overall, the balance of payments is always in balance, or equal to 0. However, this does not mean that policy-makers should ignore the persistent current account deficit.

   TRUE or FALSE

4. Deficits in the current account must be financed through even larger deficits in the capital account.

   TRUE or FALSE

5. Allowing the dollar to depreciate would lower the current account deficit.

   TRUE or FALSE

6. If there is a balance of payments surplus, there will be a tendency for the dollar to depreciate in value compared to the foreign currency.

   TRUE or FALSE

7. In a world of fixed exchange rates, a decrease in the demand for a country's exports will cause the country's currency to depreciate.

   TRUE or FALSE

8. A current account deficit may be reduced through the control of capital outflows.

   TRUE or FALSE

9. The Asian financial crisis was caused when the Chinese government began to dominate the world textile market.

   TRUE or FALSE

Multiple Choice

Check yourself. Choose the best answer. Answers are found at the end of the chapter.

1. The exchange rate between two countries is
   a. the rate at which both countries would be willing to make a trade.
   b. the value of one country's currency in terms the other.
   c. always fixed for advance industrial economies.
   d. a good measure of the comparative standards of living in both countries.

2. The balance of payment accounts:
   a. will show a deficit if exports exceed imports.
   b. will show a deficit if imports exceed exports.
   c. will never be out of balance.
   d. will be out of balance only when foreigners purchase U.S. assets.

3. Suppose that in 2006 there was a net decrease of $25 million in foreign private assets invested in the Xaphire Empire. This change would cause:
   a. an increase in Xaphire's current account.
   b. a decrease in Xaphire's current account.
   c. an increase in Xaphire's capital account.
   d. no change in Xaphire's capital account.

4. If a country has $400 million in exports, $450 million in imports, and net unilateral transfers of -$50 million, the balance in its current account must be:
   a. -$100 million.
   b. $0.
   c. $50 million.
   d. $100 million.

5. A country has a balance of -$32 billion in its capital account. In the absence of any statistical discrepancy, it must have what balance in its current account?
   a. $0.
   b. $32 billion.
   c. -$32 billion.
   d. cannot be determined without further information.

6. Suppose that Albania buys more goods and services from the rest of the world then it sells to the rest of the world. In this case,
   a. Albania's imports are greater than its exports.
   b. Albania has a current account deficit.
   c. Albania has a surplus in its capital account.
   d. Albania's overall Balance of Payments is equal to zero.
   e. all of the above.

7. For the past three decades, the United States has generally had:
   a. a deficit in its balance of payments.
   b. a surplus in its balance of payments.
   c. a deficit in its current account.
   d. a surplus in its current account.

8. The equilibrium exchange rate is:

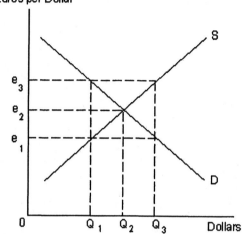

a. e_1.
b. e_2.
c. e_3.
d. between e_3 and e_1.

9. If the exchange rate is currently e_1, there will be a tendency for:

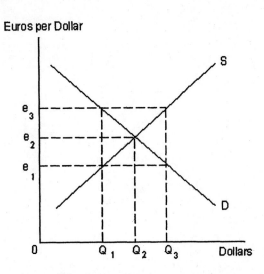

a. the exchange rate to fall and the dollar to appreciate.
b. the exchange rate to fall and the dollar to depreciate.
c. the exchange rate to increase and the dollar to appreciate.
d. the exchange rate to increase and the dollar to depreciate.

10. Suppose GDP in the United States increases relative to that in the Euro countries. This will cause:

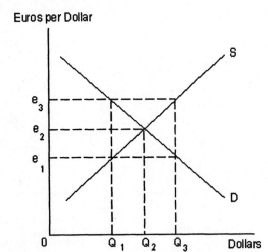

a. the supply of dollars to increase.
b. the supply of dollars to decrease.
c. the demand for dollars to decrease and the supply of dollars to increase.
d. the demand for dollars to increase and the supply of dollars to decrease.

11. If the exchange rate is currently e_3, there will be:

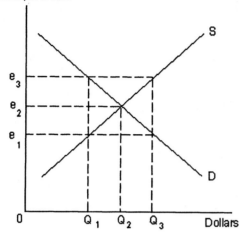

Euros per Dollar

a. a tendency for the exchange rate to increase.
b. balance of payments equilibrium.
c. balance of payments surplus.
d. balance of payments deficit.

12. Suppose the current exchange rate between the United States and Japan is $6 for 1 yen while the equilibrium exchange rate is $5 for 1 yen. It is likely that:
a. the exchange rate (yen per dollar) will fall and the relative price of U.S. exports will fall.
b. the exchange rate (yen per dollar) will fall and the relative price of U.S. exports will rise.
c. the exchange rate (yen per dollar) will rise and the relative price of U.S. exports will rise.
d. the exchange rate (yen per dollar) will rise and the relative price of U.S. exports will fall.

13. Assume that Canada's interest rate increases relative to that in other countries. This will most likely result in:
a. an appreciation of its currency that will cause both exports and imports to fall.
b. a depreciation of its currency that will cause both exports and imports to increase.
c. an appreciation of its currency that will cause imports to increase and exports to fall.
d. a depreciation of its currency that will cause imports to fall and exports to increase.

14. The demand for and supply of dollars is initially given by D_1 and S_2, respectively. A recession in the United States causes real GDP to decrease, and as a result:

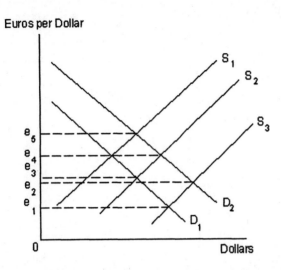

a. the supply of dollars will decrease to S_1 and the exchange rate will rise.
b. the demand for dollars will increase to D_2 and the exchange rate will increase.
c. the supply of dollars will decrease to S_1 and the demand for dollars will increase to D_2, causing the exchange rate to rise.
d. the supply of dollars will increase to S_3 and the exchange rate will fall.

15. Suppose the equilibrium exchange rate is e_4. If the economy is at full employment and monetary authorities in the United States increase the rate of growth in the money supply, what is the most likely result of this policy?

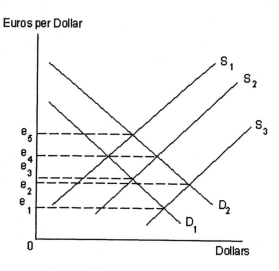

Euros per Dollar

Dollars

a. a shift in demand from D_2 to D_1 and a shift in supply from S_3 to S_2.
b. a shift in demand from D_2 to D_1 and a shift in supply from S_2 to S_3.
c. a shift in demand from D_1 to D_2 and a shift in supply from S_2 to S_3.
d. a shift in demand from D_1 to D_2 and a shift in supply from S_3 to S_1.

16. A system in which exchange rates are determined by the interaction of demand and supply is known as:
    a. a voluntary exchange rate system.
    b. a bendable exchange rate system.
    c. a flexible exchange rate system.
    d. a monitored exchange rate system.

17. Assume the Federal Reserve lets the value of the U. S. dollar fall relative to the value of the Canadian dollar. In this instance we would say:
    a. the U. S. dollar has floated.
    b. the U. S. dollar has been maintained.
    c. the U. S. dollar has been revalued.
    d. the U. S. dollar has been devalued.

18. One difference between a fixed and a flexible exchange rate system is that
    a. a flexible exchange rate system requires frequent intervention by the central bank.
    b. a fixed exchange rate system is easier to administer.
    c. under a flexible weight system, the central bank maintains targets for the exchange rate.
    d. under a fixed exchange rate system, the central bank must be ready to buy or sell domestic currency to keep the exchange rate at its target level.

19. Which of the following is an argument for a flexible exchange rate system?
    a. A flexible exchange rate system results in greater economic stability.
    b. A flexible exchange rate system allows the central bank to change exchange rates as they see fit in order to balance exports and imports.
    c. A flexible exchange rate system can result in destabilizing speculation.
    d. Less risk and certainty exist under a flexible exchange rate system.

20. When capital flows into a country that has a flexible exchange rate system,
    a. the currency will be devalued.
    b. the currency will be revalued.
    c. the currency will depreciate.
    d. the currency will appreciate.

21. An appreciation in the value of the dollar would:
    a. encourage foreigners to invest money in the United States.
    b. make U.S. goods more expensive to potential foreign consumers.
    c. increase the number of dollars it takes to buy a Euro.
    d. make it more expensive for U.S. citizens to travel abroad.

22. Under a system of flexible exchange rates, an increase in demand for a nation's currency in the foreign exchange market will:
    a. cause the nation's currency to appreciate.
    b. make it more expensive for the nation to import goods and services.
    c. lead to a deficit situation in the nation's balance on current account.
    d. make it less expensive for foreigners to buy domestically produced goods.

23. If the exchange rate of the Euro goes from 70 cents to 90 cents, then the Euro has:
    a. appreciated and residents of the ECU find U.S. goods less expensive.
    b. appreciated and residents of the ECU find U.S. goods more expensive.
    c. depreciated and residents of the ECU find U.S. goods less expensive.
    d. depreciated and residents of the ECU find U.S. goods more expensive.

24. Under which set of exchange rates would it be possible to profit by trading currencies?
    a. $1 = ¥1; ¥1 = €1; €1 = $1.
    b. $1 = ¥100; ¥1 = €0.005; €1 = $2.
    c. $1 = ¥50; ¥1 = €0.01; €1 = $2.
    d. $1 = ¥50; ¥1 = €0.01; €1 = $4.
    e. none of the above.

25. The Mexican Peso Crisis
    a. began when the Mexican peso depreciated by 20% in December 1994.
    b. was partly caused by domestic events, such as rebellions and assassinations, that led to decline in the confidence of foreign investors in the Mexican economy.
    c. led to higher interest rates and recession in the Mexican economy.
    d. all of the above.

Fill-in Questions

1. The _____ summarizes all of the economic transactions between residents of one country and those of all other countries. In the United States, there has been much concern because the current account in the balance of payments has shown a deficit for every year since 1991. A large part of this deficit has been financed by foreign investment in the United States. As a result of this increased investment, foreigners receive more income and interest from the United States while U.S. citizens receive less.

2. A(n) _____ is the number of units of one currency exchangeable for one unit of another. Today, the United States has a system of _____ . This means that exchange rates are determined by the forces of demand and supply.

3. If exchange rates are kept constant through central bank purchases and sales of foreign currencies the system is one of _____ . Under this system a balance of payments deficit or surplus may occur. If the quantity of dollars supplied exceeds the quantity of dollars demanded, there is a(n) _____ . In this case a central bank would have to buy domestic currency in order to keep the exchange rate from falling. Eventually, if it cannot continue to buy domestic currency, it will have to _____ the currency.

4. If the quantity of dollars demanded exceeds the quantity of dollars supplied, there is a(n) _____ . In order to keep the domestic currency from appreciating, the central bank will have to buy the foreign currency. It may eventually have to _____ the domestic currency.

5. If the exchange rate increases, there will be a(n) _____ of the currency, while there will be a(n) _____ of the currency if the exchange rate falls. These movements in the exchange rate are important because they alter the international prices of goods and services. For example, if the exchange rate increases and the currency appreciates, this means that a country's exports will become relatively more expensive and the quantity of exports will fall. Imports, on the other hand, become relatively less expensive and the quantity of imports will rise. Just the opposite occurs if the exchange rate falls and the currency depreciates.

Problems Applying Economic Concepts

1. Suppose you are given the following information about the demand for and supply of U. S. dollars in terms of the Yen. Plot the demand for and the supply of U.S. dollars.

Yen per U.S. dollar	Quantity Demanded	Quantity Supplied
10	200	1,000
9	300	900
8	400	800
7	500	700
6	600	600
5	700	500
4	800	400

2. Suppose you are given the following information about the demand for and supply of U. S. dollars in terms of the Yen. What is the equilibrium rate of exchange?

Yen per U.S. dollar	Quantity Demanded	Quantity Supplied
10	200	1,000
9	300	900
8	400	800
7	500	700
6	600	600
5	700	500
4	800	400

3. Suppose you are given the following information about the demand for and supply of U. S. dollars in terms of the Yen. At an exchange rate of 5 Yen per dollar, there would be excess. (a) _____ and the dollar would (b) _____. At an exchange rate of 9 Yens per dollar, there would be excess (c) _____ and the dollar would (d) _____. If the dollar appreciates, the price of U.S. exports will (e) _____ and the price of imports into the United States will (f) _____ .

Yen per U.S. dollar	Quantity Demanded	Quantity Supplied
10	200	1,000
9	300	900
8	400	800
7	500	700
6	600	600
5	700	500
4	800	400

4. Using a diagram of demand and supply, show how an increase in U.S. interest rates will affect the equilibrium exchange rate. Will this cause the dollar to appreciate or depreciate?

5. Suppose the equilibrium exchange rate is 1.75 British pounds per dollar. The exchange rate has been set at 2.00 British pounds per dollar. In this instance there will be a(n) _____. In order to maintain the rate of 2.00 British pounds per dollar, the central bank will have to _____ dollars.

6. Suppose that you wake up one morning and find the following exchange rates:

    1 dollar = 100 yen
    1 yen = 0.02 euros
    1 euro = 0.9 dollars

    Assuming that transactions costs are zero, how could you get rich in this economy? Explain.

7. Suppose that a pound of beef sells for $5 in the United States, and for €4 in France. The exchange rate is €1 = $2, and it costs $1 to ship a pound of beef between the United States and France.

    a. Can you get rich in this market? Why or why not? Explain.

    b. In the long run, what would you expect to happen to the price of beef in the U.S. and France? What would be the price differential?

8. Assume that you have $10,000 to invest in either U.S. or French bonds. The U.S. bonds pay 10% interest, while the French bonds pay 8% interest. Both bonds mature in one year. The dollar currently trades for 0.8 euros, and you expect the dollar to trade for 0.5 euros one year from now. Which bond should you purchase? (Patriotic and anti-French feelings aside.) Explain.

Problems Applying Economic Concepts Solutions

1.

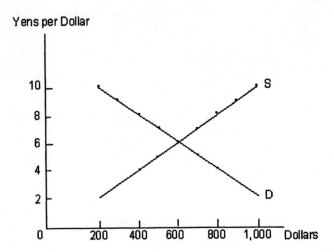

2. The equilibrium rate of exchange occurs where quantity demanded and quantity supplied are equal. Thus, the equilibrium rate of exchange is 1 euro per 1.05803 U.S. dollars (subject to change).

3.

    a. demand

    b. appreciate

    c. supply

    d. depreciate

    e. increase

    f. decrease

4. In the diagram, equilibrium is initially at point A and the equilibrium exchange rate The increase in interest rates will attract funds from abroad. This will cause the demand for dollars to increase to D2. At the same time, U.S. citizens will find it less desirable to invest in other countries. This will cause the supply of dollars to decrease to S2. The increase in demand for dollars and the decrease in the supply of dollars both work to increase the exchange rate to e2. A new equilibrium occurs at point B. The increase in the exchange rate will cause the dollar will appreciate.

Pounds per Dollar

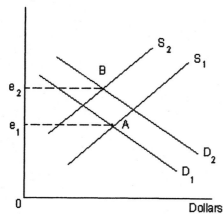

5. balance of payments deficit; buy

6. Trade $1.00 for 100 yen, 100 yen for 2 euros, and 2 euros for $1.80. Then trade $1.80 for 180 yen, 180 yen for 3.6 euros, and 3.6 euros for $3.24. As you keep trading, you accumulate more and more dollars. This is an example of international currency arbitrage.

7.

    a. Since the dollar price of a pound of beef in the United States ($5), is less than the dollar price of a pound of beef in France (€4 x 2 = $8), international arbitrageurs will profit by buying beef in the United States and then shipping the beef to France. To prove that this will result in profit:

page 2

ACTIVITY	RESULT
Buy one pound of beef in U.S.	- $5
Ship pound of beef to France	- $1
Sell beef for €4 in France	
Exchange €4 for $8	+ $8
net gain + $2	

    So a $2 profit can be made for each pound of beef shipped from the United States to France.

    b. As beef is shipped from the United States to France, then the supply of beef in the United States will fall, and the price of beef in the United States will increase. Also, the supply of beef in France will rise, so the price of beef in France will decline. The price of beef will rise in the low-priced country and fall in the high-priced country, until the only difference in prices reflect shipping costs between the two countries. Thus we would expect the price differential to fall to $1.00, or the costs of shipping beef. Once the price differential between the two countries is less than $1, then it is no longer profitable to ship beef from one country to another.

8. To calculate which bond you should purchase, consult the following table:

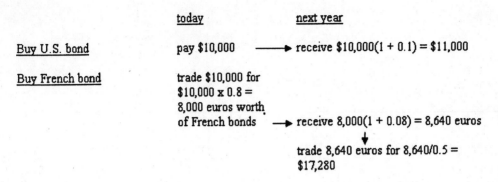

Since the U.S. bonds pay a total of $11,000 (10% return) and the French bonds pay a total of $17,280 (72.8% return), you would be better off purchasing the French bonds, unless you really hate France.

Internet Exercises

1. To find the U.S. balance of payments data, go to http://www.bea.gov. From the BEA home page, click on "Balance of Payments" under "International", and then click on "Latest News Release". After reading the news article, answer the following questions:

   a. What are the recent trends in the U.S. trade deficit in the past quarter? Why?

   b. What are the major components of the Balance of Payments that are discussed in the article? Briefly, how have these been moving in the recent past?

2. Go to the Economist magazine website to read about the Big Mac Index: http://www.economist.com/markets/Bigmac/Index.cfm.

   a. First, click on "Explanation" and "video clip". Briefly, what does the Big Mac Index measure? How?

   b. Next, click on "The Big Mac Index" for the latest available date (currently January 12, 2006). According to the table, which currencies are most overvalued? Which currencies are most undervalued? How would you expect the yen and euro to move against the dollar?

Solutions

True False Questions

1. F, False, exchange rates should be consistent with each other so that it is not possible to profit by buying a currency in a country with a low price and reselling the currency in a country with a high price. Here, you could trade a dollar for 100 yen, 100 yen for 2 euros, and 2 euros for 4 dollars, so you started with $1 and you end up with $4. If you could continue to trade at these rates, you could create an infinite amount of dollars.

   Instead, a euro should trade for 100/0.5 = 200 yen. With that set of exchange rates, it is not possible to profit by exchanging currencies.

2. T, True, as the value of the dollar falls (depreciates) it will take less yen to purchase a dollar. This means that Japanese consumers now find that the cost of American exports has declined in terms of yen, so Japan will increase its purchases of goods and services from the United States.

3. T, The current account deficit has been financed largely by foreign investment in the United States. This means that foreigners now own more of this country's assets. As a result, they receive more income and interest from the United States while citizens of this country receive less. Thus, even though the overall balance of payments always balances, there is some cause for concern when the U.S. consistently runs a deficit in its current account.

4. F, False, the overall balance of payments must always balance, or be equal to 0. This means that any deficit in the current account must be financed through a surplus in the capital account, so that the overall balance of payments is equal to 0. If a country doesn't sell exports to finance its import spending, it must sell its capital assets.

5. T, If the dollar depreciates, the relative price of exports from the United States will fall while the relative price of imports into the United States will rise. As a result, the quantity of exports will rise while the quantity of imports will fall. This change in exports and imports will cause the deficit in the current account to decrease.

6. F, A balance of payments surplus means that the quantity of dollars demanded exceeds the quantity of dollars supplied. The rest of the world's purchases of the home country's goods, services, and assets will exceed the home country's purchases of goods, services, and assets from the rest of the world. This will cause the exchange rate to rise. As the exchange rate increases, the dollar will appreciate.

7. F, Suppose demand for U.S. exports declines. In a floating exchange-rate system, the demand for dollars will fall. This will cause the exchange rate (denominated in terms of the foreign currency per dollar) to fall. The dollar will depreciate. Under a fixed exchange-rate system the exchange rate is not allowed to fall.

8. T, True, since an increase in net capital outflows (foreigners purchasing US assets) enables the US to finance its current account deficit, then controlling capital outflows would provide less foreign currency for US consumers to purchase foreign imports.

9. F, False, the Asian financial crisis started in 1997, before China gained its dominance in the world textile market. The most commonly-cited cause of the Asian financial crisis was the devaluation of the baht, the Thai currency, by the Thai central bank in July 1997.

Multiple Choice

1.	B	5.	B	9.	C
2.	C	6.	E	10.	A
3.	A	7.	C	11.	D
4.	A	8.	B	12.	A

13. C	18. D	23. A
14. A	19. A	24. D
15. B	20. C	25. D
16. C	21. B	
17. D	22. A	

Fill-in Questions

1. balance of payments
2. exchange rate; flexible exchange rates
3. fixed exchange rate; balance of payments deficit; devalue
4. balance of payments surplus; revalue
5. appreciation; depreciation